Sustainable Growth and Economic Development

To

Mera Bapu

Babaji

Sustainable Growth and Economic Development

A Case Study of Malaysia

Renuka Mahadevan

The University of Queensland, Australia

Edward Elgar
Cheltenham, UK • Northampton, MA, USA

Published by
Edward Elgar Publishing Limited
Glensanda House
Montpellier Parade
Cheltenham
Glos GL50 1UA
UK

Edward Elgar Publishing, Inc.
William Pratt House
9 Dewey Court
Northampton
Massachusetts 01060
USA

A catalogue record for this book
is available from the British Library

Library of Congress Cataloguing in Publication Data

Mahadevan, Renuka.
  Sustainable growth and economic development : a case study of Malaysia /
  by Renuka Mahadevan.
      p. cm.
  Includes bibliographical references and index.
  1. Malaysia—Economic conditions. 2. Malaysia—Economic policy. I.
Title.
    HC445.5.M3235 2007
    338.9595'07--dc22

                                                              2007011663
ISBN 978 1 84720 361 8

Printed and bound in Great Britain by MPG Books Ltd, Bodmin, Cornwall

Contents

Figures

Tables

Appendices

Abbreviations

ADB	Asian Development Bank
AFTA	ASEAN Free Trade Area
APEC	Asia Pacific Economic Cooperation
ASEAN	Association of Southeast Asian Nations
CEPT	Common Effective Preferential Tariff
DEA	Data Envelopment Analysis
ECM	Error correction model
EPU	Economic Planning Unit
FDI	Foreign direct investment
GDP	Gross domestic product
HRDF	Human Resources Development Fund
ICT	Information and communication technologies
IMF	International Monetary Fund
IMP1	First Industrial Master Plan 1986–1995
IMP2	Second Industrial Master Plan 1996–2005
IMP3	Third Industrial Master Plan 2006–2020
IP	Intellectual Property
IRPA	Intensification of Research in Priority Areas
IT	Information technology
K-economy	Knowledge economy
KDI	Knowledge-Based Economy Development Index
MARA	Majlis Amanah Rakyat (Council of Trust for the Indigenous Peoples)
MASTIC	Malaysian Science and Technology Centre
MDC	Multimedia Development Corporation
MNC	Multinational company
MITI	Ministry of International Trade and Industry
MOSTE	Ministry of Science, Technology and Environment
MP	Malaysian Plan
MSC	Multimedia Super Corridor
MyRen	Malaysian Research and Education Network
NEP	New Economic Policy 1971–1990
NDP	National Development Policy 1991–2000
NIE	Newly industrialising economy
NITC	National Information Technology Council
NRI	Networked Readiness Index

NVP	National Vision Policy 2001–2010
OECD	Organisation of Economic Cooperation and Development
OPP1	First Outline Perspective Plan 1971–1990
OPP2	Second Outline Perspective Plan 1991–2000
OPP3	Third Outline Perspective Plan 2001–2010
PLI	Poverty Line Income
R&D	Research and development
RM	Ringgit Malaysian
SARS	Severe Acute Respiratory Syndrome
SME	Small and medium enterprises
SSO	Shared services and outsourcing
TFP	Total factor productivity
TE	Technical Efficiency
TNC	Transnational corporation
TP	Technological progress
UNIDO	United Nations Industrial Development Organisation
US	United States
US$	United States Dollar
VAR	Vector Autoregressive Regression
VC	Venture capital
WEF	World Economic Forum
WTO	World Trade Organisation

Preface

Malaysia is considered a success story in terms of development among the semi-developed countries and is often being touted to join the ranks of the first-tier newly industrialising Asian economies of Singapore, South Korea, Hong Kong and Taiwan, possibly ahead of Indonesia and Thailand. However, little has been researched on Malaysia apart from her recovery from the Asian financial crisis of 1997/98. It is now timely to study this economy beyond that and analyse the direction in which the economy is being steered in its economic development strategy.

This book provides an insight into some of the efforts and actions taken by the rapidly developing economy of Malaysia towards its Vision 2020 of becoming a developed country. Can the vision become a reality and not just remain a dream? The purpose of this volume is thus to study selected key areas such as structural transformation, total factor productivity growth, human capital and technology development policies as well as poverty and income equality. In addition, the various challenges that Malaysia faces in this increasingly global environment and its move to the knowledge economy are examined.

The book uses both quantitative and qualitative methods to support the analysis and discussion. The empirical investigation is carried out using appropriate econometric techniques. The book would appeal to policymakers, academics and postgraduate students interested in applied work. The material is presented in such a way that the non-technical audience would also greatly benefit from the analysis as the focus of the book is on policymaking. Lastly, the lessons drawn from the Malaysian experience are valuable for other rapidly developing economies or developing economies interested in embarking on a similar development strategy.

In completing this book, I would like to thank Mr Dorairajau of the Department of Statistics in Kuala Lumpur for helping me with data collection and arranging for the use of the department's library facilities during my fieldwork in Malaysia. The moral support of my close friends and colleagues, John Asafu-Adjaye and Sandy Suardi, is also much appreciated.

1. Introduction

Malaysia is undoubtedly one of a handful of remarkable success stories in the developing world. Some 14 years ago, the 330 252 km^2 large economy of Malaysia with a population of about 28 million was hailed as the next Asian newly industrialising country (World Bank 1993). Despite the currency crisis in 1997/98, Malaysia has bounced back into those ranks once again. Thanks to the underlying resilience in the economy, and unconventional but successful capital controls, Malaysia coped with the crisis better than most other economies in the region. With a real GDP growth rate of 7.1 per cent in 2004, Malaysia was the fourth fastest-growing economy in Asia after China, Singapore and Hong Kong.

However, it remains to be seen if Malaysia is able to sustain its growth and development to enter the league of developed industrial nations by 2020. This particular aim was envisaged by the former Prime Minister, Dr Mahathir Mohamed, as Vision 2020, in his inaugural speech at the Malaysian Business Council Meeting in February 1991. Since then, the vision has been formalised as the National Vision Policy and the Third Outline Perspective Plan for 2001–2010 constitutes the first decade of development under Vision 2020. While nine broad challenges were put forth under this vision, one key aspiration is for the real GDP in 2020 to be eight times larger than that in 1990 and this is to be achieved with an average GDP growth of about 7 per cent until 2020.

Malaysia has come a long way from being a low-income developing economy to that of a high middle-income export-oriented economy. Her per capita GDP has more than doubled from US$1750 in 1975 to US$4650 in 2004, and Malaysia was the nineteenth largest trading nation in 2004. Although Malaysia's economic growth performance has been enviable, the vulnerability of the economy to external shocks such as the experience in 1997/98, necessitates rethinking strategies for sustainable growth and development. For instance, there is a need to move away from labour-intensive manufacturing operations from assembly-line production and make progress into higher value-added manufacturing activities which use high-skilled labour and more advanced technology. In an attempt to diversify the manufacturing base, the government started focusing on information technology and knowledge-based industrialisation as seen in the establishment of the Multimedia Super Corridor spanning 50 km from the capital, Kuala Lumpur, to its relatively new international airport at Sepang.[1]

World-class multimedia companies are encouraged to locate in the Corridor to undertake some manufacturing as well as to introduce high value-added information technology goods and services that will make Malaysia a regional information technology hub. The reliance on foreign direct investment has been reinforced further with plans to compete globally in the international market. The key challenge for Malaysia is to remain competitive and continue enjoying steady economic growth.

However, the success of the above plans clearly hinges on many other factors, both internal and external. No one should pretend that such a study of economic development is straightforward. With that thought firmly in mind, it suffices to say that the principal aim of this project is to identify some of the factors that have caused Malaysia to record impressive growth and to isolate the key factors that will play an important role in shaping future economic growth. In particular, the discussion intends to critically raise a number of policy issues and bring to light new questions for research and policy discussion.

A brief outline of the objectives of the subsequent chapters is as follows.

CHAPTER 2: INDUSTRIALISATION WITH A FOCUS ON PRIMARY PRODUCTION

Industrialisation is the fundamental policy objective in most developing countries, including Malaysia. This chapter provides an overview and analysis of this move by tracing the structural transformation process and reviewing industrial policies over time. The trends in output, employment and labour productivity of agriculture, manufacturing and services are discussed before exploring the empirical evidence on the causality links between these sectors. The inter-industry links pave the path for the renewed role of agriculture which is not without its fair share of challenges and problems in significantly contributing to economic growth.

CHAPTER 3: UNDERSTANDING THE DRIVERS OF ECONOMIC GROWTH

This chapter is divided into two parts – analysis of the productivity growth of the aggregate economy and of the manufacturing sector. The first section computes and discusses the empirical evidence on labour productivity and TFP growth of the aggregate economy, and the latter is measured by both the parametric and non–parametric measures to establish robustness. The decomposition of output growth into input growth and TFP growth provides some understanding of how well the economy is performing.

The second part of the chapter focuses on the manufacturing sector. Here, a stochastic production frontier model is estimated using a new panel data set of Malaysia's 26 three-digit manufacturing industries from 1970 to 2002. This enables the perspiration versus inspiration debate to be revisited using empirical evidence. In addition, TFP growth is decomposed into technological progress and technical efficiency in order to investigate the determinants of each of these sources of growth. This allows the dynamic relationship between the sources of TFP growth to be studied so as to highlight the importance of two crucial aspects of policymaking – the importance of weighing the trade-off in the effects of policy, and the consequent need for coherent policy coordination, both of which have been overlooked in the literature.

CHAPTER 4: HUMAN CAPITAL AND TECHNOLOGY DEVELOPMENT POLICIES

With the rapid spread and adoption of ICT technology, human capital and technology development are clearly major engines of growth. Thus the Malaysian situation with regards to education, training and research development is critically reviewed in the light of current policies and evidence. While some short- to medium-term strategies are discussed to overcome the shortage of skills, the need for a more concerted and integrated effort towards developing appropriate human capital and technology development policy as a long-term strategy is emphasised.

CHAPTER 5: LEAPFROGGING INTO THE KNOWLEDGE ECONOMY

The move towards a K-economy was inevitable for Malaysia as it was part of the plan to spearhead the economy into attaining the status of a developed country by 2020. This chapter assesses the progress of the K-economy at the macro, meso and micro levels. At the macro level, the debate of IT production versus IT use for productivity growth, the impact of ICT, the Multimedia Super Corridor and government policies favouring the expansion of ICT industries are reviewed. At the meso level, the strategic role of ICT and differences in knowledge content at the industry level are detailed using firm-level survey data. At the micro level, the IT literacy of the community at large and the availability of knowledge workers are argued to be crucial for the optimal transformation to a K-economy. In this regard, the issue of the digital divide and how ICT can help reduce poverty are also discussed.

CHAPTER 6: POVERTY AND INCOME INEQUALITY

Malaysia is often said to have enjoyed growth with equity and it has made remarkable progress in its war against poverty in particular. This chapter first reviews the trends in poverty using various strata in light of the national development plans on poverty alleviation to help understand the extent of success in reducing absolute poverty. But the country's success in reducing the incidence of absolute poverty is empirically shown to have been due more to growth than to reductions in inequality. Relative poverty has thus changed little, and an attempt is made to measure relative poverty for the first time and to discuss the unnoticed nature of the poverty transition that Malaysia has undergone. One implication of the discussion is that the current focus on hardcore poverty and absolute poverty is misplaced.

The second section on income inequality begins with an overview of trends in overall income inequality as well as inter-racial and inter-regional income inequality. This is followed by an analysis of the effect of redistributive policies on income inequality so far, and where Malaysian inequality may be heading in the future.

CHAPTER 7: CONCLUSION

By providing a summary of the findings of the previous chapters, this chapter discusses the challenges and opportunities for Malaysia in the face of globalisation. In addition, the changing role of the government in its pursuit of developed country status in the global environment is critically examined in the context of how policy has evolved and where it is heading. These analyses allow important lessons to be drawn not only for Malaysia but other rapidly developing economies as well.

NOTE

---

[1] Incidentally, this airport was the third best airport in the world in 2003.

2. Industrialisation with a Focus on Primary Production

2.1 INTRODUCTION

Since independence in 1957, the Malaysian economy has transformed itself from a commodity-based economy to one of the world's largest producers of electronic and electrical products. In fact, the Accelerated Industrialisation Drive mapped out under Vision 2020 clearly states the need to industrialise rapidly for economic growth. This is reinforced in the Package of New Strategies unveiled in May 2003 where efforts to accelerate the transition towards the production of high value-added goods and exploration into new areas where Malaysia has comparative advantage were to be increased in the light of greater uncertainties in the external environment and increased competition from new global players. Thus the importance of structural transformation and the process of policy reform underlying the continuing transition are important areas for analysis.

The chapter is organised as follows. The next two sections provide a brief overview of the macroeconomic performance and industrial policies of Malaysia. Section 2.4 outlines the trends over time in output, employment, and labour productivity of the agriculture, manufacturing and services sectors while section 2.5 presents the empirical evidence on the causality links between these sectors. Section 2.6 discusses the renewed role of the agricultural sector as a third engine of growth and the last section raises some concerns and challenges facing this sector.

2.2 MACROECONOMIC PERFORMANCE

Malaysia has often been acknowledged as one of the fast growing economies in the Asia–Pacific region. Table 2.1 shows that GDP growth has been more than 4 per cent in the decades of 1970, 1980 and 1990. After the setback in 1997/98 which lasted until the end of 2001, Malaysia has bounced back, and in 2002 recorded a GDP growth of 4.1 per cent. The growth experience has been accompanied by consistently low inflation rates and in the oil crisis years of 1974/75 and 1979/80, and the financial crisis year of 1997/98, it did not go beyond 6 per cent. Unemployment rates have also been reasonable even by developed country standards.

Table 2.1   Some macroeconomic indicators on Malaysia

Indicator	1971–80	1981–90	1991–95	1996–2000	2001–05
Real GDP growth	7.8	6.0	8.7	4.8	4.5
Inflation rate	6.0	3.2	4.0	3.2	1.8
Unemployment rate	6.6	6.7	3.9	4.0	3.5

Note: Above values are averaged over the years.

Source: Ministry of Finance, *Economic Report* (various issues).

Overall, the focus of macroeconomic management has enabled an adequate level of savings, a balance of payment surplus, a stable exchange rate, fiscal prudence and strong external reserves. Malaysia's savings rate is high with its gross domestic saving averaging about 42 per cent of GDP since 1990. This shows that monetary resources are available to expand investment capacity when needed. The current account balance is healthy and has been in surplus since 1998–2004. In 2003, the foreign debt ratio was 6.1 per cent of the total value of exports and about 80 per cent of the external debt was medium- to long-term obligations (Bank Negara 2004a). The World Bank (2004b) considers Malaysia a moderately indebted nation and debt as a share of exports is considerably lower than that for upper-middle-income economies. Lastly, from 1992 to 1997, the government budget has been in surplus, averaging 1.3 per cent of GDP. Since 1998, the Malaysian government has shown its willingness to use the budget to mitigate adverse shocks such as the 1997/98 financial crisis, the 2003 SARS epidemic, and weak international demand. It has adopted a more expansionary stance to support growth, with the budget deficit averaging 4.5 per cent of GDP between 1998 and 2003.

In general, the Malaysian economic story so far is a good news story. It is undeniable that careful planning and management has helped build Malaysia's strong economic performance since the 1970s. The challenge now for Malaysia is to maintain this momentum.

2.3 INDUSTRIAL POLICIES

First, the colonial period in the early 1950s was largely limited to export and import processing and packaging of food and simple consumer items, especially encouraged by transport cost considerations. Much of this manufacturing activity was located in Singapore, Malay's commercial centre during the British colonial period. Since its independence from Britain in 1957,[1] Malaysia has introduced various development strategies in the following phases:

1. Import Substitution (1957–67)
2. Export Development (1968–80)
3. Development of Heavy Industries (1981–84)
4. First Industrial Master Plan 1986–95
5. Second Industrial Master Plan 1996–2005
6. Third Industrial Master Plan 2006–20

The above phases can be studied under various economic policies and plans undertaken by the government. Since 1966, nine five-year economic plans which broadly fall under The First Outline Perspective Plan 1970–90, The Second Outline Perspective Plan 1991–2000, and The Third Outline Perspective Plan 2001–10, have been drawn. Underlying these perspectives, are the New Economic Policy 1970–90, the National Development Policy 1991–2000, and the National Vision Policy 2001–10.

Thus there has been substantial planning and target setting in Malaysia whose economic performance has come a long way since its traditional dependence on natural resources. Agriculture related to rubber, palm oil, rice and cocoa is also considered to have played an important role in economic growth. Like most economies, the motivation to modernise the economy led the initial impetus given to manufacturing through import substitution using generous tariff protection.

The transition to export-oriented industrialisation began in the late 1960s as the limits of import substitution (by way of the creation of relatively little new employment and the smallness of the domestic market) became apparent, and a new international division of labour emerged, particularly involving manufacturing. Two main types of export-oriented industries were developed. Resource-based industries involved the increased processing of rubber, tin, palm oil, wood products and timber primary commodities in addition to food, beverages and tobacco, chemical and chemical products for export. The non-resource export-oriented industries, on the other hand, involved textiles and garments, transport equipment, machinery, electrical and electronic products.

In the 1980s, scope for further expansion in the resource-based industries was constrained by production costs of raw materials as well as tariff, transport and other trade barriers in the more industrially developed economies, whose governments generally continued to favour the import of raw materials rather than finished products. Thus although the processing of primary commodities still continued to expand, non-resource-based export industries have been more important in generating employment and growth since the 1970s. These industries mainly involved the relocation of certain labour-intensive aspects of the manufacturing processes in the export-processing or Free Trade Zones.

The next phase from the early 1980s is less distinct because it involved not the explicit abandonment of export-oriented industrialisation, but the government's promotion of selected heavy industries, which took the form of a second round of import substitution. These industries were meant to foster strong forward and backward linkages for the development of other industries and included steel (the Perjawa plant), cement, petrochemicals, shipbuilding and repairs, the Malaysian car project (Proton) and motorcycle engine plants. The motivation for the major push for heavy industrialisation was drawn from the experience of South Korea which had vigorously promoted heavy industries from 1972 to 1979. This led to the 'Look East' strategy where massive projects with Japan on construction and joint ventures in the heavy industries took place. This was carried through a public agency, namely the Heavy Industrialisation Corporation of Malaysia. But most of these heavy industries faced major gluts on the world market from the outset (Bowie 1988). The significant protection required to support these selected ventures raised the production costs and consumer prices for other parts of the economy. Thus heavy industrialisation has involved massive government borrowings from abroad for investment and the heavy import of capital goods and long gestation periods proved unprofitable. The heavy public sector involvement during that time is said to have distorted resource allocation, drained Malaysian financial resources, and crowded out private investment (World Bank 1989). However, the 'honeymoon' period of this policy came to an abrupt end in August 1984 when the need to launch a process of privatisation and restructuring was recognised. The situation was compounded by the global economic crisis of this period and its ramifications for Malaysia through the electronics industry product cycles.

This led to the promotion of the Investment Act in 1986 to attract FDI under the First Industrial Master Plan. The New Investment Fund in 1985 and the Industrial Adjustment Fund in 1987 were set up to provide a better environment for private investment by way of reducing the public sector investment share. The aim was also to embrace a more export-orientated strategy as well as to gain access to advanced foreign technology via FDI and export-oriented manufacturing.

The general thrust of the IMP2 introduced in 1996 was to promote productivity growth as a prime objective. But unlike the earlier Master Plan, it did not promote specific products or activities, but stressed the development of entire clusters instead. The central objective of the cluster-based development was to provide higher value added goods because it is meant to be an agglomeration of inter-linked or related activities comprising industries, suppliers, critical supporting business services, requisite infrastructure and institutions.

In particular, the IMP2 identified two new growth areas – ICT industries, and industries such as drug research and bio-processes related to biotechnology. With the former in mind, the Multimedia Super Corridor (a 15 km by 40 km strip of real estate between Kuala Lumpur and a new administrative centre Putrajaya) launched in 1996 was Malaysia's first initiative to lay the foundation for the knowledge-based economy in the hope of becoming Asia's Silicon Valley. The MSC was intended to offer an excellent and conducive environment to attract knowledge-based workers and high-technology industries, especially world-class multimedia companies from the private sector to enable Malaysia to become a regional IT hub. The Bio Valley on the other hand, is located on a 500-acre site of Cyberjaya and it signifies Malaysia's initiative to contribute towards biotechnology. The IMP2 states that as an emerging technology with immense research and business potential, biotechnology has the capacity to support and steer Malaysia into a knowledge-based economy.

The IMP3 is focussed on achieving global competitiveness as this is the last league in making Malaysia's vision of becoming a developed nation by 2020. This is to be done with the services sector assuming the lead role in driving economic growth, in addition to sustaining manufacturing sector growth by way of enhancing TFP growth in the new growth areas through sufficient R&D and skilled human capital.

2.4 THE GROWTH SECTORS

Part of the growth of the Malaysian economy is often attributed to its rapid industrialisation move which considerably changed the structure of the economy. It can be seen in Figure 2.1 that there has been a decline in agricultural (comprising livestock, crops, forestry and fisheries) share over time. The agricultural sector was the main economic activity that contributed 39.3 per cent to GDP when Malaysia achieved its independence in 1957 but the contribution progressively declined to 28.8 per cent in 1970 and 8.5 per cent in 2004. Within the agricultural sector, industrial commodities have always had a major share of the value added but this too has declined over time to 60 per cent in 2003.

Manufacturing, which contributed only 14 per cent of the GDP of a predominantly agricultural and primary goods producing country in 1975, now accounts for at least 30 per cent of the economy's output. In 1987, for the first time in the nation's history, Malaysia's manufacturing sector overtook agriculture in terms of GDP share. Within manufacturing, the electronics sector[2] has grown more than eightfold in real terms, increasing its share of manufacturing output from 14 per cent in 1987 to 27 per cent in 2003. In the same year, when manufactures accounted for 79 per cent of merchandise exports, 67 per cent were electrical and electronic products. Together with industries such as textile and wearing apparel, basic metal and metal products, transport equipment, and machinery, the non-resource-based industries are the main contributors in terms of GDP value added in the manufacturing sector, accounting on average, for about 53 per cent of value added share since 1990. The resource-based industries comprise food, beverages and tobacco, chemical and chemical products, petroleum refineries, wood and paper products, rubber processing and products and non-metallic minerals.

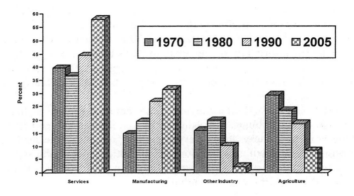

Note: Other industry includes mining, construction and utilities.

Source: Ministry of Finance, *Economic Report* (various issues).

Figure 2.1   Sectoral output shares

The services sector[3] share, on the other hand, has been quite stable over time with a contribution to GDP of about 43 per cent on average over 1975–2003. This is low compared to levels ranging between 60 per cent and 75 per cent in developed countries. The largest service subsector is the wholesale and retail trade including restaurants and hotels. Since the early 1990s, policies have been directed towards promoting the growth of the services sector both as a strategy for containing the services deficit in the balance of payments as well as for diversifying the economy. The current focus is on areas such as tourism, education, shipping, financial services, and contract and professional services.

Corresponding to the output trends in Figure 2.1, a structural shift in employment is evident in Table 2.2, with agricultural employment declining while the manufacturing and services sector experienced increases in their employment shares.

Table 2.2   *Employment by sector (%)*

Sector	1975	1985	1990	1995	2000	2005
Agriculture	43.6	31.3	26.0	19.97	15.2	12.9
Manufacturing	14.2	15.2	19.9	23.3	23.5	28.7
Services	35.5	45.1	46.5	47.7	48.9	51.0

Source: Ministry of Finance, *Economic Report* (various issues).

2.4.1 Labour Productivity Trends

Labour productivity makes a good starting point for analysis as it reflects how efficiently labour is combined with other factors of production. In addition to being intuitively appealing and relatively easy to compute, this measure is useful in showing the savings achieved over time in the use of the output per unit of labour input. From the welfare point of view, labour productivity which is linked to output per capita by labour force participation and the age structure of the population, ultimately limits per capita consumption. Therefore, this partial measure retains a role in the family of productivity measures relevant to national economic policy.

Labour productivity is measured by value added output per worker and here we compare the labour productivity trends of the three growth sectors from 1970 to 2004. Figure 2.2 shows that manufacturing labour productivity is the highest followed by that of services and agriculture. After the dip in labour productivity due to the 1997/98 crisis, the manufacturing sector was the quickest to pick up. Within the heterogeneous group of services, the transport, storage and communication services as well as the financial, insurance, real estate and business services were found to consistently experience higher labour productivity growth than manufacturing since 1984. Also, for the services sector, output and hence labour productivity is likely to be underestimated as the former is often intractable, especially producer services which are often accounted for indirectly in the manufacturing sector. Some factors that may explain inter-sectoral gaps in productivity are disparity in efficiency or wages, differences in structural characteristics of the sectors such as labour and capital intensity of activities, educational and skill level of workers, and predominance of small enterprises or the market structure of the sector.

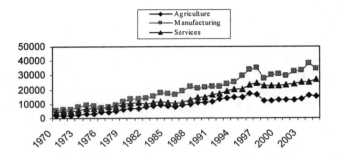

Source: Computed from *Economic Report* (various issues), Ministry of Finance.

Figure 2.2   Labour productivity (RM$ per worker)

In general, labour productivity in agriculture is low due to the following reasons. First, this sector has been experiencing a tight labour situation and consequently was dependent on foreign workers. In 1995, migrant labour was 30 per cent of the total workers employed in agriculture, and even then there was a shortage of 45 000 workers particularly tappers, harvesters and weeders. In 2005, this ratio declined to 26 per cent (MITI 2006) but the problem of out-migration of workers from agriculture to other sectors of the economy and the reluctance of younger workers to work in this sector is still acute. This leaves behind the older workers with possibly lower productivity. In addition, efforts to utilise mechanical harvesting technology in the plantation sector has met with limited success (EPU 2003). In consonance with the policy to optimise land utilisation and realise economies of scale, consolidation and rehabilitation of existing smallholdings and group farming continue to be a major programme. It must be noted that the general rising trend in agricultural labour productivity is due to the rise in the land–labour ratio rather than labour being efficiently combined with other inputs.

2.4.2   Decomposition of Economy-wide Labour Productivity Growth

Given the above trends in labour productivity, the extent to which relative labour productivity growth in the three sectors is responsible for growth in the economy-wide labour productivity is examined in this section. Improvements in resource allocation related to changes in sectoral labour productivity growth can have large effects on observed growth rates as shown by Young (1995) for Taiwan and South Korea, and Dowrick and Gemmel (1991) for developing countries. Here, an attempt is made to quantify the importance of resource allocation by decomposing annual change in aggregate labour productivity growth into within-sector (own) and between-sector (reallocation) effects as follows.

$$\Delta L \, Prod = \sum_{i=1}^{3} (\Delta SH_i \bullet \overline{L \, Prod_i}) + \sum_{i=1}^{3} (\overline{\Delta L \, Prod_i} \bullet \overline{SH_i})$$

$$\underbrace{\phantom{\sum_{i=1}^{3} (\Delta SH_i \bullet \overline{L \, Prod_i})}}_{Reallocation \; Effect} \quad \underbrace{\phantom{\sum_{i=1}^{3} (\overline{\Delta L \, Prod_i} \bullet \overline{SH_i})}}_{Own \; Effect}$$

(2.1)

where $\Delta LProd$ is the change in aggregate labour productivity growth, $LProd_i$ is the labour productivity of the *ith* sector and SH_i is the share of sector *i*'s GDP output in the economy's total GDP. The sectors considered are agriculture, manufacturing and services. The reallocation effect is the product of the change in the output share of the sector and its average labour productivity while the own labour productivity effect is the product of its average output share and the change in labour productivity of the sector. This decomposition, while not unique, allows us to quantify the degree to which more productive sectors are growing and how sectors themselves are growing more productively.

A positive reallocation effect results from an increasing share of total output in sectors with higher than average labour productivity. The own effect is positive if the mean of the output weighted within-sector labour productivity growth is positive. The own effect will be dominated by sectors with relatively large productivity changes in levels and/or large sectors with positive growth. And if the high productivity sectors have the highest productivity growth rates, then the own effect will be large.

Table 2.3   A decomposition of labour productivity growth in 1987 prices (%)

	Economy-wide productivity growth	Reallocation effect (Between sectors)	Own effect (Within sectors)
1971–79	9.8	0.5 (5.1)	9.3 (94.9)
1980–89	4.66	0.48 (10.2)	4.18 (89.8)
1990–99	4.09	0.64 (15.7)	3.45 (84.3)
2000–05	5.94	1.50 (25.3)	4.44 (74.7)
1971–2005	18.4	1.89 (10.3)	16.51 (89.7)

Note: Productivity growth is measured at the end points of the years. Percentage contribution is given in parenthesis.

The dominant source of aggregate labour productivity growth over the last three decades was the own-productivity effect, accounting for about 90 per cent of the total change. This is because, not only were the manufacturing and services productivity levels higher than the agricultural sector, but the latter also registered declines in its output share This is a rather standard development in the change of the structure of any economy. The reallocation effect between sectors, although small, has increased in importance over time as seen by the rising contribution to the change in labour productivity growth. This is the consequence of improved allocation of inputs that has occurred during the development process. Due to different rates of return on capital investment in the sectors, capital gets reallocated to the more productive sector and so does labour. This raises the economy's labour productivity growth, but how substantial or sustainable this is depends on the mobility of capital and labour, the possibility of increasing returns to these inputs as well as the developmental stage of the economy.

The small reallocation effect was due mainly to large declines in the share of the agriculture sector coupled with rising labour productivity. This reflects the movement of resources out of agriculture to manufacturing until 1990, after which services too obtained a rising share of the reallocated resources. There are however two caveats that need to be kept in mind regarding the above analysis (Chenery et al. 1986). One is the possible source of overestimation of the importance of resource allocation between sectors due to the assumption of input homogeneity. Differences in returns to labour and capital across sectors may reflect quality differences as well as disequilibrium within the economy. A reallocation of resources from sectors with low productivity to those with high returns would then reflect a reduction in the misallocation of resources and an improvement in the average quality of inputs. The effect thus includes both the reduction of disequilibrium and the upgrading of the quality of inputs. The contribution of resource allocation to growth could also be overstated if the higher productivity observed in manufacturing when it is compared to agriculture reflects, in part, a distorted domestic price structure. This could arise if government provides subsidies or incentives to expand the manufacturing sector.

Another potential source of underestimation of the importance of resource shifts lies in the static and partial nature of the measures. According to Cornwall (1977), these estimates assume that the level and rate of growth of productivity in the sector expanding inputs and output are independent of the expansion of the process itself. This rules out the possibility of various economies of scale in manufacturing and a more general and dynamic approach would explicitly recognise that resource shifts may facilitate or directly trigger higher productivity growth.

2.5   INTER-INDUSTRY CAUSALITY LINKS

There are a few ways of investigating causal links. The pioneering work of Granger (1969) was first extended by the use of Sims' (1972) forward and backward causality tests and this led to the estimation of first, the bivariate, and then the multivariate ECM which enabled the examination of short- and long-run causality relationships. However, there are some problems with the multivariate ECM for the use of causality interpretation.

First, in an ECM the significance and sometimes the signs of the coefficients that provide information on causality are known to be sensitive to the number of variables as well as the choice of the normalising cointegrating vector. While the latter task is meant to be based on economic theory, often, due to the lack of it, normalisation[4] is done on an ad hoc basis not necessarily supported by sound economic theory. The second problem is that for higher dimensional systems, the causal variables must be adequately involved in the cointegration, but often sequential strategies are not carried out to examine sufficient cointegration in the vector ECM (Giles and Williams 2000). Third, and more importantly, it has been argued by Toda and Phillips (1993) and Zapata and Rambaldi (1997) that standard Granger causality tests have non-standard asymptotic properties and thus the use of the F-test based on a VAR or ECM is not valid if the variables in the VAR are integrated or cointegrated. The issue is more complicated given the pre-testing distortions associated with prior test for cointegration such as unit root tests or if the stability and rank conditions are not fulfilled when there is more than one cointegrating vector in a multivariate model.

Thus an improved testing procedure developed by Toda and Yamamoto (1995) is used here to study the inter-industry linkages in the three growth sectors. This procedure uses the modified Wald test for restrictions on the parameters of the first k lags in a VAR ($k + d_{max}$) where k refers to lag length and d_{max} is the maximum order of integration that occurs in the system. The reason why this works is that the distributions of test statistics with non-stationary time series are singular and by over-parameterising the VAR, one can avoid singularity and obtain test statistics with the usual asymptotic distributions (Dolado and Lutkepohl 1996).

Here, three separate models (for output, employment and labour productivity) are estimated to identify causality links between the aggregate economy, agriculture, manufacturing and services sectors. To illustrate, we consider the hypothesis that there is a relationship between the growth of the variables of aggregate output, agricultural output, manufacturing output and service output. The empirical model for estimation is the following four-equation VAR model:

$$\begin{bmatrix} DAgg_t \\ DAgri_t \\ DManu_t \\ DServ_t \end{bmatrix} = \begin{bmatrix} A_{10} \\ A_{20} \\ A_{30} \\ A_{40} \end{bmatrix} + \begin{bmatrix} A_{11}(L) & A_{12}(L) & A_{13}(L) \\ A_{21}(L) & A_{22}(L) & A_{23}(L) \\ A_{31}(L) & A_{32}(L) & A_{33}(L) \\ A_{41}(L) & A_{42}(L) & A_{43}(L) \end{bmatrix} \times \begin{bmatrix} DAgg_{t-k} \\ DAgri_{t-k} \\ DManu_{t-k} \\ DServ_{t-k} \end{bmatrix} + \begin{bmatrix} \varepsilon_{1t} \\ \varepsilon_{2t} \\ \varepsilon_{3t} \\ \varepsilon_{4t} \end{bmatrix}$$

$$(2.2)$$

where
  Agg, Agri, Manu and Serv represent aggregate economy, agriculture, manufacturing, and services respectively;
  D is a difference operator;
  k represents number of lags;
  A_{i0} are the parameters representing intercept terms;
  $A_{ij}(L)$ are the polynomials in the lag operator L; and
  ε_{it} are white-noise disturbances that may be correlated.

The optimal lag length is chosen by minimising the values of the Akaike Information and Schwartz Bayesian Criteria. In order to gain efficiency through cross equation residuals (that is, by assuming that the multivariate error vector has a non-zero diagonal covariance matrix), Zellner's seemingly unrelated regression is used to obtain estimates of the VAR coefficients (Charemza and Deadman 1992). Taking a VAR model with two lags as an example and looking at equation (2.1), a given variable does not Granger-cause X if and only if all the coefficients of $A_{1j}(L)$ are equal to zero. In the reverse case, X does not Granger-cause the variable if and only if all the coefficients of $A_{j1}(L)$ are equal to zero. Therefore, in a model with two lags, the hypotheses to be tested are

$$H_0: \; a_{1j}(1) \; = \; a_{1j}(2) = \; 0 \qquad\qquad (2.3)$$
$$H_0: \; a_{j1}(1) \; = \; a_{j1}(2) = \; 0 \qquad\qquad (2.4)$$

where in equation (2.2), $a_{1j}(i)$ are the coefficients of the given variable in the first equation and $a_{j1}(i)$ are the coefficients of X in the jth equation in the VAR model of the first equation.

  Similarly, the above models were estimated for employment and labour productivity links between the sectors. The annual data used covers the period 1970–2005 on GDP and number of workers employed for agriculture, manufacturing and services obtained from the Department of Statistics, Malaysia. All variables are in constant 1987 prices and the natural logarithm of the variables is used. The empirical results are tabulated in Table 2.4. A p-value of less than 0.05 means that the null hypothesis (that the right-hand-side variable does not Granger-cause the left-hand-side variable) is not accepted at the 5 per cent level of significance.

  With GDP growth, there is a bidirectional causal relationship between the aggregate economy and both the manufacturing and services sector. This reflects the important contribution that these sectors make to the economy, and when the economy grows, an expansion in these two sectors take place. Although there is also a two-way relationship between the manufacturing and the services sectors, the causality from the services to the manufacturing sector is weaker, given by the 10 per cent level of significance.

Table 2.4   Causality results

Causality direction	Real GDP growth	Employment growth	Labour productivity growth
Agri → Agg	0.122	0.153	0.279
Manu → Agg	0.036	0.031	0.003
Serv → Agg	0.024	0.027	0.052
Agg → Agri	0.026	0.264	0.173
Agg → Manu	0.043	0.037	0.226
Agg → Serv	0.051	0.001	0.016
Agri → Manu	0.109	0.093	0.359
Manu → Agri	0.057	0.174	0.142
Agri → Serv	0.364	0.234	0.205
Serv → Agri	0.592	0.273	0.397
Manu → Serv	0.016	0.122	0.004
Serv → Manu	0.089	0.151	0.228

Note: A → B refers to the null hypothesis that A does not Granger-cause B. The above results report *p*-values based on the χ^2 statistic.

Although the manufacturing sector was initially labour-intensive, over time it has moved up the value added chain beyond processing and assembly to incorporating various services, including services for promoting brands, designs, patents, research and development, franchising, marketing and warehousing and integrated logistics. Towards this end, fiscal and other incentives have been extended to cover the service industries, resulting in an increase in the services content of the manufacturing sector. This is what Bhagwati (1984) called the 'splintering effect' where services grow due to increased production of manufactured goods. Also, with increasing specialisation, or technological progress allowing for standardisation of services or relatively lower transactions costs, industrial firms may choose to contract out their 'in-house' services, thereby increasing the link from the manufacturing to the services sector.

But services sector growth also influenced growth in the manufacturing sector albeit at a less significant level. Bhagwati (1984) explains this as the 'disembodiment effect' where goods splinter off from services, for instance, due to a technical revolution in information and communication technology. This results in products that include distributive trades (wholesale and retail of machinery, equipment and supplies), renting of office machinery and equipment including computers, telecommunications (telephone services, broadcasting, internet service provider and paging services) and computer-related activities (comprising hardware and software consultancy, data processing, database activities, maintenance and repair of computers). Other examples include R&D activities that could result in the improvement in manufacturing technology and thus an increase in industrial output. Or when banks provide low borrowing rates, there is an incentive for manufacturers to borrow and produce more. The existence of trading companies and their worldwide network can be seen to encourage greater exports of manufactured goods as producers now increasingly rely on such middlemen (who have specific knowledge) to conduct their trade for them.

These examples suggest that causality from services to the manufacturing sector is likely to take place in the later stages of an economy's development. It can thus be seen that this relationship is weaker than the causality from the manufacturing to the services sector in Malaysia. Also, services such as public administration, law and order, education and health are often independent of the growth in the manufacturing sector.

Although both manufacturing and service sectors will continue to be the twin engines of growth, any government policy biased towards either sector should not be a major concern due to these two-way causality effects. As long as one sector grows, the other sector will also grow. Thus, Malaysia's Vision 2020 commitment to retaining a manufacturing base of at least a quarter of GDP or to ensure a growth rate of 8.3 per cent for the manufacturing sector is in no way worrying. In effect, the emphasis on nurturing either sector or an expansion of one sector at the expense of the other would only matter for short-run growth.

With employment growth, the links are less clear between the manufacturing and services sectors[5] but this could be due to part-time employment especially prevalent in the services sector that may mask the significance of the relationship. On the other hand, employment growth in the aggregate economy has a two-way relationship with the manufacturing and services sectors. Not surprisingly, the small amount of employment in the agricultural sector was not influenced by or found to influence employment in the aggregate economy or the other two sectors. With labour productivity growth, there is unidirectional causality from the manufacturing to the services sector, and bidirectional causality between the manufacturing sector and the aggregate economy.

Now let us focus on the agricultural sector which is to be revitalised since 2006 under the ninth MP as the third engine of growth. The Plan emphasises large-scale commercial farming, the wider application of modern technology, production of high quality and value added products, unlocking the potential in biotechnology, increased convergence with ICT, and the participation of entrepreneurial farmers and skilled labour to boost agricultural productivity. Table 2.4 shows that output growth in this sector does not significantly lead to economic growth although the agricultural sector was the most important contributor to GDP until 1987. But the causality results show that the agricultural sector does stimulate some growth in the manufacturing sector and this would be the case when agricultural products such as rubber, timber and oil palm are processed. In terms of employment and labour productivity growth, the agricultural sector neither affects nor is affected by growth in the economy or in any other sector. While the hollowing out of the agricultural sector is a natural occurrence in a rapidly developing economy like Malaysia, this sector has nevertheless gained attention of late. In fact, after the financial crisis of 1997/98, there has been a renewed call for the sunset agricultural sector, in particular for the oil palm and domestic food production, to expand (National Economic Recovery Plan 1998).

2.6 THE RENEWED ROLE OF THE AGRICULTURAL SECTOR

Heavy reliance on the manufacturing sector as well as services such as banking and financial services increases the vulnerability to external shocks given the level of integration of the Malaysian economy in the global world. This was seen during the 1985 world recession, the early 1990s slump in the electronics market, and the 1997/98 financial crisis.[6] Thus Malaysia recognised the need to cushion the economy by exploiting her unique position of having a comparative advantage in the primary sector under the ninth MP. The development of the primary commodities sector was first given a boost not only by the existence of natural resources but also by the NEP in 1970 to achieve the twin objectives of eradicating poverty and restructuring the society as many of the poor were living in the rural areas where the primary sector activities were concentrated.

The re-engineering of traditional agriculture is to be one of the main policy planks of the Malaysian government as outlined in the Prime Minister's 2005 budget speech. The government's allocation for developing agriculture in 2006–10 has almost doubled to RM12 500 million from 2001–05. While real agricultural GDP growth per annum during 2001–2005 was 3 per cent higher than the 2 per cent target of the eighth MP, the target for 2006–10 has been set at 5 per cent per annum.

The agricultural sector is made up of crops such as oil palm, cocoa, pepper pineapple, paddy, sugar cane and coconut as well as industrial crops like tobacco, and others like forestry and timber (such as sawlogs and plywood) and minerals (tin, copper, bauxite and iron ore). This sector (excluding petroleum and gas) accounted for about 34 per cent of GDP in 1970 but its share has progressively declined to less than 10 per cent in 2003. The export earnings from the agricultural sector made up 44 per cent of total export receipts in 1982, and in 2003, this was only 14 per cent of total export revenue. The exports of major agricultural products in particular declined from 55 per cent in 1970 to 9 per cent by 1995. The decline in the price of some of the major commodities such as palm oil, rubber, cocoa and minerals subjected the commodity exports to international price fluctuations. This was partly the reason for the rapid move towards industrialisation in Malaysia.

Among the industrial commodities, initially, there was heavy dependence on tin and rubber. Rubber was the most important crop, with Malaysia being the largest producer since 1965, but from the early 1990s it has become second to Indonesia. Malaysia's share of global rubber production has decreased from 43 per cent in 1970 to 8.2 per cent in 2003. Of late, there has been increasing demand for natural rubber, particularly from China, and higher production has been possible with increased tapping and the adoption of the low intensity tapping system among smallholders. The participation of Malaysia in international commodity agreements such as the International Tin Agreement and the International Natural Rubber Agreement since 1997 has been beneficial in providing price stability in these two commodities.

Attention is focused on the production of higher value added products in the area of speciality graded rubber types which fetch a premium in the market and greater effort is being ensured to create a niche in the up-market sector. There is also continued production of other rubber products such as tubes, latex goods (condoms, gloves, catheters, foam products), general and industrial rubber goods, and footwear. Malaysia's well-diversified natural rubber market covers more than 80 destinations with no single country accounting for more than 15 per cent of its total export. The domestically produced national car of Proton since the mid 1980s has certainly created a large market for rubber tyres.

In a move to diversify production away from rubber and tin, palm oil production took precedence and production grew from 0.43 million tonnes in 1970 to 14.96 million tonnes in 2005. Government intervention was however crucial for much of its successful development. For instance, the imposition of higher duties on exports of crude palm oil in the mid 1970s stimulated massive investments in refining capacity. Intense competition, specialisation, and excess refining capacity soon resulted in rapid technical progress, taking Malaysian palm oil refining to the world technological frontier in barely a decade (Gopal 1999). In the 1980s, palm oil ranked third as a major foreign exchange earner after petroleum and forest products, but since 2000 it has overtaken forestry products to be the second largest foreign earner bringing in RM19 billion in 2005. Malaysia's world share of palm oil production has also more than doubled in this period from 21 per cent in 1970. While emerging and expanding markets such as China and India indicate strong external demand, Malaysia has also to contend with competition from soya bean oil and other oils and fats as alternatives to palm oil in addition to expanding production in Indonesia.

Since 1990, land for palm oil production has become scarce in the Peninsular, and cultivation is being concentrated in Sabah and Sarawak. In 2001, the government launched an attractive oil palm replanting package and large areas of aging palms in Malaysia have been replanted since then. More importantly, there has been a conscious move to set up palm oil-based industries to increase value added from this sector. In 2005, the commercialisation of palm oil-based biofuel at the global level took off and this looks favourable as an alternative in the environment of high energy prices, instability in the Middle East, increased demand by rapidly expanding countries such as India and China, the significance of the Kyoto Protocol, and the depletion of fossil fuels.[7] The Biodiesel Bill launched in late 2006 is necessary for a well-placed legal framework in order to attract FDI in this area. The government has made it mandatory that at least 5 per cent biodiesel is blended into diesel sold at all petrol stations. This move would enable Malaysia to save up to 500 000 tonnes of biodiesel imports (*The Sun* 1 May 2006). Biodiesel can also be produced from yet another hardy crop in Malaysia, *Jetropha Curcus*, which is a European Union-compliant feedstock for biodiesel production.

After the success in producing diesel from palm oil, and vitamin products from palm kernel, the oil palm industry has entered a new phase of using palm oil trunks which were formerly considered a waste product if they are not used as compost. Now, zero waste can be achieved as the trunks can be used in the making of laminated veneer lumber to produce various products including furniture and partition walls. This is a new alternative for plywood and these products have already made inroads in the Japanese market in June 2004. If trunks were processed and marketed widely, a conservative income estimate of RM2.5 billion a year could be generated.[8]

Furthermore, the harvesting cycle for oil palm is much faster than traditional timber or logs from forest estates. Oil palm trunks will play an important role in the timber, construction and furniture industries in future because of the depleting supply of rubber wood as well as other species of timber in Malaysia and other parts of the world. In addition, the government is concentrating on downstream production such as oleochemical products (detergents, cosmetics and personal care products) and palm kernel as well as higher value-added production such as lubricants.

In the other areas of non-food applications, oil palm products such as production of pulp and paper from oil palm fronds, production of blockboard from oil palm lumber, and the utilisation of oil palm empty fruit bunches for the production of roof tiles have also been undertaken. In food uses, various shortening and margarine blends have been formulated for local refiners. Thus some success is seen in line with the country's efforts to promote resource-based industries under the IMP2 where increased R&D efforts targeted the use of palm oil as substitute raw materials for consumer end-products.

Next to palm oil and rubber, cocoa is the third most important crop and Malaysia is the fourth largest producer after Côte d'Ivoire, Brazil and Ghana. The development of the cocoa industry was accelerated by the low commodity prices of natural rubber and palm oil in the late 1960s and early 1970s as well as the high prices of cocoa in the second half of the 1970s. But the relatively lower prices since the 1990s have led to its rapid decline in production. Land hectarage for the planting of cocoa tress nationwide had dwindled considerably from 393 000 ha in 1990 to 45 000 ha in 2005. In 2004, cocoa imports stood at more than RM1 million and this is a heavy import bill for a country capable of producing cocoa. To revive the industry, the government has agreed to provide a 100 per cent grant for cocoa farmers by allocating RM85 million (see *The New Straits Times* 5 Feb 2005). Continuous efforts are being taken to improve the quality of cocoa beans from fermenting and drying of wet beans, handling and storage, and grading for export or domestic use.

The production and export of pepper has placed Malaysia in the fourth position in the world. Although market conditions for pepper have not been encouraging, the Minimum Export Price Scheme established by other large producers such as Indonesia, India and Brazil has helped to some extent. The need to increase the level of processing and upgrade the quality of pepper by the appropriate technology and investment in equipment has been identified.

The other two smaller industries are the pineapple and tobacco industries. The former industry is largely export-oriented and the latter industry, which is heavily regulated, has been important for government revenue in the form of import and excise duties. In general, the cultivation of these crops has been possible due to good soil and favourable climatic conditions in Malaysia. However it is becoming increasingly difficult to maximise this potential in the face of competition from other countries.

The timber industry, on the other hand, exports logs, sawntimber, plywood, wooden frames and wooden furniture. The Malaysian Timber Council continues to organise activities such as seminars and technology study missions to support efforts in management and manufacturing technology in timber production. With effect from 8 June 2005, the government has banned the export of rubber wood sawn timber to alleviate the supply shortage in the country as well as to intensify the downstream value added activities of the wood-based industry such as engineered solid or hardwood flooring, windows and doors.

While fishing constituted 12.4 per cent of agricultural output, forestry and logging contributed 14 per cent in 2004. To further develop the fishing sector, the government has introduced specific measures for coastal, deep-sea fishing (more permits and training for fishermen) and aquaculture. In particular, venture capital funds totalling RM300 million have been set aside by Bank Negara in 2006 to create and develop an integrated agricultural business as well as for technical and business support. The targeted areas for investment are integrated farming and fisheries as well as agro-based ventures.

2.6.1 Challenges Faced by the Agricultural Sector

One concern is the third agricultural policy's (for 1998–2010) objective of reducing imports and being self-sufficient in food by 2010. The current lack of a strong comparative advantage in agriculture would mean the denial of trade benefits. It is best to purchase lower-value food stuff with fewer resources than it would take to produce them under self-sufficiency. This is a case of resource misallocation and would lower national income. The self-sufficiency objective is clearly a political one with little economic sense.

The second objective of the agricultural policy is to increase productivity for two reasons. The first reason is to increase rural incomes to reduce poverty. The second reason is, future agricultural output expansion is limited with the current land and labour shortage and any increase in output will have to emanate from productivity increases. This is however constrained by the uneconomic size of the smallholdings and crop farms stemming from land fragmentation and customary practices which impose a barrier to commercialisation and technological upgrading possibilities.

In this regard, the government's push to modernise agriculture includes greater commercial orientation, wider adoption of new technologies and modern management systems, and greater participation by the private sector. In fact, 43 per cent of the development expenditure on agriculture was spent on modernising agriculture over 2001–05 but many private companies regard the agricultural sector as high risk, and to combat these perceptions the 2005 government's budget included incentives such as a 100 per cent deduction on capital expenditure on machinery and equipment, pioneer status or investment tax allowance for five years, reinvestment allowance for 15 years and a 100 per cent tax exemption for food production. A sum of RM300 million has also been set aside for commercial seed capital for the private sector and government-linked companies. However, there is concern that these incentives have come too late and in too little a form to be successful.

Malaysia needs to continue to increase the value added in the agricultural sector by further developing and processing agricultural produce.[9] This will help strengthen the links between the agricultural and manufacturing sector by creating greater employment and output opportunities. As commodities and their related products are substantially produced for the export market, it is also important that the range of products produced and the market base be broadened. Thus efforts to develop new products for the new and emerging markets, while maintaining and improving existing ones, need to be intensified. These aspects will set the pace for the accelerated development of agro-industrialisation which is a balanced industrialisation-cum-agricultural development whereby agriculture needs to be linked to other sectors with an outward looking strategy for agriculture. Agro-industrialisation involves the interrelated activities of production, processing, transport, storage, financing, marketing and distribution of specific agricultural produce. To spearhead agro-industrial development one has to enhance agribusiness development and rural development through socio-economically empowered participants in an environment of favourable community needs to be pursued.

The contribution of agro-based industries to GDP is on average about 6.5 per cent over 2000–05 while that of agriculture's contribution is 8.5 per cent. But the average annual growth of the former was 4.5 per cent and the latter was 3 per cent over this period. In terms of exports, both categories make up about 7 per cent of total export earnings in 2005 although the real value added per worker is about 1.2 times higher for the agro-based industries. Thus the prospects offered by the agro-based industries should not be ignored.

To strengthen the marketing and global networking in the agricultural sector with better access to market information such as prices, logistic services, inventory management, credit, training and skills development, as well as to conduct trading on line between farmers, producers, retailers and exporters, the Supply and Demand Virtual Information System and electronic trade mechanisms need to be expanded. The internet system of Agribazaar is one good initiative of the government in this regard.

One challenge faced by the agricultural sector is however is its ageing labour force, with about 31 per cent of them in the age group of 55 years and above (Department of Statistics 2005). The younger age group is less involved in the sector as they believe that the agricultural sector provides unfavourable returns to ensure a better future. Furthermore, there is strong competition from high labour demands in the manufacturing sector, and currently foreign workers make up about 10 per cent of those employed in this sector. In addition, the size of land uses is small, uneconomical, and there is uncertainty about land status such as Temporary Own Land where land can be turned into other purposes such as housing and industrialisation (ibid.). Furthermore, 25 per cent of the agricultural workers had no education whatsoever while the majority of 45.6 per cent only had primary education and less than 1 per cent had tertiary education. This has implications for the use and adoption of modern techniques and high technology. Also, the continued import of unskilled workers to meet labour shortage discourages the move into higher value added agricultural production. As at July 2004, 25 per cent of the foreign workers were absorbed by agriculture (*Economic Report 2004/05*). The demand for such labour has led to an increasing trend in illegal unskilled workers and this is discussed in Chapter 4.

One way of securing sustained growth in the agricultural sector is to ensure more diversification, particularly in large-scale food production. Here, the government has identified eight priority sectors in agriculture for development – food manufacturing, fruit cultivation, livestock rearing, fish breeding, agro-based small and medium-scale business, cottage industries, handicraft and aquaculture.

With the exception of large palm oil and rubber plantations, most of Malaysia's agricultural industry remains small-scale with few opportunities at present to take advantage of economies of scale production. It is estimated that smallholders with an average land area of only 1.2 hectares currently contribute 70 per cent of food production (Australian Government 2005). A budget of RM1.5 billion has been allocated to benefit smallholders for 2006. It is also important that the smallholders engage in mixed cropping as opposed to monocropping in an attempt to diversify their risks. Land consolidation and rehabilitation through the group farming concept will be continued on a larger scale to accelerate the modernisation of smallholdings to increase productivity according to the ninth MP.

In a concerted effort to increase investment in large-scale agricultural and commercial activities, RM$10 million has been set aside for the development and promotion of halal products for studies in business planning, technology, market development and improving quality. This is to help intensify the establishment of Malaysia as a regional centre for the production of food and halal products. The global market for halal food is increasingly lucrative and the potential market for such products is estimated in the range of US350–400 billion (RM1330–RM1520 billion) per year based on the world Muslim population of about 1.8 million. Malaysia is well placed to capitalise on being a global hub for the halal food industry, given its credible standing as a progressive, moderate and dynamic Muslim nation. Furthermore, at the end of June 2004, an agreement containing preferential tariff concessions among 23 participants of the Organisation of Islamic Members was signed, thereby paving the path for more exports to these countries.

Halal food production is relatively small as reflected by the GDP value added manufactured food products (including edible oils and beverage) at RM10 876 million or 2.8 per cent of nominal GDP in 2003. However, halal food production zones have been identified and a special course for skills of halal accreditation has been developed and run by the Malacca Industrial Skills Development Centre since 2004. More generally, large-scale commercial production of food is being undertaken through the establishment of Permanent Food Production Parks and Aquaculture Industrial Zones in various states. The parks are aimed at creating entrepreneur farmers with a minimum income of RM3000 per month. So far, 28 such parks have been established involving 319 entrepreneur farmers and 2007 hectares of land (ninth MP). In addition, the need for a second rural development transformation comprising the restructure of villages to be compatible with both agriculture and modern industry has been identified by the 2003 Package of New Strategies. For this, an allocation of RM300 million has been set aside to improve the infrastructure and delivery system in rural areas aimed at stimulating rural economic activities. In the short to medium term, plantation activities in idle land in Peninsular Malaysia and new openings of agricultural land in East Malaysia are to be continued.

Another plan to boost the value added in the agricultural sector is to come from the use of biotechnology to support bio-processes in agro industries. In fact, the bulk of the largest government R&D grant scheme went into agriculture with an allocation that was three times that provided for manufacturing over 1996–2000. During 1996–2000, the agro industry alone received 25.6 per cent of the total amount of grants but for 2001–2005, this industry only obtained 11.4 per cent of the grants while manufacturing and construction took the bulk of 42.9 per cent (see various Malaysian Plans). There are, however, foreseeable problems in getting adequate human resource into agro research (Ministry of Agriculture 1999). The undergraduate curricula at the universities will need to be of greater breadth and diversity to provide requirements at the scientific and technological level.

So far, Malaysia has successfully applied agriculture biotechnology (agrobio) in practical genetic engineering works to improve food crops,[10] fish breeding as well as meat production and quality (Economic Report 2005/06). Research and development in agrobio has led to the development and commercialisation of products and processes such as vitamin E from palm oil, animal recombinant vaccines, new varieties and hybrids of horticulture crops, detection of virus in shrimps, and antifungal extracts from sea cucumbers. During 2001–05, of the 535 R&D projects that were undertaken by the agricultural research agencies, 90 have been commercialised while another 30 are ready to be commercialised. In 2004, it was announced that three new research institutions will be established in Biovalley, with one focusing on improving agricultural yields. Other fields such as herbal-based pharmaceuticals and treatment of tropical diseases will also be explored under biotechnology.

Malaysia's untapped rich biodiversity also offers commercialisation potential by biotechnology. There are plans to focus on the enhancement of the commercial value of the country's forest plants, medicinal plants and fragrance trees (ibid.). This can be done by welcoming strategic and international alliances in research and bio-prospecting activities. It is however noteworthy that the Malaysian Agricultural and Research Development Institute has been quite successful in its various inventions over time, and they won 2 gold, 1 silver and 2 bronze medals in the 2006 International Exhibition of Invention, as well as the New Techniques and Products Competition in Geneva.

It is undeniable that structural changes in the economy have brought about new issues and challenges which affect the continued performance of the agricultural sector, particularly those related to labour shortage (due to migration to urban areas), competing land use, increasing cost of production as well as enhanced competition in the regional and global markets resulting from trade liberalisation and globalisation. In order to remain competitive, it is imperative that these issues and challenges be addressed through the timely formulation and implementation of appropriate policies and programmes as well as by ensuring the optimal use of the country's limited resources for agricultural development.

Attention should continue to be given to foster closer co-operation and links with producing and consuming countries through bilateral, regional and multilateral arrangements. The government's role is not only crucial to deal with trade negotiations to expand and secure markets, but also in the pace that it adopts in liberalising some of its agricultural industries. For instance, the government imposed a tax of 40 per cent on rice imports as a pre-emptive measure to protect the local rice industry in December 2004 but this will be gradually reduced to 30 per cent in 2007, and 20 per cent in 2010 to comply with the AFTA scheme.[11] The price and grade control of rice laid out in 1992 is also to be reviewed with the aim of deregulating the industry (Ministry of Agriculture 1999).

On the global front, post-Doha negotiations held in late 2004 saw Malaysia continuing to insist on substantial reduction in high tariffs that pose a barrier to palm oil exports in a number of markets. As a member of the Cairns Group, Malaysia also supported the interest in seeing reductions in domestic and export subsidies in agricultural products, particularly those provided by the EU and the USA, that distort the global market and pose unfair competition.

2.7 CONCLUSION

During the process of industrialisation, neglecting the agricultural sector can constrain the development process (International Labour Office 2004) and this is especially the case for resource-rich countries. Studies on Malaysia such as Jenkins and Lai (1989) and Rahman (1998) have pointed out that industrial trade, taxation and pricing policies since the late 1950s have accorded a greater level of protection to the non-agricultural sector *vis-à-vis* the agricultural sector and hence discriminated against the latter. On the other hand, studies such as Rock (2002) show that selective interventions to stabilise the rice price and growth of agriculture more generally contributed to manufacturing growth in Malaysia, and Reinhardt (2000) provides evidence of the important role that resource-based products played in Malaysia's export-led growth development.

Unlike many countries, Malaysia is unique as it has quite successfully gone ahead with industrialisation without totally ignoring the agricultural sector. While industrialisation by way of expansion into manufacturing and services will continue to provide fast growth, the speed of growth is less important than the character of that growth for long-run development prospects, and here agriculture offers much promise. Given the proven competitiveness, heritage and long history of agricultural research and production, there have been learning-by-doing gains over time and it will be irrational not to capitalise on that by further developing this sector.

The policy thrust for agriculture should therefore take on a two-pronged approach in its diversification efforts. Horizontal diversification should focus on the promotion and expanded production of industrial crops, apart from food crops, horticulture, livestock and aquaculture. Presently, the unbalanced output mix in favour of industrial crops for agriculture is risky particularly in the event of sharp fluctuations in commodity prices. Vertical diversification should involve the production of high value added agro-based products to help move up the technology ladder within agriculture. The link with other sectors in the economy must be strengthened to benefit from possible spillover effects such as in agrotourism or the use of IT in the set up of a one-stop centralised and electronically linked database to support decision making, business development, marketing activities, advice on production and mechanisation, training programmes etc. for primary producers.

To ensure maximum benefits from the agricultural sector's diversification strategy, the necessary legal, economic and institutional provisions must be well coordinated to enable effective implementation. The proliferation of agriculture and rural development institutions at the state and federal levels since the 1960s has resulted in the duplication of functions which render some of the efforts inefficient and ineffective (Siwar and Rahman 1999) and the natural resources industry has been acknowledged to be over-regulated (Ministry of Agriculture 1999). While a substantial number of these institutions have been revamped and are continuously being restructured, efforts in this consolidation process are somewhat slow and are likely to impede the advancement of the agricultural sector.

In conclusion, for successful structural transformation of the economy, the first macro policy challenge is to find the right balance in fostering the development process in agriculture, manufacturing and services. The second policy challenge is to devise specific and appropriate ways and means to best develop each sector.

NOTES

[1] In 1957, the Federation of Malaya was formed with 11 states in the Malay Peninsula, and in 1963, Malaysia was formed by the Federation of Malaya, Sabah, Sarawak and Singapore. However, in 1965, Singapore became independent of the Federation.
[2] This refers to the production of computer peripherals, integrated circuits, semiconductor devices, printed circuit boards, audio and video equipment, opto-electronics, flexible manufactures, information and communication. Malaysia is currently the world's fifth largest exporter of semiconductors.
[3] This consists of commerce, transportation and communication, real estate, financial and business services as well as community, social and personal services including government.
[4] This procedure is to detect if there is a cointegrating relationship between a selected number of variables in a multivariate setting.
[5] The significance levels are around 12 per cent and 15 per cent.
[6] The implication of the bidirectional causality relationship between manufacturing and services established earlier is that the adverse effects experienced by any one sector will result in negative consequences for the other sector.
[7] The National Biofuel Policy was formulated in 2005 to provide guidelines on biofuel usage for all related sectors, particularly transportation, petroleum companies and palm oil industries.
[8] This was announced by the Forest Research Institute Malaysia's director-general, Datuk Dr Abdul Razak Mohamad (*The Sun* 1 May 2006).

[9] The Universiti Putra Malaysia is to be transformed into a centre of excellence for agriculture education and set the stage to develop Malaysia into a centre for processing, packaging and marketing of agricultural products for global markets.

[10] This includes regenerating and mass propagating plantlets for pineapple, banana and papaya for commercial farming.

[11] See *The Edge* 10 January 2005.

3. Understanding the Drivers of Output Growth

Productivity isn't everything, but in the long run it is almost everything. (Paul Krugman 1990)

3.1 INTRODUCTION

To attain the status of a full-fledged industrial nation under the Vision 2020, Malaysia has set itself an annual GDP growth target of 7.5 per cent through the year 2020. The figure below shows how far Malaysia has come since 1970 but, more importantly, how far it still has to go. Economic growth over the past three decades has been substantial to ensure per capita income is larger than the ASEAN3 but insufficient to reach those levels of Australia and Singapore.

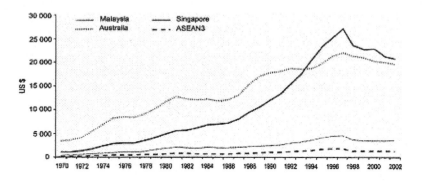

Note: ASEAN3 is the average of Indonesia, Philippines and Thailand.

Source: World Bank, *World Development Indicators 2003*.

Figure 3.1   Per capita gross national income

One reason for performing below the target growth rate is the economy's low TFP growth. Based on the premise that input growth is unable

30

to sustain output growth due to diminishing returns to factor use over time, TFP growth is the key to long-run GDP growth. In addition, the Second Industrial Master Plan 1996–2005 emphasises the need for a shift in the national development strategy, from one that used to be input-driven towards one that is productivity-driven. In light of this, it is imperative to discuss the productivity growth performance of the aggregate economy, and the manufacturing sector which is one of the key engines of growth. Unfortunately, due to poor data, a similar analysis on the agriculture and the services sectors was not undertaken.

This chapter on productivity is divided into two main parts analysing the productivity growth of the aggregate economy and the manufacturing sector. The first section reviews the main studies done on Malaysian TFP growth. The second section provides empirical evidence on labour productivity and TFP growth, the latter is measured by the parametric and non-parametric measures for robustness. The relationship between productivity growth and output also allows for a check on Verdoon's law. Lastly, the decomposition of output growth into input growth and TFP growth provides some understanding of how well the economy is performing.

The second part of the chapter focuses on the manufacturing sector. First, a stochastic production frontier model is estimated using a panel data set of Malaysia's 26 three-digit manufacturing industries from 1970 to 2002, drawn from the UNIDO. This is used to revisit the perspiration versus inspiration debate based on empirical evidence. In addition, TFP growth is decomposed into technological progress and technical efficiency in order to investigate the determinants of each of these aspects of productivity growth. This allows the dynamic relationship between the sources of TFP growth to be studied so as to highlight the importance of two crucial aspects of policy making – the importance of weighing the trade-off in the effects of policy, and the consequent need for coherent policy coordination, both of which have been overlooked in the literature. More specifically, it is shown how the failure of current policies to take explicit account of the interrelationship between the sources of TFP growth have major repercussions on the long-term objective of achieving optimal and sustainable economic growth.

3.2   A SURVEY OF TFP GROWTH STUDIES ON MALAYSIA

Table 3.1 shows a summary of the main TFP growth studies undertaken on Malaysia so far. As one would expect, the TFP growth estimates are wide ranging due to the use of different data and time periods as well as differences in methodology and models specified. Although TFP growth estimates varied widely among the studies, in general, these studies showed that Malaysia's

TFP growth is low and output growth is input-driven for both the aggregate economy and the manufacturing sector.

Table 3.1   *TFP growth estimates for Malaysia (%)*

Source	Time period	Aggregate economy	Manufac-turing sector	Agriculture sector
Abdullah (1997)	1980–90			1.37
Arnade (1998)	1961–93			1.51
Coelli and Rao (2005)	1980–2000			0.4
Collins and Bosworth (1996)	1960–73 1973–84 1984–94	1.0 0.4 1.4		
Fare and Grosskopf (2001)	1975–90 1975–96	−0.64 0.92		
Jamal and Mansor (2001)	1960–96			0.74
National Productivity Corporation of Malaysia	1980–89 1990–96 1998–2003	−0.82 0.34 0.4	2.79 1.6 3.3	−1.86 −1.33
Othman and Jusoh (2001)	1960–96			0.29
Gan and Soon (1996)	1974–78 1979–83 1984–89 1990–95	2.0 0.5 1.6 2.2		
Kawai (1994)	1970–80 1980–90	2.5 0.7		
Mahadevan (2002b)	1981–84 1986–90 1990–96		−0.82[a] 0.40[b] −0.57 0.35 −1.54 0.26	

Table 3.1 (continued)

Source	Time period	Aggregate economy	Manufac- turing sector	Agriculture sector
EPU (1996, 2006)	1971–90	1.2		
	1991–95	2.5		
	1996–2000	1.1		
	2001–05	1.3		
Nehru and Dhareshwar (1994)	1960–90	0.96[c] 0.09[d]		
Oguchi et al. (2002)	1992–96		0.95	
Okamoto (1994)	1982–85		−1.9	
	1986–90		0.3	
Sarel (1997)	1978–96	2.0		
Tham (1995)	1971–75	−1.42		
	1976–80	0.26		
	1981–87	−2.68		
Tham (1996)	1986–93		0.1	
The World Bank (1989)	1975–79		3.8	
	1981–84		−1.9	
The World Bank (1993)	1960–89	1.1		
The World Bank (2005)	1960–80	0.5		
	1980–2000	1.5		
	1980–97		−0.01	

Notes: [a] Using the stochastic frontier method.
[b] Using the data envelopment analysis method.
[c] Using the full sample of 87 countries.
[d] Using a sample of high-income countries.

To date, there are two types of studies on the productivity growth of Malaysia.[1] One is based on inter-country comparisons either using a large sample of developed and developing countries considered together, or a smaller sample of Asian countries. The World Bank (1993) study clearly shows that using different sample of countries would give different TFP growth results. As echoed by Solow (1994), these international cross-section regressions 'seem altogether too vulnerable to bias ... and above all to the recurrent suspicion that the experiences of very different national economies are not to be explained as they represented different "points" on some well-defined surface'.

In general, TFP growth of the aggregate economy is low. As can be seen, most of the studies used economy-wide data and thus the results have very broad implications for each of the sectors of the economy. Since the economy is a weighted sum of the agricultural, manufacturing and services sectors, any shift in labour from a less productive sector to a more productive sector would result in an increase in overall TFP growth without any real change in TFP growth rates of either sector. This is especially important for Malaysia which has had a substantial change in the composition of its economy with falling shares of GDP of the agricultural sector, and rising shares of the manufacturing and services sector.

The second type of productivity growth studies are intertemporal in nature and concentrate on the Malaysian economy using time series data. There are quite a few studies on the manufacturing sector which have used a wide range of estimation techniques.

To date, Ibrahim (1997a) is the only attempt to discuss patterns and variations in state manufacturing TFP growth. Using data from 1985 to 1992 on 13 Malaysian states and the Federal Territory of Kuala Lumpur, he found that TFP growth was input-driven and the leader of the pack was, unsurprisingly, Kuala Lumpur which had about 30 per cent higher TFP growth than the state of Selangor. While Melaka was found to do quite well initially, it lost its comparative advantage. Kedah and Sarawak, on the other hand, exhibited a catching-up pattern. However, there is little indication of convergence in the productivity performance of the Malaysian states, but given the limited span such inferences are inappropriate as only eight observations points were used to calculate the Tornqvist TFP growth index.

For the agricultural sector, data is rather sparse. Here too, the TFP growth estimates have generally been found to be low and land input as the largest contributor to output growth. Using a multicountry study, Coelli and Rao (2005) draw data from the Food and Agriculture Organization of the United Nations and show that all of the TFP growth was due to the use of better machinery or embodied technology and not due to technical efficiency. This figure was way below the average agricultural TFP growth of 1.9 per cent for Asia. Othman and Jusoh (2001), using data they collected from various secondary sources (but it is not clear what these are), show that TFP growth for the agriculture sector was negative for 1960–70 but has been positive and rising since then and is highest at 1.59 per cent for 1991–96.

With services, Okuda and Hashimoto (2004) and Katib and Matthews (1999) have studied the Malaysian banking sector. The first study finds a lack of economies of scope and technological progress in the banks but there was a difference in production technology between large-sized banks and small or medium-sized banks. The second study uses a panel of 20 commercial banks from 1989 to 1995 to show that average technical efficiency ranged from 68 per cent to 80 per cent and that technical inefficiency was attributed to scale inefficiency.

3.3 PRODUCTIVITY GROWTH PERFORMANCE OF THE AGGREGATE ECONOMY

Labour productivity as a partial measure only considers the use of a single input and ignores all other inputs, thereby causing misleading analyses. Thus this measure does not measure overall changes in productive capacity since it is affected by changes in the composition of inputs. For instance, improvements in labour productivity could be due to capital substitution or changes in scale economies, both of which may be unrelated to the more efficient use of labour. Or if a reduction in labour caused production bottlenecks or new capital was not utilized efficiently or intensively enough to pay its way, a labour productivity measure will show an increase even though overall efficiency declined.

Unlike the partial measure, the TFP measure considers the joint use of the production inputs and mitigates the impact of factor substitution and scale economies. But if there are important biases in the estimates of capital stock used to construct measures of TFP growth, then it is better to rely on measures of labour productivity.

Here, we compute labour productivity and TFP growth rates to enable a comparison for analysis. Value added output is used instead of gross output as data on intermediate inputs such as material costs are not available for the aggregate economy. Thus labour productivity is measured by value added GDP per worker employed. TFP growth is measured by the Tornqvist method because it is easy to compute (requiring only two data points) and allows the input shares to vary over time. To ensure robustness of the computed TFP values, both the parametric average response production function and the non-parametric Tornqvist index are used. The parametric estimation is an econometric estimation of a specific model and since it is based on the statistical properties of the error terms, it allows testing of the parameters and validation of the model.

Here, the constant returns to scale production technology underlying the Cobb–Douglas production function is chosen over the more flexible translog form which allows for varying returns to scale, for four reasons. One is that the time series data available is restricted and hence not well suited to estimate the many parameters underlying the translog production function. Second, to enable the comparison of the parametric TFP growth estimates with those from the non-parametric Tornqvist approach which is based on the constant returns to scale technology. The third reason as pointed out by Mundlak (1988) is that the Cobb–Douglas production function is a good approximation to a situation of heterogenous technology where secondary data (as is the case here) is used. Lastly, Caves and Barton (1990) and Berndt and Christensen (1973) have shown that the translog function need not be well-behaved for every possible combination of inputs and output need not increase monotonically with all inputs, and isoquants need not be convex everywhere. While methods exist for the imposition of the appropriate theoretical curvature conditions (see Diewert and Wales 1987), these are not necessarily straightforward and have their own limitations for interpretation.

3.3.1   The Tornqvist TFP Growth Measure

Consider the following Cobb–Douglas production function in natural logarithm

$$Ln\ Q = Ln\ T + w\ Ln\ L + r\ Ln\ K \tag{3.1}$$

where
  Q is real value added GDP;
  L and K are inputs of labour and capital;
  w and r ($= 1 - w$) are the shares of value added received by each factor;
  T transforms combined inputs of L and K into value added.

The Tornqvist TFP growth is then taken as

$$Ln\ (T_1/T_0) = Ln\ (Q_1/Q_0) - w\ Ln\ (L_1/L_0) - r\ Ln\ (K_1/K_0) \tag{3.2}$$

That is, TFP is calculated as a residual after subtracting from GDP growth an estimate of the amount by which GDP would have grown had inputs been transformed into value added. Factor shares are taken as the average of the share in each year. For example, $w = 0.5\ (w_0 + w_1)$. Further manipulation of the above equation would enable one to see that TFP growth equals the weighted average of the growth of output per unit of labour and output per unit of capital inputs. The growth formulae used are:

GDP growth: $Ln\ (Q_1/Q_0)$

Input growth: $0.5\ (w_0 + w_1)\ Ln\ (L_1/L_0) + 0.5\ [(1 - w_0) + (1 - w_1)]$
                   $Ln\ (K_1/K_0)$

TFP growth: GDP growth – Input growth   (3.3)

This gives a set of logarithmic growth rates which are then converted to reflect the actual growth rates.

3.3.2   TFP Growth Measure from the Average Production Function

The following is the production function to be estimated for the aggregate economy.

$$Ln\ Y = a + b\ Ln\ K + c\ Ln\ L \tag{3.4}$$

where
  Y = valued added output;
  K = capital used;
  L = labour employed;
  b is capital share; and
  c is labour share.

As the Cobb–Douglas production function has constant returns to scale technology, it is expected that $b + c = 1$. Similar to the Tornqvist method, TFP growth is then calculated as the residual output growth after input growth is netted out. That is,

$$\text{TFP Growth} = Ln\ Y - \hat{a} - \hat{b}\ Ln\ K - \hat{c}\ Ln\ L \tag{3.5}$$

3.3.3 Data Sources and Issues

The TFP growth calculations require data on value added GDP, labour, capital and wages and these were obtained from the Department of Statistics, Malaysia. All variables are in constant 1987 prices and natural logarithm is used.

Labour is measured by number of workers employed as data on hours worked is limited. In accordance to the empirical literature, capital service which is a flow concept is assumed to be proportional to the capital stock which is then depreciated. Data on capital for the aggregate economy is given by gross fixed capital formation and due to lack of data on breakdown of capital types, aggregate physical capital stock is calculated. In particular, initial capital stock for 1970 is computed by a multiple $(1/(g + d))$ of the gross fixed capital formation in 1970, where g is the long-run average growth rate of gross fixed capital formation in the first 15 years and d is the depreciation rate. Then using the conventional perpetual inventory method with a depreciation rate of 6 per cent,[2] the capital stock series was generated as

$$K_t = (1 - d)\ K_{t-1} + E_{t-1} \tag{3.6}$$

where E is the gross fixed capital formation since data on gross new investment is unavailable.

With the Tornqvist method, the share of labour is defined as the ratio of the employee compensation to GDP. These data are available from the *National Accounts Statistics* published by the Department of Statistics, where compensation represents payments of wages and salaries to their employees, pension fund, and family allowances.

3.3.4　Empirical Results

Table 3.2 shows labour productivity growth and both the parametric and non-parametric TFP growth rates for the aggregate economy over time.

Typically, labour productivity growth moves in the same direction (in terms of an increase or decrease) as TFP growth. Labour productivity growth is higher than that of TFP growth reflecting the positive influence of capital deepening. However, there is no clear trend in all of the growth rates from 1970 to 2005. Although TFP growth was positive in the decade of the 1990s this was low, and more importantly, the situation since then has worsened. The non-parametric TFP growth values are seen to be much lower than that obtained with the parametric method.

Table 3.2　Annual average productivity growth (%)

	Labour productivity	Parametric TFP growth	Non-parametric TFP growth
1971–79	4.38	0.02	−0.15
1980–89	2.66	−0.55	−0.68
1990–99	3.78	0.41	0.28
2000–05	1.32	−0.61	−0.75

3.3.5　Verdoon's Law

One hypothesis put forward in the literature is that a positive relation exists between productivity change and the rate of growth of output. Expressed in terms of labour productivity, this relation has been called Verdoon's law after P.J. Verdoon, who suggested it in 1949. Output growth can lead to higher productivity growth because it allows economies of scale to be exploited especially through trade, leading to a decrease in average cost. It was found that the correlation coefficient between GDP growth and labour productivity growth was 0.91 and that between GDP growth and TFP growth was 0.87. Thus, both productivity measures support Verdoon's law.

3.4　DECOMPOSITION OF AGGREGATE OUTPUT GROWTH

There are two TFP measures obtained from the Tornqvist method (non-parametric approach) and the average response production function (parametric approach). The average capital share of the former approach was 0.54 and that of the latter approach was 0.44 with a value 1.21 for the intercept term. While Maddison (1987) finds that historically, capital's share in the major industrial countries cluster around 0.3, Englander and Gurney

(1994) provide higher estimates. Dowling and Summers (1998) explain that for developing countries, the capital share is expected to be higher than in industrial countries, possibly over 0.4. Lastly, the diagnostics tests under the parametric estimation did not reveal any serious problems of functional misspecification or heteroscedasticity but the estimation was corrected for autocorrelation using the Cochrane-Orcutt procedure.

Table 3.3 shows the two main sources of output growth under the various approaches. There does not seem to be any major difference in the input growth or the contribution of inputs to output growth in the two approaches. It can be seen that the Malaysian economy is very much input-driven and capital input in particular is the driving force of output growth.

Table 3.3   Decomposition of aggregate output growth

	Output growth	Input growth				TFP growth	
		Non-parametric		Para-metric		Non-parametric	Para-metric
		K	L	K	L		
1971–79	8.02	6.11	2.06	5.87	2.13	−0.15	0.02
1980–89	5.66	4.68	1.66	4.49	1.72	−0.68	−0.55
1990–99	6.87	4.82	1.77	4.63	1.83	0.28	0.41
2000–05	5.14	3.55	2.34	3.19	2.56	−0.75	−0.61

Table 3.4   Contribution of factors of production (%)

	1971–90	1991–2000	1991–95 6th MP	1996–2000 7th MP	2001–05 8th MP	2006–10 9th MP (Target)
GDP growth	6.7	7.0	9.5	4.8	4.2	6.0
Labour	2.4 (36.1)	1.7 (24.3)	2.3 (23.9)	1.5 (30.8)	1.5 (33.2)	1.8 (29.9)
Capital	3.4 (50.9)	3.5 (50.2)	4.7 (50.2)	2.2 (45.2)	1.7 (37.8)	2.0 (34.3)
TFP	0.9 (13.0)	1.8 (25.5)	2.5 (25.9)	1.1 (24.0)	1.3 (29.0)	2.2 (35.8)

Notes: Figures in parenthesis are contribution to GDP in percentage. The above computations are done by the Economic Planning Unit based on the Cobb–Douglas production function.

Source: EPU (2001a, 2001b, 2003, 2006).

The computed results are compared to those under the various Malaysian Plans in Table 3.4. The Plans show that, overall, TFP growth improved from 1971 to 1995 and after a fall in the late 1990s, contributed by the financial crisis, it has increased slightly in the early 2000s unlike the above results. The contribution of TFP growth to output growth is the highest in 2001–05 and this is expected to grow in the next five years as seen by the targets set.

3.4.1 Limitations of Models Used

Problems arise when researchers take the models too literally. Thus, it is important to discuss the drawbacks underlying the models used in order to allow careful interpretation. First, the rigid assumption of constant returns to scale technology may have resulted in an underestimation of the TFP growth rate as any increasing returns to scale is discarded. Second, the way the capital stock is calculated is subject to lumpiness and may cause bias in the estimation of TFP. With the depreciation rate, it is often different for different assets but such data are not available and depreciation rates are assumed not to change over time, all of which add to inaccuracies in TFP growth computation.

Third, as capital input is not used with a constant intensity over time, it should be adjusted for capital utilisation since the use of capital is subject to cyclical factors such as in a recession or boom. To the extent that capital utilisation is overstated (or neglected to be controlled for), the measure of productive capital stock will be overstated and hence the residual TFP will be understated. When the economy moves into an upswing, output growth leads capital and labour growth as excess capacity and slackness are taken up.

Some claim that in the long run, cyclical fluctuations in the flow of services average out and one can take the ratio of the capital service flow to the capital stock to be constant and this allows the use of the perpetual inventory equation to measure capital services. In addition, effects of procyclicality on TFP growth has been raised under Verdoon's law although Sarel (1997) argues that procyclicality should not matter much over a long period such as 18 years but can be important over shorter periods such as over 5 years.

Lastly, due to data limitations, quality adjustments for labour are not considered in terms of skill level, educational qualification, age,[3] and sex distribution. If labour quality has risen as one would expect over time, the computed labour contribution will be lower than it would be otherwise. This raises TFP growth. Furthermore, with labour input, the common way is to use number of hours worked or number of workers employed. Often, the former is preferred to the latter as it accounts more accurately for part- and full-time employees in terms of actual hours worked. However, even total number of hours worked is not a satisfactory measure if a mix of skilled and unskilled workers is employed. Hours of work contributed by highly skilled workers generally contribute more to production than hours by unskilled workers.

3.5 CONCLUSION

Productivity as a possible source of economic growth is the central focus of this chapter and we sought to delineate the stylised facts at a fairly aggregate level. The determinants/sources of TFP growth are not examined here as diverging trends at a more disaggregated level may emerge thus making broad policy prescriptions at the aggregate level inaccurate.

The above exercise shows that Malaysian output growth is highly input-driven and a conservative estimate of average TFP growth over 1971–2004 is 0.03 per cent. Capital deepening in particular is the driving force and it can be expected to contribute to output growth possibly for the next decade at the very least as Malaysia's capital stock levels are significantly lower than the industialised economies and there is proof that NIEs such as Singapore and South Korea are still able to get mileage out of capital deepening.

In general, Malaysia's economic growth in the short run can be sustained provided there is sufficient external and domestic demand for its goods and services. The emphasis on TFP growth was seen in 1996 and due recognition must be given to some of the Malaysian governments efforts to raise the contribution of TFP growth to output growth. But the question as to whether enough is being done to generate significant gains still remains. Will the capital deepening benefits run out before the efforts to raise TFP growth bear fruit? This depends on how well Malaysia leapfrogs to sustain the growth momentum from this medium-term strategy. These questions present a myriad of different challenges to the Malaysian economy in balancing the costs and deliberate efforts to keep the economy from running out of steam.

3.6 THE MANUFACTURING SECTOR'S PRODUCTIVITY GROWTH

This part of the chapter focuses on the manufacturing sector. There have been quite a few studies on the manufacturing sector's productivity growth as reported in Table 3.1. As expected, results vary, but the general consensus from studies apart from the National Productivity Corporation is that TFP growth has been low and has not exceeded 1 per cent since the mid 1980s.

The possibility of the emergence of empirical regularities as more empirical work is done with different methods on the same data such as Mahadevan (2002b) should, however, not be ruled out completely. Useful perspectives can be considered with the competing models as being complementary. Different models provide different insights and the usefulness of a specific model will depend on the context and the question being asked. Different answers have no reason to give special priority in discriminating between the models or in assessing the overall impact of a parameter change. No one measure of TFP growth from either model should be taken to represent 'the right' value, given the advantages and disadvantages of the approaches to productivity measurement. Instead, if policy formulation is often the ultimate objective in productivity analysis, the trends in TFP growth should be of greater interest and considered far more reliable than the magnitude of TFP growth per se.

Here, similar to Ibrahim (1997b)[4] and the World Bank (1997), a stochastic production frontier model is estimated but it is an improvement over these studies as the latter suffer from the assumptions that production frontier shifts are necessary parallel; the technical efficiency error structure follows a distributional specification not justified by economic theory but based on statistical grounds; and technical efficiency varies at the same constant rate over time. Mahadevan's (2002b) model on the other hand relaxes all these assumptions using 3-digit industry level data from 1981 to 1996 to estimate not only technical efficiency estimates but also technical progress and TFP growth.[5]

The model here is a further improvement as it extends Mahadevan's study to 2002 (which is the most recent available at the time of computation) and is the first attempt to use the UNIDO database.[6] Second, heterogeneity in the manufacturing industries by the estimation of industry-specific input shares is allowed for. Third, instead of the value added output measure, the gross output measure is used. Often, TFP growth from the value added measure is greater than that of the gross output measure due to the upward bias created by the omission of intermediate goods such as raw and semi-finished materials, subassemblies, energy, and purchased services. If the growth rates of value added output and gross output differed greatly, this would magnify the TFP growth distortion even more. The gross output measure explicitly considers and measures the contribution of intermediate inputs which is an important component in Malaysian manufacturing.[7]

3.7 STRUCTURAL CHANGES IN THE MANUFACTURING SECTOR

The Malaysian manufacturing sector has undergone significant structural changes since the 1970s. Table 3.5 shows some summary statistics on the manufacturing sector.

The gross output shares indicate that the electrical and non-electrical machinery are important contributors and they have the highest share of intermediate inputs. These are in part due to the large presence of FDI in these industries since the mid 1980s. In particular, these industries are respon-

Table 3.5   Characteristics of Malaysian manufacturing industries (averaged over 1972–2002)

Industries	Average shares in total manufacturing (%)		RM$'000
	Gross Output	Intermediate inputs	Fixed capital assets per worker
Food products	4.89	7.17	45.76
Beverages	1.15	0.41	112.00
Tobacco	1.63	0.57	64.87
Textiles	3.07	1.01	80.82
Wearing apparel except footwear	0.32	0.05	13.97
Leather products	0.29	0.07	15.87
Footwear	0.35	2.65	24.09
Wood products except furniture	3.98	1.41	39.40
Furniture	2.02	1.29	6.62
Paper	3.65	0.81	113.98
Printing and publishing	3.11	3.79	62.17
Industrial chemicals	4.89	2.89	569.04
Other chemicals	3.06	7.47	125.69
Petroleum refineries and products of petroleum and coal	5.23	3.47	1339.86
Rubber products	5.16	2.32	36.24
Plastic products	2.35	2.66	34.46
Pottery, china and earthenware	0.58	0.08	23.96
Glass products	1.95	0.59	149.96
Non-metallic mineral products	4.36	2.87	124.47
Iron and steel	2.68	2.85	152.26
Non-ferrous metal	1.36	1.54	98.72
Fabricated metal products	5.69	2.35	36.03
Machinery except electrical	7.52	14.98	30.09
Electrical machinery	22.12	31.39	44.93
Transport equipment	4.35	6.06	57.18
Professional and scientific equipment	2.0	1.26	11.11

Source: Computed from UNIDO dataset.

sible for the production of semiconductors, integrated circuits, consumer electronics and electrical appliances. The highly capital-intensive industries are seen to comprise the petroleum refineries, industrial chemicals, and iron and steel. In the 1970s and 1980s, through the Heavy Industry Corporation Malaysia, the government ventured into a significant number of large-scale projects in these industries in a move to reduce dependency on foreign companies and in the hope this would promote backward and forward linkages in the economy. But this industrial policy was not successful and was discarded by the late 1980s.

The current industrial policy since the mid 1990s has been to attract FDI to industrial clusters set up in order to foster industrial linkages and competition in areas such as ICT. Since 2004, there has also been a deliberate attempt to establish biotechnology and nanotechnology as new engines of growth.

3.8 ESTIMATION OF THE PRODUCTION FRONTIER

This section sets out the models, data sources, and presents the estimations from the production frontier model.

3.8.1 The Stochastic Production Frontier Model

The frontier concept initiated by Farrell (1957) emphasises the idea of maximality which it embodies, and represents the 'best practice' technology. The frontier estimates a relationship that provides a benchmark of a most efficient industry. The generalised version of the random coefficient frontier model (Kalirajan and Shand 1994) can be written as:

$$Ln\ Y_{it} = \gamma_{1i} + \sum_{j=1}^{n} \gamma_{ij}\ Ln\ X_{ijt} \tag{3.7}$$

where
   i represents number of industries;
   j represents number of inputs used;
   t represents time period;
   Y = output;
   X = inputs;

   γ_{1i} = intercept term of the ith industry; and

   γ_{ij} = actual response of output to the method of application of the jth input used by the ith industry.

Since intercepts and slope coefficients can vary across industries, we can write:

$$\gamma_{ij} = \bar{\gamma}_j + u_{ij}$$

$$\gamma_{1i} = \bar{\gamma}_1 + v_{1i} \tag{3.8}$$

where

$\bar{\gamma}_j$ is the mean response coefficient of output with respect to the jth input;

u_{ij} and v_{1i} are random disturbance terms; and

$E(\gamma_{ij}) = \bar{\gamma}_j$, $E(u_{ij}) = 0$, $Var(u_{ij}) = \sigma_{uit}$ for $j = t$ and zero otherwise.

Combining equations (1) and (2):

$$Ln\, Y_{it} = \bar{\gamma}_1 + \sum_{j=1}^{k} \bar{\gamma}_j\, Ln\, X_{ijt} + \sum_{j=1}^{n} u_{ij}\, Ln\, X_{ijt} + v_{1i} \tag{3.9}$$

Following Aitken's generalised least squares method suggested by Hildreth and Houck (1968) and the estimation procedure by Griffiths (1972), the industry input-specific response coefficient estimates of the above model can be obtained. The highest magnitude of each response coefficient and intercept form the frontier coefficients of the potential production function. If γ^* are the parameter estimates of the frontier production, then, $\gamma_j^* = \max\{\gamma_{ij}\}$ where $i = 1, ..., n$ and $j = 1, ..., k$. The potential output of the industry can be realised when the best practice techniques are used and this is given by

$$Ln\, Y_{it}^* = \gamma_1^* + \sum_{j=1}^{k} \gamma_j^*\, Ln \tag{3.10}$$

Based on the above, the model to be estimated is:

$$Ln\, Y = a_0 + a_1 T + (\beta_0 + \sum_{m=1}^{7} \beta_m D_m)\, Ln\, L_{it} + (\alpha_0 + \sum_{m=1}^{7} \alpha_m D_m)\, Ln\, K_{it} +$$

$$(\gamma_0 + \sum_{m=1}^{7} \gamma_m D_m)\, Ln\, M_{it} + u_{it} + v_{it} \tag{3.11}$$

where

Y = Gross output;
T = Time trend;
D_m = Industry slope dummies grouped at the 2–digit industry level;
L = Number of workers employed;
K = Fixed capital expenditure;
M = Intermediate input;
$i = 1, ..., 26$ and $t = 1970, ..., 2002$.

The input shares of the manufacturing industries given by α, β and γ vary with the use of industry slope dummies.[8] The time trend on the other hand captures all variations that affect industries' output over time. The above model is not based on the assumption that Hicks-neutral technology underlies the shifts of the production frontier. The assumption of this particular type of technology is relaxed to allow non-neutral shifts in the production frontier such that the marginal rate of technical substitution at any input combination changes over time. This follows from Kalirajan and Shand's (1994) argument that with the same level of inputs, different levels of output are obtained by following different methods of applications. Furthermore, as this model relies on the generalised least squares estimation technique, it does not require the imposition of an ad hoc assumption on the distribution of technical efficiency which is purely based on the attractiveness of the statistical properties of the assumed distributions without any theoretical justification.

3.8.1   Data Sources and Variables

Data for the 26 3-digit manufacturing industries (see Appendix 3.1) are drawn from the United Nations Industrial Development Organisation database. These include gross output, intermediate inputs, fixed capital assets and workers employed. All data on deflators are obtained from the Department of Statistics, Malaysia. The variables are expressed in constant 1987 prices.

Gross output of all industries was deflated using the manufacturing production index. The intermediate inputs were deflated using the producer price index, and the fixed capital asset was deflated using the gross domestic fixed capital formation deflator. It is acknowledged that these deflators may not necessarily be ideal but the choice was based on the lack of more appropriate deflators.

3.8.2   Empirical Results

Initially, the more general translog model was estimated but as the second order conditions were not found to be significant, the Cobb–Douglas model was considered the better model to fit the data. Tybout (1990) explains that the Cobb–Douglas functional form allows maximum flexibility in dealing with secondary data and is demonstrated to be superior over the translog functional form in the presence of missing data and measurement problems. The coefficients obtained are summarised in Table 3.6.

Dummies for the oil price shocks in 1974 and 1975, 1979 and 1980, as well as the Asian financial crisis in 1997 and 1998 were included in the estimation. These were found to be insignificant and hence dropped from the model. The input shares are not identical across the majority of the industries as seen by the significance of the slope dummies. Intermediate input has the largest input share followed by capital and labour input shares. The null hypothesis that technical inefficiency does not exist is rejected at the 1 per cent level of significance.[9] This indicates the need to model the production behaviour using the stochastic frontier model instead of the Tornqvist index approach.

Table 3.6   Estimates of the stochastic production frontier model

Variables	Parameter	Parameter estimates
Constant	a_0	1.63 (0.891)[*]
Time Trend	a_1	1.07 (0.351)[*]
Labour (Industry 31)	β_0	0.25 (0.087)[*]
Labour (Industry 32)	β_1	−0.0034 (0.0062)[*]
Labour (Industry 33)	β_2	0.0172 (0.0011)[*]
Labour (Industry 34)	β_3	0.0141 (0.0482)
Labour (Industry 35)	β_4	0.0028 (0.0012)[*]
Labour (Industry 36)	β_5	0.0145 (0.0058)[*]
Labour (Industry 37)	β_6	0.0137 (0.0036)[*]
Labour (Industry 38)	β_7	−0.0161 (0.0041)[*]
Capital (Industry 31)	α_0	0.331 (0.0219)[*]
Capital (Industry 32)	α_1	0.0412 (0.0084)[*]
Capital (Industry 33)	α_2	0.0065 (0.0017)[*]
Capital (Industry 34)	α_3	0.0151 (0.0009)[*]
Capital (Industry 35)	α_4	0.0076 (0.0276)
Capital (Industry 36)	α_5	0.0163 (0.0044)[*]
Capital (Industry 37)	α_6	−0.0054 (0.0037)[*]
Capital (Industry 38)	α_7	0.0025 (0.0006)[*]
Intermediate Input (Industry 31)	γ_0	0.39 (0.0413)[*]
Intermediate Input (Industry 32)	γ_1	0.0316 (0.0072)[*]
Intermediate Input (Industry 33)	γ_2	0.0059 (0.0007)[*]
Intermediate Input (Industry 34)	γ_3	0.0048 (0.0021)[*]
Intermediate Input (Industry 35)	γ_4	0.0045 (0.0165)
Intermediate Input (Industry 36)	γ_5	−0.0014 (0.0028)
Intermediate Input (Industry 37)	γ_6	0.0031 (0.0008)[*]
Intermediate Input (Industry 38)	γ_7	0.0025 (0.0006)[*]

Notes: Figures in parenthesis are asymptotic standard errors.
[*] means that the coefficient is significant at the 5% level of significance.

3.9   REVISTING THE PERSPIRATION VS INSPIRATION DEBATE

The 'perspiration versus inspiration' idea was first popularised by Krugman (1994) to describe the situation of the Asian miracle economies' heavy reliance on factor accumulation. This phrase is often interchangeably used with 'accumulation versus assimilation' (Collins and Bosworth 1996). Previous studies (Krugman 1994; Collins and Bosworth 1996; Aswicahyono and Hill 2002) linking these phrases/ideas in productivity growth analysis have used the non-frontier approach in their empirical investigation.[10] This approach only considers outward shifts of the production function to represent TFP growth and the economy is assumed to be operating on the production function. But in reality, most economies are not using resources and technology fully efficiently and thus will be operating somewhere below the production function and increases in output can be obtained by shifting to a more efficient point on the production function. Thus, the inspiration factor of TFP growth should include TP and TE which represent the two types of shifts.

These shifts can be captured using the frontier model adopted here for empirical investigation. Nishimizu and Page (1982) argue that these two components comprising TFP growth are conceptually different and ignoring any one of them could result in policy misdirection. The relationship between perspiration and inspiration is established by empirically investigating the causal links between input growth, TFP growth, TP and TE. This enables the dynamic interrelationship between the sources of output growth to be studied.

Table 3.7   Sources of manufacturing output growth (%)

| Period | Output growth | Relative contribution to input growth | | | TFP growth |
		Capital	Labour	Intermediate inputs	
1971–79	8.29	32	41	27	0.94
1980–89	7.64	36	34	30	1.37
1990–99	9.89	33	28	39	0.88
2000–02	5.76	33	24	43	0.61
1971–2002	7.12	34	29	37	1.01

Note: The above are average annual growth rates.

Using the estimates in Table 3.5 and the framework set out in Mahadevan (2002b), output growth, input growth, TFP growth, TP and gains in TE are calculated for all 26 industries. Tables 3.7 and 3.8 show the results for the manufacturing sector as a whole. This is computed using a weighted approach of the share of each industry's gross output to the total gross output of all the manufacturing industries.

Throughout 1971–2002, factor accumulation (the perspiration factor) is seen to play a major role in contributing at least 80 per cent of the gross output growth in Malaysia's manufacturing sector while TFP growth (the inspiration factor) accounted for less than 20 per cent of output growth. Amongst the inputs, intermediate inputs have seen a steady increase in their share of contribution while labour share has declined and capital share has somewhat stablised contributing to a third of total input growth. Average annual TFP growth hardly exceeded 1.5 per cent although it increased slightly in the decade of 1980 but has decreased since then. Using the non-frontier approach, the World Bank (2005) study too provides similar evidence of annual TFP growth net of improvements in labour quality ranging from 0.5 per cent to about 1 per cent.

Table 3.8   Sources of manufacturing TFP growth (%)

Period	TFP growth	Technical efficiency gains	Technological progress
1971–79	0.94	−0.31	1.25
1980–89	1.37	−0.57	1.94
1990–99	0.88	−0.28	1.16
2000–02	0.61	−0.36	0.97
1971–2002	1.01	−0.40	1.41

Note: The above are average annual growth rates.

Perhaps what is more interesting is the reason for the low and declining trend in TFP growth. Table 3.8 shows that not only has TP been decreasing since 1990 but there have also been losses in TE over time. In other words, although there is technology accumulation, the gains from that shown by the production frontier's outward shifts over time have been decreasing. The situation is worsened by these gains being outweighed by the deteriorating performance in the efficient use of resources and technology.

At the disaggregated level, Table 3.9 shows that there is no discernible pattern in the TFP growth over time except for a general decline in most industries performance since 1990 or mid 1990. The annual average TFP growth over 1971–2002 is very low and does not go beyond 2.5 per cent for any one industry. Industries such as industrial chemicals, electrical machinery, and transport equipment have performed relatively better but the latter two have seen a decline in their TFP growth. The petroleum refineries and coal product industry has had negative TFP growth since 1990 and has been inefficiently using resources and technology by about 50 per cent (see Table 3.10). It is unclear if this is due to the excessive domestic use of energy given Malaysia's natural resource base and her position as a net exporter of energy. The large firms in this industry which are likely to be operating in a less competitive environment may well be comfortable with the profits earned and hence were slack in their performance. The iron and steel industry too is not particularly productive although this industry is vital for providing materials for production.

Table 3.9   Annual average TFP growth measures (%)

	1971–79	1980–89	1990–99	2000–2002	1971–2002
Food products	1.23	1.82	0.76	0.91	1.13
Beverages	0.41	0.81	1.02	0.61	0.53
Tobacco	0.83	1.06	–0.24	–0.15	–0.4
Textiles	0.89	0.76	0.21	0.52	0.51
Wearing apparel	1.08	–0.33	0.82	–0.15	0.67
Leather products	0.77	0.98	–0.64	1.19	0.93
Footwear	0.92	1.12	0.66	0.53	0.78
Wood products	0.69	–1.24	–0.74	0.31	–0.62
Furniture	0.55	–0.81	0.65	–0.22	0.18
Paper	1.28	1.34	0.87	0.68	1.09
Printing and publishing	0.67	2.24	0.74	0.26	1.23
Industrial chemicals	1.98	2.02	2.81	2.61	2.47
Other chemicals	1.39	–1.06	2.41	0.94	1.81
Petroleum refineries and products of petroleum and coal	1.26	2.15	–0.94	–1.41	–0.51
Rubber products	1.78	1.06	0.68	0.14	0.88
Plastic products	0.72	–0.58	1.04	0.86	0.79
Pottery, china and earthenware	–0.43	0.89	0.94	1.11	0.63
Glass products	0.86	0.59	0.31	0.26	0.44
Non-metallic mineral products	–0.82	0.73	–1.08	1.24	–0.55
Iron and steel	0.66	–1.16	0.15	–0.83	–0.71
Non-ferrous metal	0.13	0.77	–1.18	0.29	0.22
Fabricated metal products	0.44	1.26	0.88	–0.38	0.74
Machinery except electrical	0.98	2.19	1.36	1.06	1.67
Electrical machinery	1.93	2.79	1.83	1.11	2.01
Transport equipment	1.06	1.73	1.88	2.56	2.09
Professional and scientific equipment	–0.18	–0.44	2.67	1.82	1.36

Table 3.10   Annual average technical efficiency ratios

	1971– 79	1980– 89	1990– 99	2000– 2002	1971– 2002
Food products	0.73	0.69	0.54	0.41	0.59
Beverages	0.49	0.71	0.34	0.53	0.44
Tobacco	0.61	0.48	0.34	0.33	0.41
Textiles	0.74	0.66	0.71	0.51	0.63
Wearing apparel	0.58	0.71	0.46	0.61	0.59
Leather products	0.73	0.61	0.52	0.68	0.63
Footwear	0.64	0.78	0.62	0.81	0.71
Wood products	0.64	0.67	0.73	0.71	0.69
Furniture	0.79	0.84	0.58	0.78	0.76
Paper	0.44	0.71	0.79	0.73	0.68
Printing and publishing	0.69	0.83	0.58	0.41	0.59
Industrial chemicals	0.59	0.64	0.61	0.63	0.61
Other chemicals	0.76	0.47	0.81	0.52	0.64
Petroleum refineries and products of petroleum and coal	0.81	0.66	0.57	0.51	0.58
Rubber products	0.74	0.84	0.51	0.38	0.49
Plastic products	0.64	0.58	0.66	0.59	0.61
Pottery, china and earthenware	0.78	0.84	0.37	0.44	0.62
Glass products	0.61	0.42	0.53	0.28	0.46
Non-metallic mineral products	0.64	0.81	0.41	0.55	0.59
Iron and steel	0.36	0.71	0.63	0.64	0.54
Non-ferrous metal	0.56	0.39	0.4	0.38	0.43
Fabricated metal products	0.38	0.45	0.86	0.95	0.66
Machinery except electrical	0.88	0.77	0.74	0.64	0.71
Electrical machinery	0.79	0.84	0.66	0.57	0.72
Transport equipment	0.55	0.64	0.84	0.89	0.73
Professional and scientific equipment	0.67	0.59	0.63	0.66	0.64

Table 3.11   Annual average technological progress estimates (%)

	1971– 79	1980– 89	1990– 99	2000– 2002	1971- 2002
Food products	1.03	1.28	1.41	1.36	1.26
Beverages	0.78	0.84	0.65	0.57	0.71
Tobacco	0.86	−0.94	−0.53	0.43	−0.26
Textiles	0.71	0.88	0.93	0.64	0.78
Wearing apparel	0.71	1.07	0.91	0.79	0.86
Leather products	1.12	1.01	1.12	1.03	1.04
Footwear	0.97	1.13	1.04	0.81	0.96
Wood products	0.51	0.13	0.46	−1.31	−0.72
Furniture	0.44	0.51	0.47	0.58	0.36
Paper	1.11	0.99	0.87	0.81	0.96
Printing and publishing	2.13	1.98	1.78	1.63	1.87
Industrial chemicals	3.59	2.01	1.34	0.76	2.03
Other chemicals	2.55	2.13	1.99	1.81	2.12
Petroleum refineries and products of petroleum and coal	−0.48	0.77	−0.84	0.98	−0.31
Rubber products	1.44	1.51	1.13	1.01	1.26
Plastic products	0.86	1.31	0.93	1.27	1.08
Pottery, china and earthenware	0.76	0.88	1.02	0.91	0.88
Glass products	0.66	0.57	0.61	0.44	0.59
Non-metallic mineral products	1.48	1.06	0.74	0.68	1.03
Iron and steel	1.02	0.76	0.64	0.54	0.74
Non-ferrous metal	0.87	0.68	0.41	0.33	0.54
Fabricated metal products	0.72	0.66	0.78	0.59	0.68
Machinery except electrical	4.38	5.26	3.86	1.74	2.88
Electrical machinery	4.28	6.43	3.08	2.44	3.93
Transport equipment	0.78	0.96	1.19	1.31	1.06
Professional and scientific equipment	1.53	1.63	1.56	1.71	1.28

With TE,[11] on average, over the entire period, no manufacturing industry operated at more than 76 per cent of its maximum possible output. Thus, there is huge potential to use inputs and technology more efficiently to produce more output. A majority of the industries experienced a rise in technical inefficiency except for the transport equipment and fabricated metal products industries. The export-oriented industries such as the electrical and non-electrical machinery, and the transport equipment also performed better than the other industries.

On the TP front, Table 3.11 shows that most industries have positive but low gains. The petroleum refineries and products of petroleum and coal industry is the most capital-intensive industry but it experienced negative gains from TP. Such technological regress can be interpreted as the application of relatively labour-intensive technologies which did not show technological improvement. On the other hand, Burnside et al. (1996) explain that if capital utilisation is not corrected for (as is the case here due to lack of data), this may result in technological regress. The star performers in terms of TP are the iron and steel, and electrical and non-electrical machinery industries. In general, it can be observed that the TP estimates are higher than the TFP growth estimates and this shows that declining technical efficiency is a major cause of the low TFP growth. This is true regardless of whether they are light, medium or heavy industries.

3.9.1 Relationship between Perspiration and Inspiration

This section addresses causality links between TFP growth, TP and TE, as well as input growth to enable a link between perspiration and inspiration to be established in an empirical framework to evaluate current policies. In particular, the questions of interest are as follows: Has inspiration in Malaysian manufacturing been adversely affected by perspiration? Can Malaysia afford more perspiration before any form of inspiration takes place? How have current policies favouring perspiration and inspiration fared?

The causality model used here is based on the approach suggested by Toda and Yamamoto (1995) as explained in Chapter 2. To illustrate, we consider the hypothesis that there is a relationship between the growth of the variables of total inputs, TFP, TP and TE. The empirical model for estimation is the following 4-equation VAR model:

$$
\begin{bmatrix} \Delta X_t \\ \Delta TFP_t \\ \Delta TP_t \\ \Delta TE_t \end{bmatrix} = \begin{bmatrix} A_{10} \\ A_{20} \\ A_{30} \\ A_{40} \end{bmatrix} + \begin{bmatrix} A_{11}(L) & A_{12}(L) & A_{13}(L) \\ A_{21}(L) & A_{22}(L) & A_{23}(L) \\ A_{31}(L) & A_{32}(L) & A_{33}(L) \\ A_{41}(L) & A_{42}(L) & A_{43}(L) \end{bmatrix} \times \begin{bmatrix} \Delta X_{t-k} \\ \Delta TFP_{t-k} \\ \Delta TP_{t-k} \\ \Delta TE_{t-k} \end{bmatrix} + \begin{bmatrix} \varepsilon_{1t} \\ \varepsilon_{2t} \\ \varepsilon_{3t} \\ \varepsilon_{4t} \end{bmatrix}
$$

(3.12)

where
X refers to total inputs;
Δ is a difference operator;
k is the optimal number of lags;
A_{i0} are the parameters representing intercept terms;
$A_{ij}(L)$ are the polynomials in the lag operator L; and

ε_{it} are white-noise disturbances that may be correlated.

The unit root results (not shown here to conserve space) indicate that the first differences of the variables are stationary. This gives a maximum order of integration of one. The optimal number of lags chosen by the AIC and SBC was 2, thus a VAR of order 3 was estimated. The causality results in Table 3.12 show the *p*-value underlying the modified Wald test of the Toda and Yamamoto procedure.

Table 3.12   Causality results

Null hypothesis	*P*-value
$\Delta X \rightarrow \Delta TFP$	0.195
$\Delta TFP \rightarrow \Delta X$	0.225
$\Delta X \rightarrow \Delta TP$	0.072**
$\Delta TP \rightarrow \Delta X$	0.246
$\Delta X \rightarrow \Delta TE$	0.038*
$\Delta TE \rightarrow \Delta X$	0.662
$\Delta TP \rightarrow \Delta TE$	0.312
$\Delta TE \rightarrow \Delta TP$	0.514

Notes: $\rightarrow$ means 'does not Granger-cause'.
    * and ** denotes significance at the 5% and 10% level respectively.

It can be seen that input growth and TFP growth do not affect each other, that is, perspiration and inspiration do not appear to be causally related, but when the two types of inspiration given by TP and TE are considered, the results provide some important insights. Factor accumulation is seen to Granger-cause TP albeit at a weak level of significance. Thus, some inspiration is perspiration-driven and this is due to the embodied technology especially in capital and intermediate inputs that enable increases in output when technology is adopted. On average, these inputs in total have a high share of about 74 per cent of total merchandise imports since 1990. This is not surprising as the inflow of FDI into Malaysia is substantial and is second only to Singapore in East Asia. DeLong and Summers (1992) have emphasised the crucial contribution in such inputs generating growth as they provide the main medium through which new technologies are introduced into the production process.

However, factor accumulation has a negative significant impact on TE (although this is not shown in the table as the table reports *p*-value). In other words, when there is factor accumulation, gains from TP are obtained at the expense of TE. The high adoption rate of new technology has not been accompanied by technological mastery in the Malaysian manufacturing sector. The lack of learning-by-doing gains has hampered the exploitation of the full benefits of the adopted technology that is obtained via factor accumulation. There is also no causal relationship between TP and TE.

Interestingly, neither type of inspiration affects factor accumulation. This may seem unusual since with the advancement of technology and efficient use of resources, more inputs can be used to increase output more than proportionally. But in the case of Malaysia, both TP and TE are at very low levels and factor accumulation is already at very high levels. Thus it is not surprising that there is no causal relationship from TP or TE to input growth.

3.10 DETERMINANTS OF MANUFACTURING TFP GROWTH

Previous studies on Malaysia often undertook a regression analysis of possible factors influencing TFP growth as a single measure without recognising that different efficiency components of TFP growth are at play. This would lead to spurious results as policy options intended to improve TFP growth would be badly misdirected given that the concepts of technical change and technical efficiency are analytically different. This is especially important for Malaysia given that TP and gains from TE move in opposite directions. Factors which could help improve TE and TP, and hence TFP growth, are essentially the same. Here, we discuss some key determinants of productivity growth. The choice of factors affecting TP, TE and TFP growth are described in Table 3.13 and this is dictated by the availability of data in the UNIDO dataset.

Table 3.13   Inter-industry determinants of total factor productivity growth

Variable	Symbol	Description
Capital–labour ratio	K/L	Stock of physical capital per unit of person employed.
Female worker efficiency	FEMALE	Ratio of the number of female employees to total number of employees.
Number of firms	FIRMNO	Number of firms in industry.
Foreign ownership	FOREIGN	Share of foreign capital assets in total fixed capital assets.

The capital–labour (K/L) ratio is a measure of capital intensity of the industry and to some extent reflects technology intensity[12] as well. It is expected that an increase in this ratio would have a positive effect on TP if the capital equipment is technologically advanced. A positive effect on TE can also be expected if this results in the better use of inputs to produce more output. It is hypothesised that industries with higher capital intensities are likely to use resources more efficiently because they cannot afford the rental cost of unused capital and thus have the incentive to economise on the cost of capital. However, there is also the possibility that if the cost of capital becomes relatively cheap due to subsidised credit at low interest rates, then industries may accumulate more capital than is required and underutilise it, thereby lowering TE.

A high proportion of female workers in the work place is reflective of a low level of skill amongst workers (Booth et al. 2003; Magnani 2003) and this is more so in the manufacturing sector. Due to family commitments or lack of opportunity for females to upgrade themselves, this ratio is expected to adversely affect TE and is unlikely to affect TP as the less skilled female workers are unable to be involved in product innovation and equipment modification. More skilled workers or better educated workers raise TE as these workers contribute effectively to the acquisition and combination of productive resources and they are more receptive to new approaches to production and management. A World Bank (2005) study notes that the shortage of skills is one of the top three concerns of manufacturing firms in its survey. It has been reported that large manufacturing industries would see an increase in sales averaging at 11 per cent if skill shortages can be overcome.

The number of firms in an industry is a proxy for the industrial concentration in the industry. The larger the number of firms the lower the market power but their effect on TP and TE is unclear. In the standard industrial organisation paradigm, a high concentration ratio is expected to diminish competitive rivalry among industries with the likelihood of underutilising the production capacity of resources. But some reason that a high concentration ratio brings about sufficient greater innovation (and hence TP) to offset the adverse effects of high concentration, and that concentrated industries suffer less uncertainty of demand than other firms and can plan better for higher utilisation of productive capacities.

The foreign ownership variable is measured by the ratio of foreign-owned to total fixed assets. Dunning (1988) explains that FDI often stems from ownership advantages like specific knowledge of the use of resources due to R&D experience and/or exposure to international competition. Thus FDI can be expected to have a positive effect on TE as well as TP as the import of more advanced technology embodied in capital often accompanies FDI. However, there is mixed empirical evidence of the impact of foreign ownership on the host country.

The equations for TFP, TP and gains in TE as dependent variables are estimated in semi-logarithms with only the independent variables (except for the FOREIGN variable which is a dummy) being logged. The estimation results are summarised in Table 3.14. Although a battery of diagnostics tests did not reveal problems of misspecification, heteroscedasticity and autocorrelation, as expected, the $\overline{R}^2$ of the equations ranging from 0.6 to 0.68 are not high (but reasonable for the number of variables considered), reflecting the need for more determinants to be included in the equation.

Table 3.14   Regression results on TFP growth and its sources

Variable	TP	Gains in TE	TFP growth
Constant	1.42 *	1.67 *	0.98 *
	(0.512)	(0.648)	(0.44)
K/L	0.12 *	−0.36 **	0.26
	(0.014)	(0.212)	(0.167)
FEMALE	0.28	−0.084*	− 0.059**
	(0.191)	(0.041)	(0.031)
FIRMNO	− 0.17	− 0.451**	− 0.192
	(0.108)	(0.266)	(0.128)
FOREIGN	0.33 *	0.062	0.418**
	(0.08)	(0.042)	(0.224)

*Notes :*Figures in parenthesis are standard errors.
* and * * indicates that the estimated coefficient is significant at the 5% and 10% level of significance respectively.

The K/L ratio is seen to affect TP positively. It is possible that industries with high capital intensities have more incentive to use the best technology available or to invest in heavy capital that embodies technology. However, this ratio has a negative (although not strong since it is significant only at the 10 per cent level) impact on TE. There are two possible reasons for this. First, the speed of transformation in industries with newly adopted capital-intensive technology may have brought sufficiently high profits to weaken the incentive for industries to use the new technology efficiently. Also, in order to qualify for various incentives from the government, many industries could have accumulated capital which they did not have sufficient knowledge to use efficiently.

Second, labour as well as skill deepening did not match the rate of capital deepening. Shortage of labour has been a problem in Malaysia since the early 1990s, and by 2000 the manufacturing sector had the largest share of foreign workers but 67 per cent of them had no formal or primary education (Ministry of Finance 2004/05). Furthermore, in 1975, while 2.5 per cent of the labour force had tertiary education, this proportion only increased to about 17 per cent in 2003 (Department of Statistics). This is low compared with other NIEs, Japan and the USA. The FEMALE variable suggests a similar point in that a large proportion of females employed, means a generally low level of skill, which then adversely affects TE.

The empirical results also show that foreign ownership has a positive impact on TP as foreign-owned companies have the resources to invest in high technology capital and are able to enjoy the benefits of R&D undertaken in their home country. Using firm-level data, the World Bank (2005) found that partially or fully foreign-owned firms showed higher TFP than local firms.[13] However, foreign ownership has no apparent impact on TE. This stems from the lack of skilled workers employed and the poor competition from local firms (Noor et al. 2002). Similar results on the weak impact of FDI on TFP growth were found by Menon (1998) and Oguchi et al. (2002).

Lastly, market power as measured by the number of firms in an industry does not affect TP but improves TE. It can be said that such firms have an incentive to provide training to workers so as to ensure technology and inputs are used efficiently as the resulting benefit in the form of lower cost is a competitive advantage that is worthwhile as these firms cater to a significant market share.

With the regression results on TFP growth, there is no effect from the K/L ratio as the separate and opposing impacts of capital deepening on TP and TE counteract one another. Although the effect of FEMALE and FIRMNO on TE is negative and significant, the overall effect of these variables on TFP growth is weakened by the non-impact of these variables on TP. The same is true of the effect of foreign ownership on TFP growth but with the signs reversed. Similar factors are seen to have different effects on TP and TE as the two concepts are conceptually different and the overall effect on TFP growth is determined by the strength of these impacts on TP and TE. Studies that regress factors on TFP growth as a single entity miss out on understanding these dynamics underlying policy effects on TFP growth.

3.11   MAKING POLICY WORK

The different and sometimes opposing impacts of various factors on TP and TE make policy prescription problematic. For instance, should the Malaysian government continue providing incentives in the form of tax deductions related to capital expenditure? Should there be more aggressive wooing of FDI? Being aware of the trade-offs in the consequences of these actions on TP and TE is a first step towards finding a solution to such policy-making conundrums. The next step is to ensure policy coherence so that implemented policies do not pull in different directions and at the very least do not undermine the attainment of the two (in this case) or more objectives it involves. This requires careful coordination of policies so that they work hand in hand to provide maximum benefits.

For the Malaysian manufacturing sector, maximising TP at the expense of improving technical efficiency or vice versa is not an optimal strategy.

Tables 3.9 to 3.11 make it quite clear that TP has slowed in many industries while technical inefficiency has been rising, and the result has been low and even negative TFP growth. Furthermore, TP can be expected to continue to decline in the long run, because the scope for obtaining newer and more advanced technology becomes more limited as Malaysia itself moves closer to international best practice in a range of industries.

This is not to say, for example, that capital deepening embodying new technology should not be encouraged because it raises TP. Rather, the form this takes in providing increasing rates of return should be the focus. One solution is for Malaysia to concentrate on higher value added manufacturing operations at the top end of the technology ladder. Evidence from Narayanan and Wah (2000), and Noor et al. (2002) suggest there is continued involvement in assembly-line production and medium-level value added manufacturing activities in the electronics and electrical sector which is the driving force in the manufacturing sector. Thus, incentives provided need to be sufficiently strong to encourage both local and foreign producers in upgrading to higher value added production.

While the Malaysian government has attempted to do this with the establishment of the Multimedia Super Corridor in 1996, various technology parks since 1990 and the BioValley in 2004, these industrial clusters have yet to show success (Jussawalla and Taylor 2003; Wahab 2003). In fact, there is concern that leapfrogging into these areas without sufficient learning-by-doing gains can bring more harm than benefit in the long run in spite of the short-run advantages Malaysia would enjoy as a later-comer in this field. This represents a slack in policy coherence as the mechanisms to support the transformation to the high valued added activities are not sufficiently in place.

One such support stems from the level of R&D undertaken within an economy which is reflective of the absorptive capacity of the economy. With increasing R&D expenditure, the availability of better technology or modifying existing technology in the long run is a good possibility. But research intensity, as measured by the share of R&D expenditure in GDP, has increased rather slowly from 0.37 per cent in 1992 to 0.65 per cent in 2002. The targets set by the National Plan of Action of 1990 of 1.5 per cent in 1995 and 2 per cent in 2000 proved to be unrealistic and have been revised downwards, with the 1995 target of 1.5 per cent by 2010. Thus, Malaysia is still in its infancy stage of building its R&D capacity. Not only are India and China's ratios of 0.78 per cent and 1.09 per cent respectively in 2001 higher, but Malaysia does not come anywhere near that of the first-tier newly industrialising countries' average of at least 2.4 per cent in 2002 (MASTIC 2004).

Another example of poor policy coherence is seen in the slow pace of the improvements in the quantity and quality of the labour force. It has been argued earlier that capital deepening must be accompanied by sufficient labour and skill deepening to allow a more effective adaptation and application of new technology. But the increase in education expenditure as a percentage of GDP has not been rapid in Malaysia, the 1980–99 average being only 5.4 per cent compared with an average of 5.3 per cent in the 1970s. At 6.6 per cent, the figure for 2000–03 does show some improvement but more remains to be done. The 2010 target to have 35 per cent of the workforce with tertiary level education is still below the levels already achieved in 2003 by developed countries such as Japan (36 per cent), the United States (41 per cent), Ireland (43 per cent) and Finland (36 per cent).[14]

Lack of training is another problem yet to be addressed by appropriate policy even though industrial training accounts for the bulk of the government's development allocation for training, and this allocation has increased from $RM580 million in 1991–95 to $RM3760 million in 2001–05. Tan and Gill (2000) report that public training institutes continue to play a relatively minor role in meeting the in-service training needs of private firms since their focus is on pre-employment training. Tan and Gill also find that only one fifth of the manufacturing firms in their extensive survey provide formal training while half the firms rely on informal training. Neither are private firms enthusiastic about providing training even with the help of a matching grant from the government established in 1992. Official statistics indicate that, in 2002, only 56 per cent of the Human Resources Development Fund set aside for this purpose has been utilised (Ministry of Human Resources Annual Report 2004).

Recognising the lack of domestic skills, the Malaysian government must be given credit for its short- and medium- term efforts to improve the quantity and quality of the labour force as seen in its foreign worker policy and brain gain initiatives at the same time. Unfortunately, even in these attempts, there is a lack of policy coherence. For instance, Pillai (1995) describes Malaysia's foreign labour policy as having 'many twists and turns', and after 1991 it possessed a 'stop–go' quality. This was attributed to various unpredictable changes reflecting a reaction to short-term needs and comprising frequent changes in foreign worker levy and the application of different criteria of employment in different sectors. The share of unskilled workers among foreign workers has always been more than 90 per cent and this does not augur well for the upgrade to higher value added manufacturing activities.

With regard to attracting skilled foreign labour, the government must also coordinate policies to stem brain drain and implement 'brain gain' initiatives. While there are no official data on out-migration available,[15] Pillai (1995) estimates that at least 40 000 Malaysians or on average 5 000 per year migrated to Australia, New Zealand, Canada and the US between 1983 and 1990. To encourage Malaysians to return home, since 2001 there have been exemptions from income tax, duty-free import of motorcars and possessions from abroad, and the granting of permanent resident status to spouses and children. By September 2001, 356 applications were received from professionals working overseas (Economic Report 2001/02) and as of 2004, the programme has granted approvals to 246 Malaysian experts overseas. The need to re-examine the efficiency of Malaysia's 'brain gain' initiatives and to develop a compelling value proposition to attract, develop and retain talented Malaysians both within and outside the country has recently been recognised by the Malaysian government.[16]

Lastly, the policy variable that affects TP but not TE is FDI. Most FDI in Malaysia is export-oriented and although FDI brings in better technology, it does not necessarily ensure that the technology and the inputs are efficiently used. Thus the government needs to be selective about the type of FDI Malaysia is attracting for three reasons. First, to sustain TP, FDI must be in higher value added activities as well as be encouraged to undertake R&D in Malaysia. In this regard, important lessons can be learnt from Singapore which has successfully provided the environment for its MNCs to be involved in product and process innovation domestically (Amsden et al. 2001). This requires policy coherence in ensuring that appropriate infrastructure and a ready pool of R&D personnel are available.

Second, there must be some form of formal agreement that foreign owned firms provide training to their locally employed workers where necessary. While this would inevitably discourage FDI given the competition from other economies without such an imposition, in the long run this loss of such FDI might be small price to pay. Third, government must take on greater efforts to benefit from spillover FDI effects by encouraging and providing strong incentives for MNCs to foster backward and forward linkages with local firms. This will improve the productivity growth of domestic firms as well. Narayanan and Wah (2000) note that uncoordinated approaches and limited absorptive capacity of the economy may have undermined potential spillover effects from FDI.

3.12 CONCLUSION

The need for coherent policy coordination both in the micro (in this case, the manufacturing sector) and macro context (the related general government policies) has been discussed to highlight the complexity of policy making. For maximum and sustainable TFP growth, appropriate policies must be implemented to ensure that the adoption of better technology also brings technological mastery in the form of improved technical efficiency. But policy prescription is not made easy as capital deepening and foreign ownership are found to increase technological progress but decrease technical efficiency, while greater market power does not promote the former but positively affects the latter.

Hence capital deepening must be accompanied by increases in the quality and quantity of the workforce and improvements in these areas must move in tandem. Human capital investment (related to both education and training) and technology development policies need to be aligned to productivity growth needs. This requires a reassessment of a whole range of factors – foreign worker policies, provision of hard and soft infrastructure as well as incentives conducive for higher levels of R&D in the private sector, training incentives to continuously upgrade workers, 'brain gain' initiatives, and selective FDI policies based on high valued added activities and potential to foster backward and forward linkages with the local firms.

There is also a need for business accelerator programmes to foster entrepreneurship as it is not possible to keep relying on foreign talent if the domestic sector's participation remains limited, as this will adversely affect the building of its own technological capabilities. Current industrial policy to spearhead the economy by leapfrogging into biotechnology and information and communication technologies without having a strong base of local talent and support may only bring productivity growth in the short run. Such rapid structural transformation will bring technological progress but does not allow sufficient learning-by-doing gains for long-term benefits. The current situation of 'too little too late' must be addressed soon or unsustainable productivity growth will become a permanent feature of the Malaysian economy.

Although necessary, policy coherence is not sufficient for sustained productivity growth. Effective mechanisms for monitoring and evaluation must also be in place for lessons to be learnt and practice to be continually improved in the light of new information, changing circumstances and feedback on their impacts. This requires transparency and accountability on the part of the Malaysian government in objectively assessing their policy initiatives. Great care needs to be exercised in the timing as well as sequencing of the chosen polices. Thus, best practice policy initiatives rely on good policy coherence which rests on the challenge of integrating policies and ideas appropriately, all of which require a change in the mindset of the policymakers themselves.

NOTES

[1] For a detailed critique of some of the studies in the table, refer to Mahadevan (2002a).

[2] This setting is not crucial as using various alternative depreciation rates does not substantially change the results.

[3] But adjustment by age-related productivity differences across labour is not without its limitations as it depends on whether age is expected to increase or decrease productivity and this varies across industries and occupations.

[4] This study used 3-digit industry level data from 1983 to 1991 with no consideration of differences in technology among the 28 manufacturing industries. Also, technological progress was simplistically captured by a time trend with the surprising result that it was found to be insignificant.

[5] Technological progress results from the advanced technology embodied in capital and is represented by outward shifts in the production frontier over time. Increased technical efficiency, on the other hand, results from the more efficient use of technology and inputs (due to the accumulation of knowledge in the learning-by-

doing process, diffusion of new technology, improved managerial practice, etc.) and is represented by movements towards the production frontier.

[6] The Malaysian Department of Statistics provides data on manufacturing industries at the 5-digit level since 2000. This makes it cumbersome to reconcile the data before 2000 which is at the 3-digit level.

[7] The ratio of the value of intermediate inputs to GDP (in nominal terms) in Malaysia has been as high as 0.8 on average, since 1995.

[8] The estimation using dummies at the 3-digit level did not provide plausible and significant input shares. Hence dummies at the 2-digit level were used.

[9] The test statistic for this is 118.38 and the critical value following the chi-square distribution is 6.63.

[10] See Mahadevan (2004) for an exposition on the various empirical methods underlying the frontier and non-frontier approach of TFP growth computation.

[11] The TE ratio is given by the ratio of industry's actual realised output to that of its potential output computed using the frontier input share estimates.

[12] This is seen when measures of K/L ratios for the manufacturing industries are compared with the OECD product classification for technology profile for Malaysia in UNIDO (1985).

[13] The World Bank study used the non-frontier approach to measure TFP growth which is synonymous to TP since firms are assumed to be technically efficient under this approach.

[14] See MASTIC (2004).

[15] Mainly because Malaysia does not have a formal policy nor does it impose controls on nationals working abroad.

[16] Labour Day Speech on 1 May 2004 by Dr Fong Chan Onn, Minister of Human Resources.

Appendix 3.1 MALAYSIA'S MANUFACTURING INDUSTRIES

Industry code	Manufacturing industries
311	Food products
313	Beverages
314	Tobacco
321	Textiles
322	Wearing apparel
323	Leather products
324	Footwear
331	Wood products except furniture
332	Furniture
341	Paper
342	Printing and publishing
351	Industrial chemicals
352	Other chemicals
353/54	Petroleum refineries and miscellaneous products of petroleum and coal
355	Rubber products
356	Plastic products
361	Pottery, china and earthenware
362	Glass products
369	Non-metallic mineral products
371	Iron and steel
372	Non-ferrous metal
381	Fabricated metal products
382	Machinery except electrical
383	Electrical machinery
384	Transport equipment
385	Professional and scientific equipment

Source: UNIDO dataset.

4. Human Capital and Technology Development Policies

4.1 INTRODUCTION

In the face of rapid globalisation and the spread of ICT technology, human capital and technology development are increasingly viewed as major engines of growth. This chapter critically reviews current policies related to these two aspects and traces the ongoing changes in Malaysia. In the light of this, some attention is drawn to how economic policy thinking can be guided by the Neo-Schumpeterian growth theory in the area of evolutionary economics. Also, while some short- to medium-term strategies are discussed to overcome the shortage of skills, the need for a long-term strategy integrating human capital and technology development policy in a broader setting is emphasised.

4.2 HUMAN CAPITAL INVESTMENT

There is no shortage of evidence on human capital's important role in the burgeoning literature on the drivers of economic growth. People are Malaysia's abundant human resource and it is necessary to ensure that maximum benefit is derived by using this resource efficiently. This in part depends on the education and training obtained by its populace. Table 4.1 below shows that Malaysia has paid close attention to raising the educational level of their workers.

As an economy develops, its workforce is expected to see a decrease in the proportion of workers with less education and this is seen in the category of no formal education and primary education in Table 4.1. While there is an increase in the proportion of those with tertiary education, this is somewhat insufficient to meet the growing demand of the highly skilled workforce. By 2010, this target is set at 35 per cent of the labour force but this is still low compared to the levels achieved by developed countries in 2003 such as Japan (36 per cent), the United States (41 per cent), Ireland (43 per cent) and Finland (36 per cent). In addition, there is an education mismatch especially at the tertiary level. The findings of the World Bank (2005) study indicate that 70 per cent of the managers in their firm-level survey highlighted the insufficient supply of university graduates and that the shortage of graduates has led to a sub-optimal hiring policy among firms. About 40 per cent of the unemployed are in areas that are not of interest to manufacturing activity. There is also a wide wage disparity between workers depending on the qualifications. The World Bank reports that the rate of return for tertiary education is nearly 18 per cent versus 9.5 per cent for secondary education, and only 4.5 per cent for primary education in Malaysia.

Table 4.1   Distribution of labour force by level of education (%)

	No formal education	Primary	Secondary (Upper and lower)	Tertiary (Form 6 and above)
1975	17.7	51.1	28.7	2.5
1980	14.5	44.5	37.0	3.8
1985	13.6	38.8	43.0	4.6
1990	4.6	38.8	51.0	5.6
1995	8.6	27.6	52.7	11.1
2000	6.1	26.1	53.8	13.9
2001	5.7	24.1	54.9	15.3
2002	5.4	23.9	54.5	16.6
2003	4.8	22.7	55.3	17.5
2004	4.7	21.9	55.1	18.3

Source: Labour Force Survey, Reports from Department of Statistics, and
EPU (2006).

In terms of government expenditure on education, Table 4.2 shows that there has been a slight but consistent rise in the proportion of GDP spent on education, followed by a decline in the decade of the 1990s, and finally an increase since 2001. This compares well with the ratio of 5 per cent in most OECD countries. In terms of government expenditure on education, the pattern is quite different.

The development allocation for education rose from RM17 948.5 million for 1995–2000 to RM18 660 million for 2000–05. Concomitant with the increase in these funds, there has been an increase in the number of people having access to education at all levels as seen in Table 4.3. This has also met with an improvement in the pupil-teacher ratio as evidenced by the decline of 31 in 1970 to 17.2 in 2005 in the primary schools, and in the secondary schools, it fell from 23.3 to 16.3 in the same years.

However, educational expansion has not had a significant effect on the occupational distribution of workers (see Table 4.4). This indicates that educational expansion had moved individuals up the educational ladder without altering their relative position on the occupational ladder. For example, the proportion of individuals in high skill occupations did not increased significantly despite a substantial increase in the educational composition of the labour force.

Table 4.2   Education expenditure ratio (%)

	Ratio of GDP	Ratio of total government expenditure
1970–74	5.22	19.64
1975–79	5.59	18.94
1980–84	5.73	15.18
1985–89	5.77	18.03
1990–94	5.20	19.52
1995–99	4.84	21.53
2000	3.27	13.29
2001	7.41	25.04
2002	8.13	28.10
2003	7.49	25.77
2004	8.64	23.57

Note: Averages were computed over the years before 2000.

Source: Computed from *Economic Report* (various issues), Ministry of Finance.

Table 4.3   Student enrolment in local public institutions

	1990	1995	2000	2005
Primary	2 445 600	2 799 359	2 945 906	3 044 977
Secondary (upper & lower)	1 315 680	1 627 874	1 942 746	2 093 847
Certificate	10 130	13 556	23 816	37 931
Diploma	32 020	46 480	91 398	98 953
First degree and post-graduate	58 440	87 891	198 160	253 504

Source: Five-Year Malaysia Plans, EPU.

Although there has been regular focus on the level of government expenditure on education, little attention has been paid to the actual features and consequences of human capital investment. Here we consider the need for a comprehensive investment programme of primary and pre-primary education. Heckman (1999) outlines a strong argument for early intervention based on skill begets skill, and argues for an investment strategy that lays a strong foundation for the formation of cognitive and non-cognitive skills in early childhood. He stresses that non-cognitive skills and motivation are important determinants of success and this is related to the need to cultivate and develop entrepreneurship qualities. This is easier than trying to address the dearth of entrepreneurs at a later stage with incentives and training, as it is more difficult to remedy entrenched values and attitudes. The pre-school and primary syllabus needs to be carefully examined to ensure that the subject matter allows for creativity instead of merely drilling students with cognitive skills. In essence, an intertemporal perspective on education is required and policies pertaining to early investment in education and teaching will maximise the potential for ongoing learning and skill upgrading through later stages in life.

Table 4.4   Employment by major occupational groups (000 persons)

	1980	1990	2000	2005
Professional, technical and related workers	150 (3.1%)	588 (8.8%)	1019.8 (11%)	1314 (12.1%)
Administrative and related workers	58 (1.2%)	160 (2.4%)	389.4 (4.2%)	543 (5%)
Clerical and related workers	140 (2.9%)	655 (9.8%)	1029.1 (11.1%)	1216.2 (11.2%)
Sales workers	416 (8.6%)	769 (11.5%)	1019.8 (11%)	1227.1 (11.3%)
Service workers	416 (8.6%)	775 (11.6%)	1094 (11.8%)	1346.6 (12.4%)
Production and related workers	914 (18.9%)	1845 (27.6%)	3041 (32.8%)	3355.4 (30.9%)
Agricultural workers	2718 (56.2%)	1892 (28.3%)	1678.1 (18.1%)	1856.6 (17.1%)
Total	4835	6686	9271.2	10858.9

Note: Percentage shares are given in parenthesis.

Source: Five-Year Malaysia Plans, EPU.

Another problem in Malaysia's education system has been the continued emphasis on obtaining good grades by equipping students with exam-specific skills at the expense of training students to, think through, analyse, reflect and question, when it comes to problem solving. At the tertiary level, students expect to be spoonfed with printed lecture notes and the proliferation of websites for various subject matters has affected the exploratory side to learning or at least changed the course of it. The concept of working or building up ideas and thought processes from base level information or primary level data to some extent is hampered by the information on the Internet. That is not to say that modern technology has not enhanced learning, but rather, different means of teaching and testing must be devised in accordance to the new mode to ensure critical thinking in students. This is required to instill an inquisitive and inquiring mind that is not seeking straight answers, and in the event will not hesitate to overcome challenges in the ever changing business environment.

The lack of interest in science and technology subjects also needs to be addressed at an early stage in schools. In part, this is due to the rudimentary and textbook-oriented approach in the teaching of mathematics and science. Appropriate modifications are needed to involve students intellectually and practically to see the usefulness of these subjects and to develop an appreciation for science. The MASTIC (2005) however reports that 45.5 per cent of the people interviewed felt that the quality of science and mathematics education in the schools was not satisfactory and 32.4 per cent felt that the teaching of science was too academic. Malaysians also perceive themselves as having a weak knowledge of issues in science and technology and 42.3 per cent of the respondents thought that science subjects are tough.

Table 4.5 shows that science and technical graduates accounted for only 52 per cent of the total number of graduates during the period 2001–05, of which 21 per cent are from technical courses. While this is an improvement over time, the arts and humanities courses still remained popular. However, in the cohort of secondary students, the proportion of science stream students increased from 32.2 per cent in 2000 to 45.6 per cent in 2005 (EPU 2006). Particularly in the field of engineering, Malaysia is said to need 210 000 engineers to support the country's development by 2020, but there were only about 52 000 engineers as at the end of 2003.[1] Thus greater effort should be taken to increase enrolment and output at higher levels in science and technical fields especially in ICT courses to cater to the need of qualified manpower towards the knowledge-based economy.

Table 4.5   Output of degree courses (number of students)

	1991–95	1996–2000	2001–05
Arts, humanities, social science	49 018	87 882	161 102
	(62%)	(58%)	(48%)
Medicine, agricultural science	19 642	38 273	100 967
and pure science	(25%)	(26%)	(31%)
Technical, architecture, and	10 508	24 343	70 650
engineering	(13%)	(16%)	(21%)

Source: Five-Year Malaysia Plans, EPU.

Parents' attitude and values attached towards the prestige of professions such as doctors, lawyers, accountants, business managers, and teachers also has some bearing on the choice of the careers of their children. While engineering is highly regarded, there are those who perceive a technical education as a blue-collar job with poor rewards and image, and thus encourage their children in completing their formal education even though they are not academically inclined. Currently, the vocational stream is an option but there is an increasing move to adopt the German education system to stream students, where the less academically inclined students automatically enter the vocational stream.[2] These students are then trained under an apprentice scheme, and companies can adopt and sponsor them for further skills upgrading. Upon completion of their training, these students will serve the companies. This system is also seen to work well in Australia.

Thus, the role of the vocational schools deserves more attention than is currently provided to develop the pool of skilled blue-collar workers needed for the industry, and at the same time reduce the dependence on foreign labour. Also, rather than view investment in education just in terms of the level of education or type of education (academic or vocational), there is a need to understand the clear complementarities that exist among different levels and types of education at different stages of development.

Another concern is the lack of English proficiency among workers. The World Bank (2005) survey notes that this is a problem across all types of occupations and is highlighted as the first most important skill lacking in workers. English must be progressively brought back as a medium of instruction in all subjects. The teaching of mathematics and science in English began only in 2003[3] and students entering university are now required to take the Malaysian University English Test although passing it is not compulsory. The second required skill noted by the World Bank is that of communications skills. Following Becker's (1964) definition, both these skills are general skills that can be taught in school because they are not firm-specific.

Lastly, large financial commitments to achieving marginal improvements in class size or expenditure per student can be less effective than investments to enhance school quality from low levels in a smaller range of schools in the less developed states of Malaysia. This is now being addressed by the Education Development Plan 2001–2010 which is a conscious effort to increase access to and equity in education. First, there is an expansion of the pre-school education programme for *orang asli* and natives from remote areas in Sabah and Sarawak. Second, at least 80 per cent of the newly constructed 234 primary schools are in rural areas. During the period from 2001 to July 2004, a total of RM13.5 billion was expended for rural schools and the provision of broadband internet services in schools, including 10 000 schools in rural areas, is high on the agenda (2005 Budget Speech in September 2004). The second phase of this plan is to implement a centralised school project in Sabah and Sarawak to facilitate students with transportation problems, providing them with educational facilities such as hostels, a conducive educational environment, and adequately trained teachers. The education development expenditure as at 31 July 2004 shows that urban development took up 32 per cent while rural development took up 68 per cent of the expenditure (*Economic Report 2004/05*).

4.2.1   Training

To improve the quality of education in school, training must also be provided to the educators. In fact, under the ninth MP, the target has been set to ensure that all secondary school teachers and 25 per cent of primary school teachers have a first degree by 2010. However, it is not clear why the development allocation for teacher education has been halved to RM577.7 million for 2006–10 from the development expenditure for 2000–05. In particular, to cater to the high demand for engineers, for instance, to increase the flow of 3000 engineers per year requires 12 000 students in a 4–year programme and with a student teacher ratio of 15:1 this requires a good 800 teachers with appropriate engineering and science qualifications at the postgraduate level. In January 2004, 31 000 students were pursuing postgraduate degrees in local universities, representing only 17 per cent of the student population in universities. The government has targeted to increase the figure to 40 per cent by 2010 to meet the growing needs of the economy.

Economic rationalists have however viewed public sector education and training as inefficient and wasteful because it is not sufficiently exposed to the rigour of the market and competition. Thus, the private sector was allowed to step in as seen by Malaysia's efforts to liberalise its education sector. As early as 1995, a Private Education Department and the National Accreditation Board were set up within the Ministry of Education to regulate and monitor private education institutions. At the same time, the University Act and University College Act were also amended for the establishment of higher education institutions. The number of private providers in tertiary education grew from 156 in 1992 to 532 in 2005 (EPU 2006). There was also a proliferation of the twinning programmes being set up between local educational institutes and overseas universities, and five overseas universities have already set up campus in Malaysia.[4] There is also the Open University of Malaysia set up in August 2000, and the first virtual university,[5] Universiti Tun Abdul Razak, began in January 2005. It allows greater flexibility for mature age students to continue their education and its strength lies in its close relationship with the 11 public universities. A number of privatised public enterprises such as Telekom, Tenaga Nasional and Petronas have been allowed to set up their own technical universities to cater to the industrial needs of the economy.

In order to produce local graduates who are equipped with the required skills, there has to be close collaboration between the universities and other institutions to organise, conduct or restructure courses that are considered relevant, essential and practice-oriented to cater to the needs of the industry.[6] To address this concern, all local undergraduates would be required to do a minimum of four months internship and industrial attachment (ninth MP). In addition, the Graduate Training Scheme launched in August 2005 aims to equip local graduates who have been unemployed since 2003 with specialised skills. In 2005, 7992 graduates were trained. The Graduate Reskilling Scheme, on the other hand, is targeted at engineering and selected technical graduates with no previous employment history. By the end of 2005, 2370 graduates had participated in the various courses. Another programme is the Graduate Apprenticeship Program, which was initiated in 2005, and benefited 9225 graduates within nine months of the same year.

While the World Bank (2005) notes that the shortage of skills is one of the top three concerns of both the manufacturing and services firms, one emerging skill demand by employers has been for the workers to possess different types of skills in addition to higher skills. For instance, interest is now in personnel equipped with managerial and entrepreneurial expertise although they possess technical skills. This is due to manufacturing companies extending their activities towards distribution, sales and marketing. Such a lack of local expertise has been highlighted by a 2001 survey undertaken by the Socio-economic and Environmental Research Institute (an independent think-tank in Malaysia) where 75 per cent of the respondents in Penang indicated that they had to bring in 101 foreign experts for a wide range of services, both technical and managerial in nature. This is partly attributable to the lack of training institutes that provide a good combination of both types of courses. To address this problem, two positive steps have been taken.

One is the introduction of techno-entrepreneurship courses introduced to all science, technology and engineering undergraduates with the introduction of an annual techno-entrepreneurship competition in 2003, but it is too early to tell how effective this scheme is. The Technopreneurs Association of Malaysia, which was formed in 2003, has also designed a one-year mentor programme for firms requiring help in addition to an education initiative programme aimed at providing awareness and promoting entrepreneurship (courses include business planning, marketing savvy and venture funding) amongst local universities and college students. The other step is the significant increase in the development allocation for management training in the second half of the decade of 2000 as seen in Table 4.6. Also, industrial training takes the bulk of the training funds and has almost doubled from the late 1990s to the early 2000s with only a slight increase for 2006–10.

The changing trend from resource-based to manufacturing- and knowledge-based employment means the shelf life of a worker's knowledge and skills are becoming shorter as a result of rapid continuing technological changes. It was estimated that 50 per cent of what is learnt in school becomes obsolete in five years in the field of electrical engineering and the shelf life of current knowledge is two and a half years.[7] Training and retraining is therefore crucial to make workers multi-skilled and versatile to be able to cope with these changes. In 2000, industrial training institutes under the Ministry of Human Resources provided training to 20 881 trainees in various fields such as IT, computer engineering, communication skills and English. By the end of 2005, there were 30 such industrial institutes which catered for 38 765 trainees.

Table 4.6   *Development allocation for training (RM million)*

Program	1991–95	1996–2000	2001–05	2006–10
Training	777	2237.3	4000	4792.8
Industrial training	580	1876.0	3760	4103.6
Commercial training	27	71.3	100	179.5
Management training	140	290.0	140	509.5

Source: Five-Year Malaysia Plans, EPU.

To help workers develop necessary skills, the Human Resources Development Fund (HRDF) was established in 1993 with a matching grant from the government. Eligible employers with 50 or more employees are required to contribute 1 per cent of their payroll to HRDF. But official statistics indicate that only slightly more than 50 per cent of the grant from HRDF has been utilised (Ministry of Human Resources Annual Report 1998). The World Bank (2005) notes that, although the HRDF is considered critical by firms in their decision to train, the HRDF is slow (taking as long as five weeks) to reimburse claims sent in by firms. If the processing were more efficient, 84 per cent of the firms sampled would have provided more training to their workers. The HRDF has now been expanded to include training in manufacturing-related services such as logistics, market support and ICT. The utilisation period of the fund has also been extended from two to five years.

To encourage SMEs in particular to participate in the training schemes, the Double Deduction Incentive Scheme, established in 1988, allowed companies to subtract double the cost of training expenditures from gross income before taxes. But the scheme was unsuccessful and replaced by the HRDF. Business organisations such as the Federation of Malaysian Employers and the Federation of Malaysian Manufacturers have set up their own training centres as well. In addition, the Technical Skills Development and Industrial Skills Enhancement Programs are implemented by the 12 state-level skills development centres to help address the shortage of skilled manpower. On average, these centres have been training about 30 000 people since 2000 (MITI 2003). A double session programme is also to be implemented in polytechnics, MARA and industrial training institutes' community colleges to create an additional 30 000 places by 2008 (2005 Budget Speech). To date, since 1992, five advanced training centres in collaboration with the foreign governments of Germany, France, Britain, Spain and Japan have been set up, and as at the end of 2003, 14 732 people have been trained (MITI 2003). It is however important to monitor the design and delivery of the various training courses to evaluate their relevance to the needs of the industry.

Table 4.7 shows evidence of poor take-up of the skill development and technology support programmes. The World Bank (2005) reports that 45 per cent of managers believed that the programmes do not offer services relevant to their firms needs while 37 per cent do not know how to make the first contact with these institutions. But in general, those who have used the programmes said they were satisfied with them. Not surprisingly, more large firms than SMES sent their workers for skills upgrade at the institutions.

Table 4.7   Use of support institutions by firms interviewed

	Skills development institutions	Technology support institutions	Technology incentives
SMEs	14.7%	14.5%	1.2%
Large firms	39.1%	17.4%	11.4%

Source: World Bank (2005).

Previous studies on training in Malaysia such as Tan and Batra (1995) have shown that as early as the 1990s, training by firms was insufficient. Tan and Gill (2000) however report that foreign firms were more likely to provide in-house training than local firms, and that SMEs do not train because of high labour turnover, lack of knowledge about how to train and limited resources for training. The World Bank (2005), on the other hand, reports that 42 per cent of manufacturing firms provide some formal training for their employees.

One possibility is for local companies to carry out joint training programmes with their MNC joint venture partners. This would create a win–win situation where the foreign partners would benefit from work performed by the local workers while the local workers would benefit from the transfer of technology and know-how from them. While the electronics firms in the Klang Valley have performed poorly in this aspect, those in Peneng have had significant success in building a supplier chain under the Global Supplier Program[8] in 1999 by the Penang Skills Development Centre (Best 2001; Rasiah 2002). The Industrial Linkage Program is a federal level initiative that was launched in 1996 to focus on technology transfer and industrial deepening.[9] In 2004, only 27 per cent of the registered 1051 SMEs have been linked to MNCs and large companies (MITI 2004).

Another aspect that is lacking is extensive interaction among employer organisations, the government and the firms. There is a clear need for synergy between all relevant institutions to establish a cooperative system with close involvement and partnership to decide what is needed and how best it can be done. For the system to be flexible and responsive, continuous assessment and evaluation of the existing training and education system must be in place to ensure little mismatch in skill needs and development, transparency and safeguarding of standards in the assessment and certification of skills, and a positive structure of incentives to take up training. The Dual System Project introduced in 2003 is a collaborative effort in this direction, involving both the public and private sector to implement apprentice schemes and to review curriculum development and existing training programmes regularly. Lack of coordination also raises questions about how efficiently resources are being allocated across training institutions, and hinders an in-depth analysis into the take-up of the various government training incentives and schemes.

4.3 SHORT- TO MEDIUM-TERM STRATEGIES

Malaysia's strategy of moving rapidly to a more developed society hinges to a significant extent on ensuring labour is appropriately skilled and available in sufficient numbers. In the interim period, however, the government has in place measures such as importing foreign labour and addressing the brain drain problem, both of which are discussed later. But for some reason the government's efforts in enticing more women into the workforce to alleviate some of the shortage in labour have not been aggressive. The female labour force participation rate has been in the range of 43 per cent and 50 per cent in the period 1970–2005 and this is low compared to other developed countries. One reason for this may lie in the low pay for Malaysian women relative to Malaysian men, or constraints arising from family and household responsibilities. Ismail and Zin (2003) provide evidence that the earnings of male workers in the electrical and electronics, wood-based and food industries were significantly higher than those of female workers. Opportunities for educating and training women to break out of the low-skill trap may partly help in alleviating labour shortages, especially in the rapidly expanding ICT sector where women are under-represented.

4.3.1 Foreign Labour

Malaysia has a long history of importing foreign labour which has contributed to economic growth by alleviating labour shortages in selected sectors of the economy. This was manifested in the rubber and agricultural plantations in the 1980s, and by 1989 spread to the main industrial urban centres of the country and by the mid 1990s was reported throughout the country. The shortages covered unskilled, semi-skilled and a whole range of skilled occupations.

It has now been made clear that export-oriented manufacturers (with more than 50 per cent of their output meant for export) are eligible to hire foreign workers, while domestic-oriented businesses need to have a minimum paid up capital of RM100 000 and total sales of RM2 million to hire on the basis of one foreign worker to one domestic worker. Any company with a foreign paid up capital of US$2 million and above will automatically be allowed five expatriates posts including key posts. Other MNCs are allowed to bring in required expatriates in areas where there is a shortage of trained Malaysians to do the job.

Table 4.8 shows that the number of legal foreign workers has increased to 1.8 million in 2005 from about 136 000 in the early 1980s. Foreign workers with work permits accounted for 9.5 per cent of the labour force in 2003 and the ratio of foreign workers to local labour increased from 9.3:100 in 2000 to 11.7:100 in 2003 (EPU 2003). In fact, the Ministry of Human Resources Labour Report 1987–88 states that as early as 1984, Malaysia had 500 000 foreign workers including the illegal foreign workers. Pillai (1995) estimated this number to be 1.2 million by 1991. The proportion of foreign workers in the manufacturing sector has risen from 10 per cent in 1990 to 30 per cent by mid 2004 (*Economic Report 2004/05*).

Table 4.8   Number of foreign workers

	Legal workers	Including illegal workers	Expatriate workers
Early 1980s	136 000	500 000 (1984)	12 000 (1986)
1990	290 000	1 200 000 (1991)	61 269 (1993)
1995	852 700	n.a.	n.a.
1997	700 000	n.a.	n.a.
2000	813 300	2 000 000	70 245
2002	769 566	n.a.	n.a.
2003	1 225 400	n.a.	n.a.
2004	1 300 000	2 500 000	74 343
2005	1 815 238	n.a.	35 500

Note: Expatriate workers comprise professional, managerial and technical workers.

Source: Pillai (1995), Five-Year Malaysia Plans, EPU, *The Star* 12 January 2004, and *Economic Report* 2004/05, Ministry of Finance.

With the steady increase in the number of foreign workers over time, the number and importance of expatriates (who constitute professional, technical and supervisor, administrative and managerial and skilled workers) have also increased with higher economic growth, the international division of labour and FDI. In 2000, there were 70 245 expatriates comprising 9.4 per cent of foreign workers, and in 2004 this number rose to 74 343 workers who only comprise 3 per cent of foreign workers, indicating a very high proportion of unskilled workers. In terms of educational attainment, foreign workers with no formal education or primary education background accounted for 67 per cent of the total foreign workforce as of July 2004. The import and easy availability of unskilled workers has been reported to discourage the move to higher value added manufacturing activities.

The increasing trend in illegal workers (who are mainly unskilled) is indeed very worrying and their presence has put stress on public amenities and services. The problem is trying to control the influx of illegal unskilled foreign workers who are attracted to Malaysia due to relatively higher wages *vis-à-vis* their homeland. As illegals, they have no access to the legal system in the country and thus many conflicts are resolved internally among themselves and this may be a root cause of social strife and many criminal activities among them. Their involvement in criminal activities, their persistent illegal entry and their propensity to violate the law are serious threats to the security and political stability of the country. Pillai (1995) notes that there are also fears that the continued influx from Bangladesh and Indonesia could disrupt the country's delicate ethnic balance, increase the strength of bumiputra-based political parties, and upset political and economic power-sharing now largely based on ethnic proportions in the population.

4.3.2 Brain Drain

There are no official data on out-migration available mainly because Malaysia does not have a formal migration policy nor does it impose controls on nationals working abroad. However, Pillai (1995) estimated that at least 40 000 Malaysians or on average 5000 per year migrated to Australia, New Zealand, Canada and the US between 1983 and 1990. While Malaysians who have migrated long ago are rather reluctant to return, the younger generation, particularly those who have and are going abroad to pursue their studies, are increasingly planning not to return. According to some critical analyses, the positive discrimination of Malays may damage Malaysia's competitiveness because many Chinese and Indian students go abroad to study and do not return. But Malaysia is in need of highly skilled workers to meet the labour shortage and to create an indigenous base of talent in science and technology including areas of biotechnology and ICT. Thus Malaysian citizens working abroad are being enticed to return home and serve the nation.

The first attempt at the brain gain programme to lure highly skilled personnel, both foreign and Malaysian, started in 1995. This programme attracted 94 (24 Malaysians and 70 foreigners) scientists but they all returned to their home/host countries by 2004. In 2001, another programme known as the Returnees Program aimed at attracting only highly skilled Malaysians has also met with limited success. Since 2002, there have been exemptions from income tax, duty-free import of motor cars and possessions from abroad, and the granting of permanent residents to spouses and children. However, the impediments that are discouraging these Malaysians from returning include the career prospects, the education and healthcare provisions for their families, the social and cultural environment as well as the overall quality of life in Malaysia. Besides having to undertake a high pay cut, returnees are also required to work for five years in Malaysia or the incentives would be forfeited. Also applicants are expected to have working experience to qualify, and this means they would have been established in their career and built their families overseas which makes it more difficult to relocate. While there is an estimated 30 000 Malaysians working abroad, only 665 had applied from 2001 to August 2004. Of these, 279 applications were approved but only 165 had taken up the offer and returned (MASTIC 2005a).

While there appears to be a need to re-examine the efficiency of Malaysia's 'brain gain' initiatives and to develop a compelling value proposition to attract, develop and retain talented Malaysians both within and outside the country, the reality is that it is a difficult task to do at this time and age.[10] Perhaps it is best to nip the problem in its bud by attempting to discourage people from leaving in the first place by providing equal job and educational opportunities.

4.4 RESEARCH AND DEVELOPMENT

In the 1950s and 1960s, countries generally designed *science* polices in response to the link between science and economic growth. In the 1960s and 1970s, this came to be more usually described as science *and technology* policies, a response to the realisation that technology did not equal science. From the late 1980s into the 1990s, there was a further name change to *innovation* policy as some awareness spread that innovation involved more than R&D alone. Here, we use the term technology policy to refer to policies that stimulate the economy by fostering both innovation and R&D.

The First National Science and Technology Policy devised in 1986, was followed by the Industrial Technology Development: A National Plan of Action in 1990, and the most recent is the Second National Science and Technology Policy in 2002. Thus, there has been a long gap between the last two policies. A cursory look at the 55 recommendations in the recent policy show that there has been some movement forward but the recommendations appear relatively broad-based with a limited number of targets such as:

1. International procurement operations centres should be given incentives to set up in Malaysia to strengthen linkages between purchasers and suppliers to encourage R&D and product development programmes.
2. Develop a system of commercially driven engineering and services support to meet the requirements of industrialisation.
3. Competence in industrial, engineering and product design so that ideas can be translated to workable systems.
4. Require public sector R&D institutes to draw up five-year budget plans detailing their programmes and priorities.
5. Establish five regional science centres by 2010 to elevate science and technology awareness among the population.

While all the plans showed some sense of direction, there were no clear time frames set to achieve the targets set out. Part of the previous efforts towards these targets are seen in the rapid establishment of the MSC in 1996, the various Technology Parks since the early 1990s,[11] and the BioValley in 2004, to provide the environment for undertaking R&D and innovation. While it may still be too early to judge, at least at this stage, these clusters lack dynamism, and technology management is not effective and well coordinated unlike the Silicon Valley or Taiwan's Hsinchu Science Park

Like most developing countries, Malaysia is a latecomer where R&D is concerned, and is still in the infancy stage of building its R&D capacity. There are several reasons for this. First, initial priority was given to the building of Malaysia's strength in the primary sector which led to the establishment of research institutions focusing on agriculture (mainly rubber, oil palm and rice) cultivation technology and productivity in IMP1 drawn up in 1985. Given this emphasis, the institutional mechanism to foster research in industrial technology was relatively inadequate in the early 1990s. Second, local manufacturing was initially protected for a domestic market and lacked the competitive pressures to undertake R&D. Third, as a result of export expansion, these activities were dominated almost entirely by foreigners, particularly in key sectors like electronic and electrical products in the 1990s. This may have lulled the government into leaving R&D primarily in the hands of private entrepreneurs, who in this case were largely foreigners.

Table 4.9   National R&D indicators

	1992	1994	1996	1998	2000	2002	2005
Amount spent on R&D (RM million)	550.7	611.2	549.1	1127	1671.5	2500.6	4300
Cost of R&D/GDP	0.37	0.34	0.22	0.39	0.49	0.69	0.9
Researchers per 10 000 labour force	2.1	5.8	5.1	7.0	15.6	18.0	25.0
Full-time researchers per 10 000 labour force	2.1	2.9	2.2	3.8	6.7	7.2	n.a.

Source: MASTIC (2004) and EPU (2006).

The importance of R&D for industrial technological development was recognised by the National Plan of Action of 1990 which set a target of R&D expenditure to GDP ratio of 1.5 per cent by 1995, and 2 per cent by 2000. But both targets are a far cry from reality as seen in Table 4.9. Although R&D expenditure doubled in some years and has gradually risen over time, the R&D to GDP ratio is still very low. In 2002, a new target was set to reach an R&D/GDP ratio of 1.5 per cent by 2010. The advanced economies of the US, Japan and some European countries lead the world in the proportion of GDP spent on R&D with the OECD average of 2.23 per cent in 2003 (EPU 2006). As seen in Table 4.10, the Asian first-tier NIES of Korea, Taiwan and Singapore also surpass Malaysia's research intensity by three to four times.

Although Malaysia fares better than its peers in the second-tier NIEs of Thailand and Indonesia, it lags behind China and India which are fast en route to becoming economic powers in the East.

While Table 4.9 shows that the number of researchers, full-time and otherwise, has improved, Malaysia pales in comparison with the other countries (see Figure 4.1). It can be seen that Finland's 15.45 is one of the highest in terms of number of researchers per 1000 labour force, followed by Japan, Singapore and South Korea. Malaysia is ranked among one of the lowest and is surpassed by the emerging economies of South Africa, China, the Czech Republic and Argentina. In an effort to enhance national capacity in R&D and to achieve a competent workforce, a target of 50 researchers per 10 000 labour force has been set to be reached by 2010.

Table 4.10   Comparison of research intensity

Countries	R&D expenditure/ GDP
Malaysia (2002)	0.69
USA (2002)	2.72
Australia (2001)	1.53
Finland (2001)	3.42
Ireland (2001)	1.16
Italy (2000)	1.07
Spain (2001)	0.96
Hungary (2001)	0.95
Portugal (2002)	0.78
Japan (2002)	3.07
Korea (2002)	2.53
Taiwan (2002)	2.30
Singapore (2002)	2.15
China (2001)	1.09
India (2001)	0.78
Thailand (2002)	0.24
Indonesia (2002)	0.05
Philippines (2002)	0.11
Brazil (2000)	1.05
Chile (2001)	0.54
South Africa (2001)	0.77

Source: UNESCO Institute of Statistics, and Taiwan 2003 Annual Statistics.

The problem with R&D is that it is a risky venture that may take a long time to bear any fruits. In addition, non-rivalry and full excludability of advances in knowledge mean that there are spillover effects to other firms. This implies that the private sector's incentive to engage in R&D will be less than is socially optimal. Dowrick's (2004) evidence and a few other studies point to the fact that the social rate of return on national R&D (50–60 per cent) is higher than the private rate of return (20–30 per cent). Thus, quite often, government involvement in R&D is high.

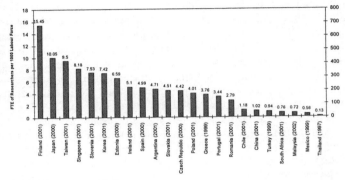

Source: MASTIC (2004).

Figure 4.1   Full-time researchers per 1000 labour force

In fact, the public sector to private sector R&D expenditure ratio was 80:20 in 1992 although this has declined (see Table 4.11). This was however made possible by the large government grants allocated to the private sector.

Table 4.11   R&D expenditure by type of sector (RM million)

	1992	1994	1996	1998	2000	2002	2005
Total R&D	550.7	608.3	549.2	1127	1671.5	2500.6	4300
Private Sector	246.3	292.6	400.1	746.1	967.9	1633.1	2800
Public Sector	304.4	315.7	149.1	380.9	703.6	867.5	1500
Government Research Institutes	253.7	164.8	108.7	247.3	417.5	507.1	n.a.
Institutes of Higher Learning	50.7	150.9	40.4	133.6	286.1	360.4	n.a

Source: MASTIC (2004) and EPU (2006).

The 1990 National Action Plan envisaged the share of private sector R&D expenditure to rise to at least 60 per cent of the total R&D expenditure by 2000, and this is close to the 57.9 per cent attained. It is encouraging to note that there is an increasingly greater proportion of Malaysian owned and controlled companies than their foreign counterparts undertaking R&D unlike the early 1990s where it was mainly undertaken by the MNCs. For local companies, manufacturing R&D took up the largest expenditure at about RM242.7 million (about 75 per cent of total expenditure), followed by transport equipment (RM164.6 million, Proton in particular), and the services sector with RM40.1 million. For foreign companies, 98 per cent of their R&D expenditure was in the manufacturing sector. Not surprisingly, R&D was found to be highly correlated with firms with high sales revenue and employment size. It was found that 63.7 per cent of total R&D expenditure was undertaken by firms with more than 2000 employees (MASTIC 2004).

Overall, Malaysia's R&D focused on applied research followed by experimental research. This was true for both the private and public sector institutions. Figure 4.2 shows that applied R&D has always taken up at least 40 per cent of R&D activities. This type of research on products is undertaken to acquire new knowledge directed primarily towards a specific practical aim or objective such as to suit local taste and/or process to achieve greater economies of scale and scope. This could result in a technologically improved product which is an existing product whose performance has been significantly enhanced or upgraded.

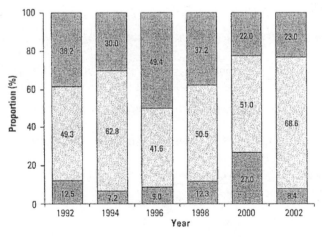

Source: MASTIC (2004).

Figure 4.2   Proportion of expenditure by type of research in 2002

Experimental development, which constitutes more than 25 per cent on average, involves systematic work using existing knowledge for the purpose of creating new or improved materials, products or devices, to installing new processes, systems and services, or to improving substantially those already produced or installed. On the other hand, very little basic research was conducted, as basic research is experimental or theoretical work undertaken primarily to acquire new knowledge without a specific application. As it is carried out without looking for any long-term economic or social benefits other than advancement of knowledge, one can expect such research to be limited and very costly without sufficient returns. Thus, the government should take a major role in the development of basic research capabilities that can provide more radical or breakthrough solutions to achieve more durable competitive advantages. Without a concomitant investment in basic research, the R&D strategy may run the risk of producing too many 'me too' types of start-ups that lack technological depth and hence are likely to be short-lived. The Scientific Advancement Grant Allocation is provided to promising researchers at institutions of higher learning to work on basic research and this is part of the overall endeavour towards realising the long-term objective of having Malaysians conferred the Nobel scientific award.

More generally, what are some of the determinants of technological activity? Here, we draw on the World Bank's (2005) study for some empirical evidence related to three types of technological activity given by adoption (update of machinery and/or the introduction of a substantially new technology), adaption (upgrades major product line and/or enter new markets due to quality or cost improvements) and creation (obtaining patents or copyrights for process or product technology). Table 4.12 shows only the statistically significant factors in a probit regression model[12] using factors such as exporter status, foreign ownership, firm size, innovation staff, collaboration between firms, firm and institution, and firm and university.

Table 4.12   Determinants of technological activity

Adoption	Adaptation	Creation
In-house skilled resources	Firm-firm collaboration	Firm size
Firm size	Exporter	Firm-institution collaboration
Exporter	Use of fiscal incentives	Use of fiscal incentives

Source: Adapted from the World Bank (2005).

It can be seen that firm size, exporter status and in-house skilled resources can increase the probability of undertaking adoption. Interestingly, foreign ownership and collaborative efforts do not drive this decision. On the other hand, inter-firm collaboration and the status of being an exporter raises the possibility of adaptation. Interestingly, 60 per cent of collaborating domestic firms are members of a business association. It appears that smaller firms see the need to work together for joint benefits and the opportunities provided by business associations for interaction and problem solving can have positive results in reducing transactional costs as well. For creative activity, in-house skilled resources or foreign ownership or exporter status are no longer sufficient. There has to be firm–institution collaboration where such interaction clearly identifies the needs of the firm so that the institution carries out relevant and applicable research with commercial value.

Now we turn to the question of what are some of the problems faced by firms undertaking R&D? The MASTIC (2004) reports that factors limiting R&D were lack of skilled R&D personnel, unclear procedures of application, narrow scope of eligibility, limited financial resources, lack of infrastructure such as space and equipment for R&D, lack of R&D management know-how, and unawareness and even lack of government incentives for R&D. Here we review some of these factors.

The government's commitments to increase R&D allocation can be seen in Table 4.13 but one can gather from the ninth MP that only 67.8 per cent of the R&D funds allocated for 2001–05 were used although numerous R&D schemes are provided by the government. Why is this the case and how effective are these allocations?

Table 4.13   R&D allocations by Malaysian Plan (RM million)

	5th Plan 1986–90	6th Plan 1991–95	7th Plan 1996–2000	8th Plan 2000–05	9th Plan 2006–10
Amount	400	600	938	1366	1581.6

Source: Five-Year Malaysia Plans, EPU.

Some incentives provided by the government do not preclude the foreign firms and these include a 100 per cent tax exemption of statutory income for five years, or investment tax allowance of 100 per cent on qualifying capital expenditure. A company can also apply for double tax deduction on its revenue for non-capital expenditure for research approved by the Ministry of Finance. The double deduction for R&D expenses has also been extended to activities undertaken overseas and this includes training of Malaysian staff as well. After the Pioneer Status period, there will be a consideration for a second round Pioneer Status for another five years or Investment Tax Allowance for a further ten years.

However, the fall in foreign share in R&D (noted by MASTIC 2004) means that foreign companies are taking their R&D elsewhere. It can be expected that MNC's local R&D activity is less advanced than that undertaken at their corporate headquarters. Another likely reason for this is that, currently, most R&D schemes offered by the Malaysian government are only for locally controlled and owned companies with at least 50 per cent or 30 per cent local equity holding depending on the type of grant. The government's attempt to develop indigenous capability at the expense of excluding foreign-dominated companies from undertaking more R&D may be too high a price to pay. This is in direct contrast to Singapore's strategy. Amsden et al. (2001) reports that Singapore has been rather successful in getting their MNCs to undertake R&D by providing generous government support in the form of laboratories and the protection of intellectual property and financial incentives. It was further reported that for every S$1 invested in R&D by a MNC between 1991 and 1999, the Singapore government invested 30 cents.

The Malaysian government's R&D schemes with various shareholder restrictions include the MSC R&D Grant Scheme (established specifically for companies of MSC status aimed at multimedia applications), the Technology Acquisition Fund and the Industrial Technical Assistance Fund. Yet another is the Demonstrator Application Grant Scheme established to encourage short-term R&D of less than 12 months in IT and multimedia applications compatible with local culture and the promotion of the development of local software and content industries for enhanced community livelihood.

Other R&D grants offered by the government are the Intensification of Research in Priority Areas, the Commercialisation of Research and Development Fund and the Industry Research and Development Grant. While the latter two are once again made available only to Malaysian and Malaysian-majority owned firms, the former grant received about 70 per cent of the R&D budget allocation under the eighth MP as greater priority was given to projects with commercial potential and which are market-driven in line with the strategic needs of the nation. The catch with all these grants is that they require the private sector to conduct R&D with the involvement of public sector organisations such as the universities and government research institutions. Several studies have noted the poor take-up on the part of firms (Kondo 1999; Jomo 2003; Rasiah 2004; World Bank 2005). The World Bank reports that only 15 per cent of firms used research institutes. The lack of or relevance of the services offered by these institutions to the firm's needs is the primary reason for this while the lack of technical capability in-house to interact with the institutes was the second reason. Firm–institution collaboration was especially necessary for the process of creation (see Table 4.12).

Nevertheless, it appears that a majority of the research institutes act as catalysts rather than getting involved to a large extent in collaborative work unless they are approached by the firms themselves. Furthermore, Mani (2002) notes that out of the 33 government research institutes, only the Standards and Industrial Research Institute and the Malaysian Institute for Microelectronic Systems are devoted to industrial technology research. They suggest that the research institutes be established according to scientific disciplines to be more effective as is the case in South Korea, Taiwan and Singapore.

Ernst (2002), on the other hand, warns that firm level upgrading will soon reach its limits without firm linkages with support industries, universities and research institutes. Since the pace at which this is happening is rather slow, Malaysia should strengthen linkages with overseas universities that can help upgrade research, development and design capabilities in Malaysian universities and research institutes. As of 2004, Malaysia has signed a memorandum of understanding on bilateral cooperation specifically on science and technology affairs between the Malaysian government and 13 foreign countries. The role of policy in this vision of the growth process is an enabling one by creating the circumstances where firms and institutions can quickly and accurately take on opportunities. Greater emphasis is also given to enhancing R&D to foster closer collaboration among local researchers in universities and research institutions via the Malaysian Research and Education Network (MyREN) to create an environment or formal means of sharing and exchanging ideas via interaction with others in a similar field. It is also intended that MyREN will be connected to research communities in South East Asia and serve as the region's hub to link with the Trans-European Information Network, the Pan-European Research Network and other counterparts around the globe (EPU 2006).

For collaboration between firms and universities, government or research institutions, end-user needs must be clearly understood and correctly identified, and best-practice research management principles must be in place (Thiruchelvam 1999). A new Reach Out Program and the establishment of the National Innovation Council in 2004 chaired by the Prime Minister is an indication of the high level commitment to having a centre for sharing best practices and experiences in science and technology as well as to enhance the commercialisation and diffusion of research findings generated from public funded research organisations. But Tham and Ragayah (2006) draw attention to the lack of effective government coordination due to replication of duties in ministries and various government agencies that appear to have resulted in some rivalry and unclear designated duties. This is not to say that no success has been achieved.

For instance, the government has in place nine technology incubator centres, some of which have met with successful outcomes.[13] Under this arrangement, the university provides office space, use of equipment, consultancy services and training to the tenant companies. In return, the company outsources its R&D through contract and collaborative arrangements, obtains expert advice on technology, marketing and finance. During 2001–05, a total of 400 companies have benefited from these services (EPU 2006).

As part of the government's ongoing emphasis on R&D, in early 2006 four universities have been designated as 'research universities' and the ministry is expecting to look at R&D-oriented universities abroad to come up with a suitable structure for governing these universities. Overseas expertise can also be sought by approaching specialized research institutes abroad to design courses catering to the specific needs and capabilities of Malaysia's clusters. For instance, in the field of electronics there exist well-regarded institutes such as Taiwan's Industrial Technology Research Institute, Korea's Electronic and Telecommunications Research Institute, the Korea Advanced Institute Science and Technology, and the Indian Institute of Information Technology.

It is also noteworthy that since 2002, a monitoring unit has been in place to foster accountability and assess the effectiveness of the management of these various grants. So far, the outcome from the use of government R&D funds appears quite encouraging as reported by EPU (2006). For instance, an evaluation of R&D projects under the IRPA programme during the seventh MP revealed that only 3.4 per cent of the projects were commercialised during the eighth MP. An evaluation of 1233 completed IRPA projects implemented during the eighth MP indicated the filing of 544 IP rights such as patents, industrial designs and copyrights as well as 4872 publications including national and international papers. These projects also provided opportunities for capacity building, and were instrumental in producing 92 PhDs, 338 Masters Graduates, and enhancing the capabilities of 765 research staff in new and emerging technologies. An evaluation of the 65 completed projects under the Industry Research and Development Grant Scheme indicated that 26 projects or 40 per cent were commercialised and 24 IP rights were filed. During the eighth MP period, the MSC R&D Scheme saw the commercialisation of 27 projects.

From the view point of the firms, how useful and effective have the government incentives and grant schemes been? The MASTIC (2003) reports that 33 per cent (23 per cent) of the companies interviewed considered government grants to be highly (moderately) decisive for their innovation efforts while an almost equal proportion of 31 per cent considered it irrelevant for their innovation attempts. Around 96 per cent of the innovating firms reported that they did not receive any government support or incentives. Empirical evidence from the World Bank (2005) in Table 4.12 shows that fiscal incentives are a significant determinant of technological activities but firms surveyed lamented that the delivery of fiscal incentives by the government was not satisfactory (ibid.). Notably, 25 per cent of all firms surveyed who had heard of the fiscal incentives chose not to use them because of the complicated process of applications and approvals. However, amongst the firms who used the fiscal incentives, satisfaction was high. The MASTIC (2004) also report of firms' unawareness of government incentives; procedures of application of the incentives are not clear and that scope of eligibility is narrow, in addition to the lack of infrastructure such as space and equipment for R&D, and lack of R&D management know-how. The majority of researchers in the private sector in 2002 had a bachelor's degree (68.5 per cent) followed by masters degree (10.1 per cent) and PhD degrees (2.4 per cent). Thus it is not surprising that 93.4 per cent of R&D outsourcing activities involved the private sector of which 75.3 per cent was sourced overseas (MASTIC 2005a).

Thus, in addition to much-needed attempts on the part of the government to provide the appropriate hardware in terms of grants and various schemes, there still exists the problem of creating the software needed to go in hand. One strategy is for foreign-based Malaysian scientists to be designated 'R&D outposts' who advise the Malaysian government on technical and business trends and help design policies to take advantage of them (World Bank 2005). For instance, the Chinese Institute of Engineers founded in 1979 by a small group of Taiwanese engineers in Silicon Valley organises an annual seminar in collaboration with its counterpart organisation in Taiwan and provides consultative services to the Taiwanese government. This resonates with the Indian IT success story where immigrants have not returned to India but have facilitated outsourcing of service development to origin. They have not only been a source of knowledge for their home countries but they have also been a source of contacts within their countries for US firms and for links to foreign capital markets (Arora et al. 2001).

4.4.1   Innovation as part of R&D

Following the footsteps of South Korea, Taiwan and Singapore, it is encouraging that Malaysia is intending to set up a National Innovation System that will involve a set of distinct processes involving institutions that jointly as well as individually contribute to the development and diffusion of new technologies. It will provide the framework within which government forms and implements policies to influence the innovation process (MOSTE 2003).

The Malaysian government's commitments towards improving innovation in the manufacturing sector can be seen in the three National Surveys of Innovation undertaken so far. The most recent survey of 2000–01 notes that about 72 per cent of most innovating firms were involved in both product and process innovation rather than in only one or the other. Product innovation is a new product or service whose technological characteristics or intended uses differ significantly from those of previously produced products. Such innovations can involve radically new technologies, or be based on combining existing technologies in new uses, or can be derived from the use of new knowledge.

Process innovation, on the other hand, is the adoption of technologically new or significantly improved production method including methods of product delivery such as changes in equipment, production organisation or a combination of these changes and may be derived from the use of new knowledge. The results of the survey noted in Table 4.14 show that some 81 per cent of all innovating firms cited improvement of product quality as an important objective of innovation. There is also interest in extending the product range but about 51 per cent of the firms are moderately or not interested in increasing their market share to get into new markets. However, with process innovation, improving production flexibility is considered quite important. The World Bank (2005) survey also shows similar results with more firms attempting to upgrade existing products and entering new markets due to quality or cost improvements related to changes in processes of production rather than introducing a substantially new technology.

Only 35 per cent of the firms interviewed in the manufacturing sector by MASTIC were innovating and not surprisingly, about 45 per cent of the firms perceived economic risks were very high in innovation. In terms of factors hampering innovation, the most important factor is the high cost of innovation in terms of infrastructure and facilities rather than labour cost which only 30 per cent of the firms thought was an important component. In addition, lack of personnel, and information on technology and markets were also a hindrance.

Table 4.14   *Objectives for innovation by level of importance (percentage of firms interviewed)*

	High	Medium	Low/Irrelevant
Government grants, loans and incentives	33.0	23.0	31.0
Improve product quality	81.4	16.3	2.3
Extend product range	47.3	41.8	10.9
Increase market share or open new market	48.2	28.8	23.0
Improve production flexibility	44.7	34.6	10.1
Reduce labour costs	30.5	42.6	26.9

Source: MASTIC (2003).

Although foreign ownership presence is greater amongst innovating firms than non-innovating firms, the majority of innovating firms tend to be locally-owned firms and this augurs well for the Malaysian economy. Interestingly, innovation is carried out by firms of all sizes. Some 45 per cent of innovating firms are small firms (with less than 50 employees) while medium-sized (50–249 employees) and large-sized firms (more than 249 employees) account for 27 per cent and 25 per cent respectively of total innovating firms. The impact of innovation is also often measured by the number of patents and industrial design granted as seen in Table 4.15 below.

It can be seen that patents to non-residents outweigh those granted to residents and there is no trend in improvements in this regard. The inventor awards look quite promising although the breakdown for residents and non-residents is not available. One could however argue that it is not important who invents or obtains the patents as what matters is the extent of diffusion in the economy and the type of healthy competitive environment this brings about to encourage other firms in pursuing this path.

Another measure of the impact of innovation is to evaluate the extent to which firms have been able to harness the fruits of innovation in terms of product development, efficient use of R&D, technological breakthrough and commercialisation of new technologies. The findings of the more recent survey are summarised in Figure 4.3.

Table 4.15   Patents and inventor awards

Year	Patents to residents	Patents to non-residents	Patent ratio Resident/Total	International inventor awards*
1990	20	498	0.04	n.a.
1991	29	1021	0.03	n.a.
1992	10	1124	0.01	n.a.
1993	14	1270	0.01	5
1994	21	1608	0.01	10
1995	29	1724	0.02	3
1996	79	1722	0.04	6
1997	52	734	0.07	7
1998	21	545	0.04	10
1999	39	682	0.05	19
2000	24	381	0.06	21
2001	18	1452	0.01	27
2002	32	1460	0.02	45
2003	n.a.	n.a.	n.a.	12
2004	n.a.	n.a.	n.a.	16
2005	37	2471	0.015	n.a.

Note: A patent is an exclusive right granted for an invention which is a product or process that provides a new way of doing things something or offers a new technical solution to a problem. *This is at the Geneva International Invention Exhibition/Competition.

Source: MASTIC (2004) and EPU (2006).

There are significant variations in the impact of innovation on an industry's turnover, and these range from as low as 15 per cent to as high as 70 per cent. For most industries, the impact of innovation on turnover was within the range of 20–50 per cent. Overall, the information in Figure 4.3 appears encouraging but it is still early to assess the situation as technological innovation and diffusion are dynamic processes with long lead and lag times. Survey data at a given point in time at best gives a snapshot of the situation. However, the World Bank (2005) provides the first suggestive evidence of innovative activity for Malaysian manufacturing productivity growth. It was found that 44 per cent of firms in industries with rapid TFP growth adopt new technologies and adapt them to their own needs.

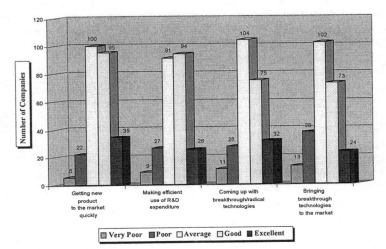

Source: MASTIC (2003).

Figure 4.3   Effectiveness and efficiency measures

Other indicators of scientific knowledge creation and diffusion are publications in the areas of sciences, social sciences and humanities. Table 4.16 provides evidence of Malaysia's performance lagging behind the developed countries and the Asian NIEs as it was ranked 55 among 178 nations. In terms of Malaysia's scientific papers in international journals that covered 59 fields of research, there has been a slow growth in its output but a steady growth after 1990 as seen in Table 4.17. However, the gap between Malaysia and developed countries remains large in the area of science and engineering as Malaysia's articles in these fields were around 22, well below the 400–1100 levels observed in developed countries.

While public funding has benefited some (mostly domestic-owned and controlled) firms that have managed to access these funds, other firms can look to venture capital for the provision of risk capital. Venture capital was first introduced in Malaysia in 1984, and even after 20 years it is still in its infancy stage as the venture capital industry remains small and risk-averse in their attitude. Although the number of venture capital companies has increased from 20 in 1995 to 38 in 2004, according to Fikri (2004), there are only about 20 active venture capital firms. The firms are either backed by government, a private firm, and institution- or bank-backed. Tham and Ragayah (2006) explain that venture capital companies have not contributed substantially to overcoming the financing problems in technology development in the country. The companies are reluctant to provide seed capital financing[14] and are mainly involved in funding acquisitions or buy-out financing or second-stage financing (such as early adoption of the product and progressing towards commercialisation). In addition, there exists a shortage of skilled personnel in both government and private institutions to effectively assess the risk and returns in the application of funds.

Table 4.16   Percentage share of world papers, 1981–2000

Countries	Ratio
USA	37.64
UK	9.06
Japan	8.13
Germany	8.02
France	5.78
Canada	4.87
Italy	3.33
USSR	2.65
Australia	2.58
South Korea	0.77
Taiwan	0.77
Singapore	0.25
Thailand	0.11
Malaysia	0.08
Philippines	0.05
Indonesia	0.04

Source: MASTIC (2005a).

Table 4.17   Malaysian papers in international journals

Year	Number of Papers
Before 1973	44
1980	117
1990	851
1995	1555
2000	1930
2002	2016
2005[1]	2293

Note: [1] is an estimate.

Source: MASTIC (2004) and EPU (2006).

While public funding has benefited some (mostly domestic-owned and controlled) firms that have managed to access these funds, other firms can look to venture capital for the provision of risk capital. Venture capital was first introduced in Malaysia in 1984, and even after 20 years it is still in its infancy stage as the venture capital industry remains small and risk-averse in their attitude. Although the number of venture capital companies has increased from 20 in 1995 to 38 in 2004, according to Fikri (2004), there are only about 20 active venture capital firms. The firms are either backed by government, a private firm, and institution- or bank-backed. Tham and Ragayah (2006) explain that venture capital companies have not contributed substantially to overcoming the financing problems in technology development in the country. The companies are reluctant to provide seed capital financing[15] and are mainly involved in funding acquisitions or buy-out financing or second-stage financing (such as early adoption of the product and progressing towards commercialisation). In addition, there exists a shortage of skilled personnel in both government and private institutions to effectively assess the risk and returns in the application of funds.

One way in which public policy can stimulate the provision of risk capital is to relax listing requirements on the national stock exchange, making it easier for new ventures to access the market for start-ups without stringent track records.[16] Efforts towards this objective as well as the deepening of the capital market are progressing (see Tham and Ragayah 2006) but the results have been rather slow to come. Another reason is that the Malaysian Stock Exchange of Securities and Automated Quotation (MESDAQ) is relatively new since its launch in 1997 and the timing could not be worse in the wake of the 1997/98 financial crisis. Thus, it has taken a while for MESDAQ to establish itself and perform its role well in the area of venture capital. Perhaps the opening of the capital market in 2005 to wholly foreign-owned futures broking and venture capital companies can expect increase funding and expertise to promote investments.

Lastly, the government has also taken on the view that patents play an important role in promoting innovation and therefore greater care and emphasis on the framework of intellectual property right is necessary (EPU 2006). According to Kondo (1999), IP rights protection systems are fairly well established in Malaysia except for trade secrets and integrated circuits. The Intellectual Property Corporation of Malaysia was established in 2003 to improve contractual certainty to combat piracy and protect content creators in an attempt to boost licensing. If IP rights are well defined, firms are likely to compete fiercely for skilled labour. In fact, a majority of the firms reported that they would increase R&D efforts if the IP right regime was strengthened (World Bank 2005).

But restructuring intellectual property to make sure that the knowledge commons are protected whilst the appropriate rewards to entrepreneurs are ensured may be a difficult balance to achieve. Strong IP can block the knowledge flow and thereby block new knowledge creation as well. While strengthening IP rights may increase R&D in forms (dynamic benefits), it would also impose a cost (static costs) in the form or raising the cost of technology access for producers and result in higher prices for consumers. Thus, Dempsey (1999) argues that in most instances, weaker IP will improve the overall pace of innovation.

4.5 CONCLUSION

The Malaysian experience shows that capital deepening must be accompanied by sufficient labour and skill deepening in conjunction with an effective technology development programme to allow a more effective adaptation and application of new technology. While human capital and technology development policies are necessary, they are not sufficient conditions for growth. These polices need to be well coordinated and integrated into a broader setting with other support policies. These include the nurturing of network cohesion, the extension of R&D schemes to MNCs, a reexamination of foreign worker policy and strengthening links with foreign research institutions, etc.

Human capital development can be achieved by the two-pronged model of academic and vocational schools to harness employment potential, and business accelerator programmes to foster entrepreneurship. In Malaysia's current environment of rapid structural transformation, leapfrogging without having a strong base of local talent and support will only bring short-run economic growth. To avoid this, there must be a change in the mindset of people, and the proposed changes to the education and training system need to be carefully implemented. As the Prime Minister, Abdullah Badawi, notes:[17]

> we need nothing less than an 'education revolution' to ensure that our aspirations instill a new performance culture of the public and private sectors ... to nurture a new kind of human capital that is equal to the tasks and challenges ahead.

With technology development policies, Malaysia had a late and slow start. But it must be acknowledged that for a developing country, the optimal strategy may not necessarily be to focus excessive efforts in R&D and innovation especially in inventing products and processes at the technological frontier (Dahlman et al. 1987). What is important is acquiring the capabilities needed for efficient production and investment. To make this work, it is necessary to combine foreign and local technology elements. The dependence on foreign technology transfer is however a double-edged sword as it may be a quick way of progressing but with short-term gains. For instance, a more sustained approach to upgrading technology from original equipment manufacturing to original design manufacturing and original brand manufacturing is required. But the acquisition of technological capabilities does not merely come from experience, although experience is important. It comes from the conscious efforts to monitor what is being done, to try new things, to keep track of developments and to accumulate skills.

In general, given Malaysia's sound macroeconomic fundamentals, there is little reason for Malaysia not to succeed in the path of technologically-driven development. The challenge is determined by the provision of an enabling environment by the government as well as the political will and governance structure in place to undertake and manage appropriate policies for sustainable growth.

NOTES

[1] Opening Speech at the Conference on Engineering Education 2004 as reported in *The Sun* 15 December 2004.

[2] The counter argument to the streaming system has been that it wrongly disadvantages students who are late developers where formal education is concerned.

[3] Sometime in the 1970s, Bahasa Melayu replaced English as the medium of instruction in schools. This was a political decision to help address the poverty and income inequality problem in the Malay community that resulted in the 1969 racial riots.

[4] These include Swinburne and Curtin University campuses in Sarawak, and Monash, Nottingham and FTMS-DeMontfort University campuses in Kuala Lumpur.

[5] This is the nation's first electronic-learning institution combining the face-to-face classes with the effective use of web-based courseware and online tutorials.

[6] The Malaysian Employers' Federation and academics criticise the higher educational system and local fresh graduates for not meeting employers' needs (*The New Straits Times* 28 January 2002). A survey undertaken by the Knowledge Worker Exchange Sendiran Berhad, a Multimedia Development Corporation subsidiary, revealed that graduates from local institutes of higher learning lack depth in their IT skills and English language proficiency and that mismatch of skills still continues (*The New Straits Times* 15 Februray 2004).

[7] See Penang's Socio-economic and Environmental Research Institute's Occasional Paper Series that can downloaded at http://www.seri.com.my/oldsite/occational%20papers/HumanResourceIssuesChalleng esProspectsForGrowth.PDF

[8] This is to develop and upgrade capability of local companies through training and smart partnerships with MNCs and this involves training in critical skills and linkage with MNCs.

[9] Singapore too has a similar programme, the Local Industries Upgrading Program, but the level of commitment on the part of the government to make this successful is noteworthy in its efforts to employ full-time procurement experts for specific periods with the adopted firms to help them upgrade their production and management capabilities to the required standards.

[10] For instance, the Korean government was able to offer of a very attractive incentive package for Korean-American scientists and engineers to return home through the 1970s.

[11] These include the Kulim High-tech Park in Kedah established in 1993 and the Technology Park Malaysia in Selangor, established in 1995.

[12] This model is appropriate as the dependent variable is based on a 'yes' and 'no' answer to the question of whether the firm undertakes the particular type of technological activity.

[13] These are documented by EPU (2005a) for Universiti Putra Malaysia, Universiti Kebangsaan Malaysia, Universiti Sains Malaysia and Universiti Teknologi Malaysia.

[14] The government has however established the Cradle Investment Program in 2003 under the purview of the Malaysian Venture Capital Management Berhad in an attempt to do this.

[15] The government has however established the Cradle Investment Program in 2003 under the purview of the Malaysian Venture Capital Management Berhad in an attempt to do this.

[16] While this presumes that venture capital contributes to the creation of high technology activities, it could well be that venture capital sources may be encouraged by the emergence/existence of technological activities instead.

[17] Speech by Prime Minister Badawi at the National Economic Action Council on January 2004 in Putrajaya, Malaysia.

5. Leapfrogging into the Knowledge Economy

5.1 THE KNOWLEDGE-BASED SOCIETY

The advent of globalisation as a process that led to the creation of the borderless world, made the move towards the K-economy rather compelling for Malaysia. Several definitions of a K-economy exist within various organisations such as APEC, OECD and the World Bank. The Economic Planning Unit of Malaysia defines a K-economy as one where the generation and utilisation of knowledge contribute significantly to economic growth and wealth creation. The OPP3 indicates that the nucleus of the K-economy will be the capacity of human capital to create, innovate, generate and exploit new ideas as well as apply technology and exercise superior entrepreneurial skills.

The World Development Report 1999 states that today's most technologically advanced economies are truly knowledge-based. Malaysia decided to lock itself into the fast expanding global information revolution and aspire to become an information society as part of its plan of attaining the status of a developed economy as set out in its Vision 2020. This is to help regain the erosion of its competitive advantage in manufacturing with the entry of low-cost players in the industry like China, India and Vietnam where cheap labour is abundant. In assessing Malaysia's readiness to become a K-based economy, the Global Competitiveness Report 2005–06 ranked Malaysia 25th among 117 developed and developing countries based on the Technology Index. This is however a narrow measure of the optimal transformation to a knowledge society which is a multi-dimensional concept. The purpose of this chapter is to provide a broad assessment by evaluating Malaysia's leapfrogging tendency from an industrial society to a knowledge society and discussing some of the challenges and prospects faced in this transition.

First, a distinction needs to be made between an information/new economy and a knowledge/digital economy. Appendix 5.1 provides the Malaysian perspective towards these terminologies. Broadly speaking, the former is dependent on IT while the latter is more than that and includes communications and media. Generally, ICT encompasses all those technologies that enable handling of information and facilitate different forms of communication among human actors, between human beings and electronic systems, and among electronic systems (Hamelink 1997). Heeks (2000) argues that in order to understand ICT and its social processes and contexts, there is a need to take a systemic view of the technology as seen in Figure 5.1. There are separate elements: the technology itself, and the information on which it operates, purposeful activity, and people to undertake those processes. All of these make up the information system that exists within an environment of institutions and of influencing factors (political, economic, socio-cultural, technical and cultural).

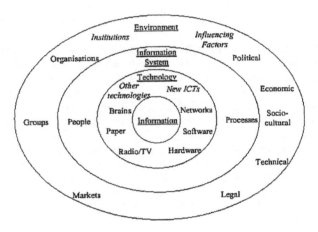

Source: Heeks (2000).

Figure 5.1   A systematic view of ICT

Based on the above general definition, a knowledge society can be defined as one that achieves various goals at the three levels depicted in Figure 5.2. At the national/macro level, there are industrial clusters comprising valued added industries producing goods and services competitively using ICT to form the basis of productivity growth in knowledge-driven economy. At the meso level, various industries comprising firms involved with ICT operate to support the production and consumption of ICT-related products and services. Finally at the micro level, two broad categories at the grass root levels are considered – the knowledge workers and the community at large. This is where human capital investment policies play a major role in ensuring that the K-economy is well supported by the quality and quantity of the right type of labour. The second group consists of the non-knowledge workers in the community who need to be bought up to date with having access and knowing how to use IT so as to avoid the digital divide that arises between the information rich and information poor. That is, there must be qualitative transformation of the community to improve its life with ICT.

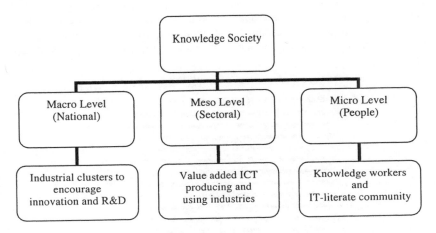

Figure 5.2 The knowledge-based society

Thus the successful transition to a knowledge society depends on the balance of development at all three levels. Achieving the right balance is important to ensure that all the three levels work hand in hand to support the activities of each level for optimal growth. The rest of the chapter discusses the three levels underlying the knowledge society.

5.2 THE K-ECONOMY AT THE NATIONAL LEVEL

The foundation for a K-economy in Malaysia was laid with the formulation of the National IT Agenda in 1996, and in 2002, the Knowledge-Based Economy Master Plan was formulated to affect the transition in the areas of human resource, physical and institutional infrastructure, and science and technology capability. To monitor the progress of the economy's move towards a K-economy, the Malaysian government developed the Knowledge-Based Economy Development Index, developed from 21 selected factors, namely, computer infrastructure, education and training, R&D and technology. Figure 5.3 shows that Malaysia's position of 17 out of 22 has not changed from 2000 to 2005 but the overall score has improved significantly from 2413 to 3014. The most significant aspect of improvement was found in computer infrastructure which registered an improvement of 196.4 per cent in terms of scores between 2000 and 2005, followed by R&D and technology at 29.5 per cent and education and training at 22.8 per cent.

Unlike the KDI, the Networked Readiness Index not only uses a larger sample of at least 100 countries but also takes a different approach to cross country comparison. This index attempts to compare the country's degree of preparation to participate in and benefit from ICT development. Based on data for 64 variables, the index separates the dimensions of environment, readiness, and usage to provide a different set of information for assessment.

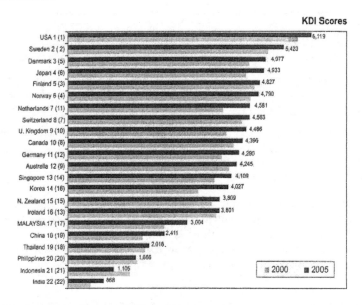

Note: Numbers in brackets are 2000 rankings

Source: Economic Planning Unit

Figure 5.3   The knowledge-based economy index, 2000 and 2005

With respect to the environment for the IT and communications industries, information is assembled on various relevant elements:

- the market assessment evaluates human resources and business relationships in relation to their ability to support a knowledge-based society – issues such as venture capital availability, competition in telecommunications, spending on education and information technology, etc;
- the political regulatory environment involves the nature of the legal system and regulations and their application in connection to fostering IT

development – legal framework, government restrictions on internet control, etc;

- infrastructure availability and quality to support adoption and use of IT technologies – number of telephone lines, switch capacity, local availability of specialised IT services, etc.

With respect to readiness, the underlying data measures:

- consumer readiness to adopt and utilise IT – availability of internet access and broadband, literacy and education, cost of communications, etc.;
- business readiness to make use of IT methods in management, supply chain operations, and marketing – capacity for innovation, business internet sophistications, quality of IT training programmes;
- government readiness to use IT in its various operations – government prioritisation of IT, competence of government officials, government online services.

In terms of usage, the focus is on the following:

- consumer use that is measured in terms of the level of adoption and usage of various types of consumer IT – use of online payment systems, use of various types of consumer electronic equipment, household spending on electronics, number of broadband subscriber lines;
- business usage that is concerned with the adoption, utilisation and range of business uses of IT measured by per cent of businesses using e-commerce, use of internet for business coordination, and use of e-mail.
- government usage that is concerned with the level of IT use in government operations and relations to its citizens – use of internet-based transactions with government, government online services, and government success with IT promotion.

The wide range of IT development in East Asia is readily apparent in Tables 5.1 and 5.2. Some East Asian countries such as Singapore, Taiwan and South Korea are seen to be far in advance, leading even some of the most mature countries. In some respects, Singapore is number one. Others like Vietnam, Indonesia and the Philippines are very much at the tail end of the readiness scale. In most cases, high income corresponds to a high ranking in IT readiness. High rankings in readiness also typically correspond to high rankings for the component indexes such as infrastructure and usage. It is most interesting consequently to note the following discrepancies:

- Among developed countries, Japan is not as highly ranked as the United States and other countries with approximately equivalent income. This

may reflect lags in the policy/regulatory index and in IT usage by government.
- In East Asia, Singapore is a leader in all categories, though government is especially highly ranked, number one in market environment, and government readiness and usage. Singapore appears to benefit from the strong government push on IT to develop a 'wired island'.
- Korea and Taiwan have a relatively high ranking with respect to individual usage, probably reflecting their high rates of consumer connectivity and infrastructure.
- China has considerably higher standing in government usage than in consumer and business use. That is consistent with its relatively low readiness index, suggesting that consumers and businesses lag behind. On the other hand, China is a large heterogeneous country and computer readiness in major urban centres like Shanghai is much further along and rural areas may be much further behind than the national average figures indicate.
- Malaysia's infrastructure in terms of environment is relatively speaking a far cry at the 60th position.

Table 5.1   Rankings of the networked readiness index

	NRI 2005	NRI 2003	Environment 2005	Readiness 2005	Usage 2005
China	50	51	52	50	49
Hong Kong	11	18	11	13	9
Indonesia	68	73	63	61	75
Malaysia	24	25	22	24	24
Philippines	70	69	73	75	59
Singapore	2	2	3	1	2
South Korea	14	20	25	7	7
Taiwan	7	17	10	8	5
Thailand	34	38	38	32	34
Vietnam	75	68	81	76	68
United States	1	1	2	2	6
Japan	16	12	18	14	16

Notes: NRI stands for Networked Readiness Index. Figures for 2005 include 115 while that for 2003 are based on 102 countries.

Source: The Global Information Technology Report from the World Economic Forum, various issues.

Table 5.2 Components of the networked readiness index 2005

	Environment			Readiness			Usage		
	Market	Political regulatory	Infrastructure	Individual	Business	Govern-ment	Individual	Business	Govern-ment
China	43	55	68	65	48	40	63	59	30
Hong Kong	2	19	20	9	23	6	6	18	10
Indonesia	48	64	99	67	54	55	59	67	86
Malaysia	6	17	60	22	24	12	44	24	7
Philippines	69	67	94	100	64	39	80	45	68
Singapore	1	2	15	1	12	1	14	10	1
South Korea	15	28	24	19	20	4	5	14	6
Taiwan	3	25	13	4	16	9	9	9	4
Thailand	28	37	75	43	32	27	59	37	24
Vietnam	75	73	92	85	82	68	91	74	47
USA	4	4	2	14	1	2	12	1	9
Japan	12	20	16	13	9	17	19	2	31

Note: Figures are based on 115 countries.

Source: The Global Information Technology Report 2005/06.

Malaysia has also made vast improvements in becoming an information society as seen by more standard types of ICT indicators in Table 5.3. Although fixed direct lines have declined, there has been a very significant rise in cellular phones. Within a decade, the number of computers and internet users too saw a substantial increase.

Table 5.3   Selected ICT indicators

Service per 100 population	1995	2000	2005
Fixed direct exchange line	16.1	19.7	17.2
Internet users	1.4	7.1	13.9
Mobile phones	4.2	21.8	74.1
Computers	3.73	9.4	21.8

Source: ICT Services Statistics 2004 (Department of Statistics) and EPU (2006).

Table 5.4 shows that Malaysia lags behind other developed countries although she is ahead of the developing countries in telephone subscription. In terms of internet usage, Malaysia is not too far off from the levels of the developed countries, and with mobile phones, usage in Malaysia is higher than Canada and close to the US, but lower than other developed economies.

Table 5.4   Service per 100 inhabitants in 2004

	Telephone subscribers	Internet users	Mobile phones
Malaysia	62.36	39.7	58.7
Australia	126.18	65.3	82.6
Canada	107.04	63.0	47.2
China	42.38	7.2	25.5
Germany	144.25	42.4	86.4
Indonesia	12.68	3.75	13.5
Italy	150.16	50.3	109.4
Japan	115.09	58.7	71.6
New Zealand	109.67	82.0	77.5
Singapore	130.28	56.1	89.5
Sweden	162.45	75.5	103.2
Thailand	49.91	11.0	44.1
UK	143.13	63.3	102.8
USA	116.96	62.3	61.0

Source: International Telecommunication Union Website.

5.2.1 Institutional Support

Nagy (2003) explains that countries which adopt an inactive or reactive rather than an adaptive and pro-active posture are likely to lose out on the opportunity to leapfrog. These countries may be simply locked out or marginalised. The Malaysian government was clearly proactive when it picked the ICT sector as one of the growth sectors in 1996 and since then has provided institutional support and funds to help expand this sector. In 2001, the government implemented the RosettaNet Standard, a system which enables local companies to communicate with their trading partners and conduct business electronically through common codes for sourcing parts and components. The government has also taken the lead with its flagship applications and computerisation funds set aside for schools and government agencies. The second largest allocation has been set aside to bridge the digital gap through the provision of internet services and other forms of information and telecommunication services in the rural areas and schools. In addition, some funds have also been set aside for various grants to promote ICT content and entrepreneurship development. Table 5.5 gives an indication of the extent of expenditure in these areas.

Table 5.5   Development funds (RM million) for ICT-related programmes

Programme	Eighth MP expenditure	Ninth MP allocation
Computerisation of government agencies	2125.0	5734.2
Bridging the Digital divide	2433.1	3710.2
School	2145.1	3279.2
Communications infrastructure service	254.0	150.0
Telecentres	18.1	101.0
ICT training services	15.9	180.0
ICT funding	1125.6	1493.0
MSC multimedia applications	1153.1	1100.5
e-Government	537.7	572.7
Smart school	363.9	169.8
Telehealth	91.8	60.0
Government multipurpose card	159.7	298.0
MSC development	320.8	377.0
ICT R&D	727.5	474.0
Total	7885.1	12888.9

Source: EPU (2006).

In addition, to boost the development of the ICT industrial cluster, the government set up a venture capital fund (Malaysian Venture Capital

Management Berhad) in 2001 to channel funds in the form of interest-free soft loans for a period of ten years. As venture capitalists are often sceptical of investing in companies, the government introduced MESDAQ (Malaysian Exchange of Securities Dealing and Automated Quotation, the equivalent of Nesdaq in the United States) which is a stock exchange where firms can be listed even though they have limited or no assets as long as they have growth potential in the technology sector. With the introduction of MESDAQ's support for technology-based firms, risk will be minimised. The Malaysian Debt Venture Berhad set up in 2002 provided another source of financing companies in ICT. However, venture capital is still in its infancy stages in Malaysia, with a very small proportion of private venture capital companies.

5.2.2 Impact of ICT

For the last two hundred years, neo-classical economics recognised capital and labour as the main factors of production in the production-based economy, but today technology and knowledge are the key factors of production in the K-economy. Here, we take a close look at the impact of ICT on Malaysian output and TFP growth, seen in Table 5.6.

Although the real rate of return on ICT capital stock was three times higher than the non-ICT capital stock, its share of GDP hardly changed over time. Subsequently, the contribution of ICT capital stock to GDP growth was small relative to non-ICT capital stock although the former increased over time, possibly due to the higher returns to the use of ICT. A decomposition of ICT capital stock's contribution to GDP growth showed that telecommunications constitute a large part of ICT followed by hardware. The software component's contribution to GDP growth was rather small, reflecting perhaps a shortage of ICT professionals. In terms of TFP growth, the evidence strongly supports the contribution of the ICT sector to total TFP growth. Not only did ICT sector's TFP growth remain positive unlike all other sectors' TFP growth, but its contribution to total TFP growth grew very substantially from 32 per cent to about 311 per cent in the late 1990s, and that helped to keep the total TFP growth less negative than it would have otherwise been.

One interesting observation is that it was not telecommunications (although this component was more responsible for GDP growth) but hardware which drove the ICT sectors' TFP growth. This is not surprising as telecommunications has a wider application than hardware in other sectors and hence shows up in the broader measure of GDP growth emanating from all sectors as opposed to just the ICT sectors alone. One point to note is that although the internet has a fairly long history, often the internet era as such is said to have come into place when the full-scale use of the internet was triggered by the World Wide Web and the Microsoft Windows 95 operating system. Hence it can be expected that the late 1990s would have more impact than the early 1990s.

A recent study by Gholami et al. (2006) has shown that ICT (measured by annual investment in telecommunications) can indirectly affect economic growth via FDI. For Malaysia, in the short run, ICT is found to Granger-cause FDI, suggesting that ICT infrastructure is an important factor in attracting foreign investors. This is especially the case since the establishment of MSC. Also, since studies exist to show that FDI contributes to economic growth, it can be further inferred that increases in information and knowledge may result in efficient collaboration and coordination; telecommunications and IT increases information availability and accuracy and provides better conditions for business. Geography and distance are found to be less important in production location decisions as communications and transactions costs continue to fall.

Table 5.6   Impact of ICT

	1990–94	1995–99
As a share of GDP		
Non-ICT capital stock	1.631	1.869
ICT capital stock	0.088	0.083
Hardware	0.013	0.012
Software	0.007	0.005
Telecommunications	0.067	0.066
Income share		
Non-ICT capital stock	0.260	0.288
ICT capital stock	0.026	0.027
Labour	0.714	0.685
Real return on capital stock		
Non-ICT capital stock	0.159	0.154
ICT capital stock	0.326	0.448
Contribution to growth		
GDP	9.396	5.118
TFP	−1.727	−1.116
Labour	6.913	3.299
Non-ICT capital stock	3.783	2.367
ICT capital stock	0.427	0.566
Hardware	0.169	0.341
Software	0.047	0.011
Telecommunications	0.210	0.214
Composition of TFP growth		
Total TFP	−1.727	−1.116
All other sectors	−2.288	−4.586
ICT Sector	0.562	3.471
Hardware	0.527	3.328
Telecommunications	0.035	0.143

Source: Lee and Khatri (2003).

Another indirect effect of ICT on economic growth is discussed by Lee (2005) who shows that international knowledge spillover effects result directly via telecommunications infrastructure. The role of telecommunications as a medium for knowledge diffusion across countries is emphasised, with substantial differences existing in intangible knowledge or information diffusion through the use of the telephone, fax, e-mail and the internet.

One view is that the link between ICT and productivity growth results from ICT production and not ICT use. Another view is that countries using ICT stand to gain a lot more than those merely producing ICT equipment. The evidence from various studies remains mixed on this issue. Wolff (2002), on the other hand, reports a study on the computer sector in the US as showing very high productivity spillovers between the computer-producing sector and sectors using computers. Both Australia and Hong Kong are high users of ICT but low producers of ICT. As importers of ICT, they have benefited from terms of trade effects as ICT prices have declined. South Korea, on the other hand, is an ICT-producing economy whose ICT industry's contribution to GDP rose from a mere 4.5 per cent in 1990 to about 50 per cent by 2000.

Facilitating the greater use of ICT by creating a flexible environment enabling firms to restructure in appropriate ways to tap the full potential of ICT will generate network economies with increasing returns and spillover benefits that change the way the economy grows. Interactive processes alone place new demands on firms and open up opportunities only for those that can respond to the need for increased flexibility. Proponents of IT-related growth believe in the strong positive linkages between IT and the other sectors in the face of structural change and organisational structures well suited to the effective implementation of IT which brings about spillover gains. Part of the problem in capturing effects on IT and ICT investment is attributable to the inherent measurement problems and time lag effects. Other sceptics say there is a need for a simultaneous increase in education and skills for productivity growth effects of ICT.

Dedrick and Kraemer (1998) have argued that East Asian countries, because of inadequate diffusion and adoption of advanced ICT in much of the non-manufacturing service sectors, have become trapped in low margin electronics manufacturing and lack the ability to move into high margin service sectors such as software development, innovative design and IT services. Rather than being complementary, ICT production may divert resources away from ICT diffusion activities. Wong (2002) provides evidence for the Asian countries that high involvement in ICT production has little or no positive spillover effect on ICT diffusion (in services, and use within community). He concludes that unlike the advanced Asian economies, the developing Asian countries such as Malaysia may have over-emphasised industrial policy to favour electronics manufacturing at the expense of promoting ICT diffusion in services sectors.

5.2.3 Industrial Clusters

In a knowledge-based economy, having knowledge is not enough; it must be shared, and in some regions this has brought about clusters of firms that network and communicate to raise the overall knowledge levels that they can draw upon. The best known cluster is California's Silicon Valley where a large agglomeration of high-tech firms makes it the world's most vibrant technology region. Firms in related industries often cluster together in a particular region, allowing them to take advantage of common resources (for example, a workforce trained in particular skills; technical institutes; a common supplier base). This is not only more cost effective but helps boost the synergies and cross-firm learning that can transform low-performing clusters into high-performing ones. For example, states can fund industry training programmes through groups of firms with the same skill needs as opposed to making grants to individual firms. The government can also reorient other programmes, such as manufacturing extension, business finance, business assistance and technology transfer, around clusters.

In Malaysia, one could say that there are three industrial clusters – the Technology Park Malaysia, the Multimedia Super Corridor and BioValley – all of which aim to provide a conductive environment for R&D and innovation and drawing on knowledge workers. It is unclear at this stage if the plans to create an ICT SME cluster in Cyberjaya (EPU 2003) will still go ahead. But it is doubtful if the idea of an SME park will work (Wahab 2003). First, is the current failure to attract large firms to Cyberjaya. Second, it is more costly for SMEs to relocate and operate in Cyberjaya. Third, is the general feeling that the government is not doing enough to help SMEs and there is little reason to believe in location-specific benefits unless specific programmes are in place to hook them with MNCs. But those who have already established links with MNCs will have no incentive to relocate. While there is a real need to foster linkages, this process must be strictly monitored, otherwise it may meet with limited success as is the case with the manufacturing industries.

However, Taiwan was able to do this with their SMEs through strong government intervention when FDI was encouraged, hence breeding efficient SMEs which have led to higher TFP growth (Chuang and Lin 1999). A similar attempt is being made under the MSC-Technopreneur Development Flagship which was set up in 2004. This flagship identified 3201 ICT SMEs to participate in the ICT-SME Development Lifecycle Program. There are also a number of ICT-related financial schemes to further accelerate the utilisation of ICT, especially by SMEs. The Demonstrator Applications Grant Scheme provided funds for short-term projects targeted at creating, developing and promoting new ICT applications for specific uses, particularly at the community levels. By the end of 2004, there were 16 incubator companies set up for a joint mentoring and nurturing programme with several foreign companies where projects were initiated to facilitate local ICT and multimedia SMEs to enrich their business concepts and plans by assisting start-up companies in the areas of communications, multimedia and intelligent systems.

The Multimedia Super Corridor

The MSC (a 15 km by 40 km strip of real estate between Kuala Lumpur and a relatively new administrative center, Putrajaya) which was launched in 1996 was Malaysia's first initiative to lay the foundation for the knowledge-based economy in the hope of becoming Asia's Silicon Valley. The MSC is intended to offer an excellent and conducive environment to attract knowledge-based workers and high-technology industries, especially world-class multimedia companies from the private sector to enable Malaysia to become a regional IT hub. At the same time, the Multimedia Development Corporation was also established as a one-stop agency to promote and manage the implementation of related programmes and projects in this industrial cluster whose development approach not only emphasises the growth of the manufacturing sector per se but the concomitant growth of the supporting industries such as the services sector.[1] The plan underlying MSC is divided into three phases, as shown in Table 5.7.

Table 5.7   Plans underlying MSC

Phase 1: 1996–2003	Phase 2: 2004–10	Phase 3: 2011–20
1. Establish Cyberjaya and Putrajaya as world-class intelligent cities. 2. Establish cyberlaws. 3. Launch seven flagship applications. 4. Attract 50 world-class companies.	1. Establish more intelligent cities. 2. Link MSC to other cities and the world. 3. Establish cluster of 250 world-class companies.	1. Establish more intelligent cities. 2. Transform Malaysia into a knowledge-based society. 3. Establish cluster of 500 world-class companies.

In the first phase of the MSC development, two intelligent cities, Cyberjaya and Putrajaya, were established with the MSC, and run as seven separate flagships applications – the Electronic Government, Multipurpose Card, Smart Schools, Telemedicine, R&D cluster, Technopreneur Development and E-business.[2] The strategic focus of phase two from 2004 to 2010, otherwise known as MSC's Next Leap, will be on developing a web of corridors by linking MSC to other parts of the country. In June 2004, the Bayan Lepas area in Penang and the Kulim High Tech Park in Kedah were conferred MSC Cybercity status as these were in an advanced state of readiness to become intelligent cities, thus enabling new MSC-status companies to be based in the northern region. As part of the gradual roll out of the MSC to the rest of the country, another cybercity is to be identified in Pahang in the near future, while there are plans to establish such cities in Perak, Malacca, Johor and Sarawak in the distant future. This is to enable a cluster of high-quality companies to harness the power of ICT as a tool in business services, consumer and product services such as health, education, fashion apparel and textiles, bio-medical products, aerospace/defence, automotive, electronics, industrial machinery, agricultural and food processing, energy and processed materials. It is projected that the number of MSC-status companies will increase to 4000 and generate 100 000 jobs by 2010 (ninth MP).

Phase three from 2011 to 2020, on the other hand, is to establish links to 12 intelligent cities on the global information highway, extend the corridor to the entire nation, and establish a cluster of 500 world-class companies. In addition, Malaysia is expected to achieve the status of a net exporter of ICT products and services.

There are, however, mixed views on the success of MSC so far and these different views are due in part to the fact that the outcomes of the MSC are measured in different ways and thus have different meanings and interpretations to different people and different interest groups. It is also difficult to benchmark MSC against other world-class projects because of dissimilarities in their objectives and scopes. Furthermore, most studies on MSC had either been done in confidence and/or conducted by foreign consultants appointed by the government or by the MDC and, as such, public accessibility to critical studies on the MSC are rarely available.

Gloomy assessments of the MSC were particularly evident in 1997 and 1998 during the Asian economic meltdown. Despite this setback which slowed down the pace of infrastructural development and affected FDI into MSC due to investors adopting a wait-and-see attitude given capital controls, the pegging of the ringgit, political instability due to the sacking of the former Deputy Prime Minister, Anwar Ibrahim, and the technology bubble burst in 2002, there have been some positive outcomes. Malaysia has been able to mobilise a nation-building project as important as MSC, and cyber laws,[3] multimedia infrastructure and various flagship applications are already in place. The MSC has also had some success in hard infrastructure development and rapidly increased the number of MSC-status companies from 94 in 1997 to 886 in 2003, surpassing the target of 500 as set out in the Knowledge-based Economy Master Plan of 2002. However, with regard to content development and the extent of cutting edge products and services, these have yet to reach expected levels (EPU 2006). But phase one's target of attracting 50 world-class companies by 2003 has been almost met, since by the end of August 2003 MSC had attracted 59 world-class companies although only 47 of them were active then. Also, by 2003, a total of 276 IPs were registered, and in 2004 alone another 119 were registered, consisting of industrial design, patents and trade marks. While it is quite encouraging to note that a total of RM670 million was spent on R&D in 2004, which is a 56 per cent increment over 2003, 73 per cent of the MSC-status companies however affirmed that they were involved only in process development related to industry applications.

In terms of employment, in 2000 the total number of workers employed in MSC stood at 11 911, of which 82.6 per cent were knowledge workers. In 2004 the number had more than doubled to 27 288 positions, of which 90 per cent were knowledge workers and 88 per cent of these workers were Malaysians (EPU 2006; MSC Impact Survey 2005). In terms of educational qualification, 57 per cent of the staff in MSC status companies have at least a first degree, 7 per cent have a Masters and 1 per cent have PhDs.

On the negative side, Malaysia faces stiff competition from Singapore, Japan and South Korea and has still not attracted substantial interest from global technology companies like Bangalore or Singapore has. In 2003, of the 868 MSC-status companies, only 667 were active and these were largely made up of small and medium-sized companies with paid-up capital of less than RM500 000 (MSC Impact Survey 2004). As at the end of 2005, 1421 companies[4] have been given MSC status of which only 70 were MNCs. For the year 2004, 190 company applications were approved as having MSC status of which only six were international world-class companies. As at the end of 2004, only 78 per cent of the 984 companies that have been awarded MSC status were active.

The former Prime Minister, Mahathir Mohamad, who pioneered the idea of MSC has admitted that the MSC has not met up to expectations (Jussawalla and Taylor 2003). However, the MSC project alongside various other traits in Malaysia led Huff (2001) to propose that Malaysia's ability to create 'the cultural and institutional conditions conducive to creativity and innovation make it a vanguard model not only for the Muslim World, but perhaps for all developing countries'. Indergaard (2003), on the other hand, explains how the Malaysian state has implemented some measures of developmental discipline in MSC that may be slow but steady in creating an enduring foundation for digital industry.

Close to MSC is Cyberjaya, a software development centre complete with the state-run Multimedia University (established in 1998), another greenfield site developed from scratch. As an infrastructure project it is a good effort, but it remains an underutilized industrial park because there is limited success in relocating MSC status companies to Cyberjaya as the majority remain in the more developed areas of the Klang Valley in cities such as Kuala Lumpur, Petaling Jaya and Shah Alam, citing that Cyberjaya ecosystems lack attractive incentives (Wahab 2003). This is an obstacle to the intended synergy expected of a cluster strategy which is further aggravated by the shortage of knowledge workers. The latter has been an ongoing problem from the very start, indicating that little is being done to attract and retain foreign and local talent, a case of putting the horse before the cart. To enforce the clustering strategy, MSC companies are forced to have a presence in

Cyberjaya or risk having their MSC status revoked. But surely, the MSC status should be an attribute of the business and process of a company rather than where they are located.

Thus, the MSC appears to be a grandiose project reflecting a vision for the future but the question is, is the scope of MSC too large and targets set too broad? This might have resulted in MSC's slow progress. The domain focus needs to be identified to make the best use of limited resources. For instance, Taiwan decided on semiconductors while Bangalore decided on software, but Malaysia is keen to try many aspects in the hope that something will work. However, in its second phase, MSC appears to be more focused or at least has identified a niche in the shared services and outsourcing industry. This is discussed in the next section.

Lastly, there is a lack of feedback in institutions and competence development in the surrounding society of MSC (Wahab 2003). The author reports on the management crisis of MSC which is based on a top-down approach run by bureaucrats and thinkers who do not have the right experience. The following are some of the findings of Wahab which to date is the most comprehensive study[5] assessing the MSC at least in its first stage:

- Linkage between universities and industry is weak and internship arrangements have not been successful and there is a breakdown of communication.
- Openness and transparency is required in the granting of tenders by the government which is said to favour giant corporations and consortiums instead of providing it to the best-qualified companies. In fact, once the contract is secured by the consortium, work is then subcontracted to companies with expertise while retaining a major chunk.
- The avenue or environment among firms and institutions to share and exchange ideas that underlies the dynamism of clusters is poorly implemented.[6]
- Lack of strong management and support for SMEs in the MSC in terms of testing and marketing their products in the local and export markets.

Drawing upon the complexity approach in evolutionary economics, Wahab (2003) urges for a bottom-up approach where platforms are created that allow interactive communication and empowerment of staff within the MSC and MDC organisations and companies to make decisions and provide constructive criticism. This will enhance the ability to constantly realign policies and nurture conditions (adaptive and innovative actions) to match the changing circumstances in the ever dynamic information age.

Biotechnology
Biotechnology was only identified in the late 1990s as one of the key enabling technologies that would help transform Malaysia into a knowledge-

based economy (*Economic Report 2005/06*). This field is touted to be the next big wave after the ICT revolution. To signify this realisation, BioValley was officially launched in 2003 following the government's initial announcement of this initiative in 2001. It is located on an 800-acre site within the MSC. However, it is said to be a sorry testament of the country's venture so far into the sector and the Malaysian Biotechnology Industry Organisation has only about 30 members involved in biopharmaceuticals, oleochemical and food manufacturing.[7] Furthermore, Malaysia faces shortages of botanists, taxonomists, zoologists, chemists and experts in medical sciences. There is also very strong competition from Singapore's Biopolis which has been running successfully since the mid 1990s. Since 2000, Singapore has spent at least RM4.6 billion on this sector and some of it has been spent to lure some famous scientists in this area. Today Singapore is said to have a pipeline that runs from the basic fundamental scientists all the way to the point of care.[8]

The Malaysian government, however, views biotechnology as having a major catalytic role in supporting a wide spectrum of biotechnology activities such as drug research in the pharmaceutical sector, and bio-processes in agro-based industries to improve value added in the agricultural sector as well as bioinformatics and industrial technology. To streamline and coordinate biotechnology research, seven Biotechnology Cooperative Centres have been set up in the various research organisations to improve cooperation and reduce duplication. The biotechnology sector is expected to contribute 5 per cent to GDP by 2020 and create 17 000 jobs by 2010. Various schemes and tax incentives have been set up by the government as early as 2001 for the commercialisation of biotechnology research findings (see Economic Report 2005/06). So far, over 2001–05, the government has already spent RM574.4 million to develop the biotechnology sector in the areas of R&D initiatives, a commercialisation fund, and business and entrepreneurship development. For 2006–10, an allocation of RM2 billion has been set aside of which 45.9 per cent will cater for physical infrastructure development and the remaining is to be used for soft infrastructure.

The National Biotechnology Policy was launched in April 2005 to provide guidelines to spearhead the development of the biotechnology industry. The targets over a 15-year period underlying the policy are listed in Table 5.8. In the first phase, capacity building includes education and training of knowledge workers, developing intellectual property and a legal framework, and developing Malaysian branding as well as industry and job creation. In the next phase, science development will be intensified for commercialisation through new product development, developing spin-off companies, strengthening branding, and developing technology licensing capabilities. The last phase will concentrate on building international recognition by consolidating strength and capabilities in technology development, strengthening innovation and technology licensing and promoting Malaysian global companies.

Table 5.8   Targets of the biotechnology policy

	Phase 1 (2005–10)	Phase 2 (2010–15)	Phase 3 (2015–20)
Policy statements	Capacity building	Creating business out of science	Turning Malaysia into global player
Employment creation	40 000	80 000	160 000
Establishment of firms	25	25	50
Contribution to GDP (%)	2.5	4.0	5.0

Source: Adapted from *Economic Report 2005/06*.

By the end of 2004, a total of 37 companies (26 Malaysian-owned and 11 foreign-owned) were approved to undertake activities in the biotechnology industry (MITI Report 2004). But as at March 2005, despite the hype, biotechnology has not taken off in a big way. It remains an undeveloped plot of land with only three companies committed to setting up operations there.[9] Industry sources lament the lack of a clear direction and this has resulted in investors adopting a wait-and-see attitude. There are no biosafety rules or regulatory framework set out. Neither is there flexibility for open field trials and pre-commercialisation. There also needs to be a one-stop shop for biotech which can provide permits, approvals and give good advice as speed and convenience are important. Banks and venture capitalists need to be educated on the funding aspects of biotech, an area that is unknown to them.

5.3   THE K-ECONOMY AT THE MESO LEVEL

The meso or intermediate level discusses ICT at the industry or sectoral level. Recognising the strategic role of ICT, investment in ICT has expanded at an average annual rate of 4.7 per cent over 2000–05 in industries. While this is a fall in the annual growth trend from 23.9 per cent in 1990–95 and 9.2 per cent in 1996–2005, it is nevertheless quite significant. The contribution of ICT to GDP increased from 5 per cent in 1995 to 8.7 per cent in 2004 while the total export value of ICT products and components was RM19.8 billion in 2002.

Table 5.9 shows how ICT expenditure in the various sectors in the economy has rapidly expanded since 1990 with the manufacturing sector taking the largest share since 2000. The manufacturing industries in ICT comprise office machinery, wire and cable, electronic valves and tubes, TV and radio transmitters and telephone, TV and radio receivers, instruments and appliances. Of these, electronic valves and tubes constitute about 50 per cent of value added of the ICT sector.

Table 5.9   ICT expenditure by sector (RM million)

	1990	1995	2000	2003	2000	2005
Banking and finance	507	1026	827	1101	1894 (4.8)[1]	2845 (8.8)
Manufacturing	78	494	1182	1416	12188 (47.5)	14367 (44.6)
Government	156	380	532	865	1389 (5.4)	2245 (7.0)
Telecommuni-cations	–	–	473	629		
Distribution	91	304	650	865	1585 (6.2)[2]	1870 (5.8)
Oil and gas	234	380	296	393		
Utilities	39	266	236	315	378 (1.5)	470 (1.5)
Professional ICT services	–	125	236	314		
Healthcare	–	–	59	79		
Education and research	52	114	236	314		
Transportation	39	114	177	236	1221 (4.8)[3]	1770 (5.5)
Home	–	76	473	629	6314 (24.6)	8104 (25.1)
Agriculture	–	–	–	–	200 (0.8)	138 (0.4)
Mining	–	–	–	–	222 (0.9)	234 (0.7)
Total		3773	5377	7864		

Notes: The last two columns have different components included in each category and hence differ from those in the first four columns. Percentage distribution is given in parenthesis.
[1] refers to financial and business services.
[2] refers to wholesale and retail trade.
[3] refers to transport and communication.

Source: Five-year Malaysia Plans, EPU.

The government, banking and services and distribution services follow quite closely in terms of high shares in ICT expenditure. The ICT expenditure in the government sector was largely due to increased computerisation and IT infrastructure deployment within various agencies. In fact, the Networked Readiness Index for Malaysian government usage was given a ranking of 7 out of 115 countries in 2005. From 1995 to 2000, the biggest increase in ICT expenditure however came from homes. The number of personal computers installed per 1000 population has steadily risen from 29.5 in 1995 to 218 within a decade.

In particular, the extent of ICT involvement in Malaysia has enabled the successful operation of contact centre service providers (also known as call centres or SSO firms) given its rank of the third most attractive location for business process outsourcing after Indian and China by A.T. Kearney's 2005 Offshore Location Attractiveness Index. A 2005 survey by Deloitte entitled, 'The Asian Advantage in the Outsourcing Revolution' ranked Malaysia as number one, ahead of Bangalore in customer support and back-office processing services. Although Bangalore has been able to attract outsourcing business from the US and Europe, it is grappling with poor infrastructure such as power shortages, traffic jams, inadequate roads and a shortage of hotel rooms to house customers and outsourcing industry executives.[10] Malaysia has the potential to become the regional contact centre for the Asia-Pacific region because of Malaysian's ability to speak several languages although Malaysia (which has over five centres employing 12 000 people) may be currently more expensive than India (has over 300 centres and employs about 350 000 workers) or the Philippines (over 250 centres).[11]

The SSO industry, which is thriving as many MNCs are outsourcing their customer service operations to cut costs, does not merely handle calls, it also provides premium customer service through face-to-face kiosks, e-mail, SMS, fax and snail mail. It has been reported that at the end of 2005, 400 of the Fortune 500 companies utilised such offshore services. The rapid growth and inherent advantage of the MSC attracted the SSO industry into Malaysia.

By the end of 2004, 48 companies in this industry were given MSC status, and the SSO industry earned a total of RM2.04 billion and accounted for 12 000 or 40 per cent of total jobs in MSC (*Economic Report 2005/06*). The contract centre industry is however suffering from an image problem as a contract centre agent is seen as a low level clerical job. Nevertheless, one advantage is that call centre workers can operate at home and allow flexibility and part-time work, and this could attract female workers unable to leave home for work due to family responsibilities. Companies can also save on rent and in-office equipment.

The SSO industry has been earmarked to be a leading industry within MSC and the phases of this industry have been identified as shown in Table 5.10.

Table 5.10   Phases of the shared services and outsourcing industry

First wave	Current wave	Next wave
Technology infrastructure • automated systems that support business applications spanning across various countries. Business applications • software development and maintenance services of ICT-based applications used by businesses.	Business processes • customer relations management • human resource training • a variety of front office and back office service functions.	Business management and integration • management of high impact, large-scale projects and divisional operations. Business transformation • high value service activities requiring executives and technologists experienced in specific global industries.

Source: Adapted from *Economic Report 2005/06*.

The first wave deals with IT outsourcing which provides customer support and device management while the current wave is concerned with business process outsourcing which deals with customer relations management as well as administration and finance. The next wave relates to knowledge process outsourcing and this requires highly skilled human resources to deal with a more complex and demanding environment.

5.3.1   The Malaysian Knowledge Content (MyKe) Study[12]

The main objective of this study was to assess the knowledge readiness at the industry level and it was based on a comprehensive nationwide survey undertaken by the EPU. The survey which consists of a random sample of 1819 firms from 18 industries (10 in manufacturing and 8 in services) was conducted in 2003.

The knowledge content measurement model in Table 5.11 from the MyKe study identifies four knowledge enablers and four knowledge actions that bring about innovation and economic performance. Various proxies detailed in EPU (2005) were used to measure these two components. Based on the above criteria of the two components, the total knowledge content levels for various industries were computed as seen in Figure 5.4. It can be seen that, overall, the IT services, chemical, telecommunications, education, and financial services industries exhibited better knowledge readiness. It was also found that in terms of knowledge leadership, the electrical and electronics, chemicals, autoparts and IT experienced above average[13] levels while transportation services, textile and wood-based manufacturing, all of which are domestic-oriented, scored rather low in terms of human capabilities, knowledge acquisition, knowledge utilisation and knowledge sharing. Industries with high knowledge generation were chemicals, IT, telecommunications and business services. The former two industries together with finance and education were rated highly for knowledge sharing and innovation output.

Table 5.11   Knowledge content measurement model

Knowledge enablers	Knowledge actions
Human capabilities • ability of workers to participate actively in knowledge-intensive activities	Knowledge generation • through R&D, process learning and other mechanisms
Knowledge leadership • commitment of management in knowledge-driven efforts	Knowledge acquisition • compilation of information, particularly from external sources
Technology/Infostructure • use of advanced technology such as systems, processes and components and infostructure refers to computing and networking facilities	Knowledge sharing • extent of knowledge shared or transferred and organisation structures and mechanisms which encourage information sharing
Knowledge environment • external aspects (policies, sector structure and dynamics) that influence firm behaviour	Knowledge utilisation • ways and extent to which knowledge is used and capitalised in firms' practices and decision making

Source: EPU (2005).

An inter-firm and intra-industry analysis based on the knowledge categories in Figure 5.4 sheds light on specific characteristics of firms and industries with regards to knowledge gaps. This gap is measured as a ratio of the respective knowledge content measure for different types of firms and for intra-industry comparison, and by the ratio of the knowledge content measure of the top 5 per cent of firms to the median knowledge content score for that industry. Table 5.12 summarises these results from the MyKe study.

Sum of Knowledge Enablers and Knowledge Actions Measures (Max=21)

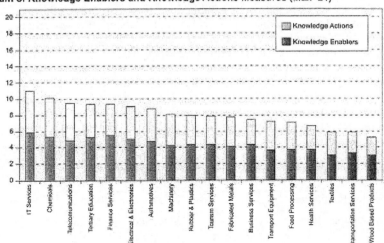

Source: Economic Planning Unit.

Figure 5.4   Aggregate knowledge content measures by industry, 2002

It can be seen that the knowledge gap between large firms and SMEs is relatively small in food processing, rubber and plastics, business services and automotive industries. This gap is greatest in health, wood, transportation equipment, textile and tourism. The top 5 per cent of SMEs have profiles of knowledge and technology use similar to the top 5 per cent of large firms, suggesting the emergence of knowledge-intensive SMEs. On average, domestic firms in education services have a higher knowledge content measure than their foreign counterparts. However, in all other industries, domestic firms lag behind foreign firms and the largest gap is in business services, food processing, machinery, textile and transportation services.

The three industries with the widest knowledge gap content between the top 5 per cent and median firms, regardless of size, are textiles, wood and transportation. The narrowest gap in knowledge content was found in the lead industry of the manufacturing sector, the electrical and electronics industry. In most industries, the predominant source of knowledge acquisition in firms was knowledge gained on-the-job and through experience and this is perhaps a reflection of the level of specialisation required. On the whole, service industries have greater accumulated experience in ICT than manufacturing industries. In terms of the use of e-commerce, only 22 per cent of firms on average used the internet to receive or place orders. This is a worry given that e-commerce presents opportunities for business to increase productivity and improve competitiveness. The biggest users of e-commerce are in the industries of tourism (48 per cent), electrical and electronics (37 per cent), and IT services (32 per cent).

Table 5.12   Knowledge content gap rankings

	Within each industry		By industry
	SME/Large firms	Domestic/ Foreign	
Food	2	17	11
Chemicals	8	8	3
Rubber and plastics	3	13	8
Wood	17	2	17
Fabricated metals	13	7	14
Automotive	5	4	6
Transport equipment	16	9	12
Textile	15	14	18
Electrical and electronics	10	11	1
Machinery	12	16	9
Education	9	1	10
Transportation	11	15	16
Finance	1	3	5
Tourism	14	12	2
Telecommunications	7	5	7
Health	18	10	15
IT services	6	6	4
Business	4	18	13

Note: A rank of 1 indicates the smallest gap.

Source: Adapted from EPU (2005).

While the above is a snapshot analysis of the current situation, it is nevertheless important to continue with such analysis on a regular basis to keep track of Malaysian industries progress in its knowledge content and readiness. On a cross-country basis, Table 5.2 shows that Malaysia business readiness ranking of 24 is not far off from the first-tier Asian NIEs. But there are concerns that the environment may impede further progress on this front. For instance, the support systems in terms of human resources and infrastructure do not offer great promise in terms of catching up to the first-tier Asian NIEs.

5.4   THE K-ECONOMY AT THE MICRO LEVEL

The fundamental requirement for a successful K-economy at the micro level is the availability of knowledge workers, and the IT literacy of the community at large. Currently, there is a disparity between the information-and-knowledge rich and the information-and-knowledge poor in the urban and rural areas. This disparity is called the digital divide, a new form of poverty that cut across not only income but also geographic, ethnic, and even gender lines.[14]

The 'information haves' are defined as those who have subscribed to individual dial-up lines and thus have access to the internet and these people were found mainly to be in the more urban and developed states of Selangor, Kuala Lumpur, Johor, Sarawak and Penang – in fact these states accounted for 73.5 per cent of the internet subscribers. One prerequisite for access to IT is electricity and Table 5.13 shows that the supply of electricity to rural areas especially to Sabah and Sarawak has been improving over time although about 20 per cent of the population in Sarawak and 27 per cent of Sabah's population have no electricity supply.

Table 5.13   Rural electrification coverage by region (%)

Region	1990	2000	2005
Malaysia	80	89.5	92.9
Peninsular Malaysia	91	97.5	98.6
Sabah	48	67.1	72.8
Sarawak	50	66.9	80.8

Source: Five-Year Malaysia Plans, EPU.

In discussing issues of the digital divide, one has to recognise that even if comprehensive free access is equitably provided to all citizens, there is no guarantee that all will use ICT. There will always be segments of any society that will not want to avail themselves of the technology of the content because of a myriad of reasons including complacency and sheer unwillingness to adapt to change. In essence, the real difference between the info-poor and info-rich is the inequality of physical and financial access to ICT and in the actual usage of sources of information in a society. One can have the best access to ICT but it will be of no use if the individual citizen does not see value in this for his conduct of daily life, work or play. It is the aggregate of individuals who make the nation which must see the benefits and importantly use ICT.

Evidence from a survey by Faziharudean and Mitomo (2003) shows that rural respondents lack informal education in ICT as 60 per cent of them did not have a chance to attend ICT classes as compared to 61 per cent of the urban respondents who attended ICT classes. To get the younger generation started early, the SchoolNet project was piloted in 1998 to enable every school, including those located in rural areas, to access the internet, thus opening opportunities for students to gain knowledge through the internet. The establishment of Smart Schools represents the government's effort in redesigning the whole educational process as well as school management to help students prepare for the information era. The Smart School pilot project (1999–2002) involved 87 primary and secondary schools, of which 35 were located in rural areas. Both of these projects went full swing in 2004 and the plan is for every primary and secondary school to be converted into a Smart School by 2010.

In general, when compared with other countries, Malaysia has done quite well for being ranked 21st in internet users, 37th in internet hosts and 35th in secure servers in 2005 out of 62 countries by A.T. Kearney, a global consulting firm.[15] There is a lot more potential to increase IT literacy in the future, given that one-third of the population was below 14 years in 2005, with a median age of 23.3 years. Opportunities are there to provide early exposure to ICTs through appropriate programmes/projects in order to develop the potential human capital for the knowledge economy. In 2004, about 4.7 per cent of the labour force had no formal education while 4.3 per cent of the population were 65 years and above. These groups are to some extent marginalised in the use of ICT. To increase ICT literacy among households, subsidies and loans are provided under the One Home One Personal Computer project since 2003. There should also be an e-learning web site in all the other three languages (Chinese, Malay and Tamil) to cater to the needs of the non-English speaking community. This is to provide a continuous interactive learning platform where some of the features include simulations of e-transactions such as shopping, banking services, online travel and bookings, and general interest information such as hobbies and recipes. The difficulty partly lies in the public consisting of diverse groups of individuals and we need to use different approaches in getting their participation and interest in being IT literate. For instance, the rural folk and low income group will need to be taught specific IT applications that would directly benefit them.

Given the importance of the TV and radio in the Malaysian community, advantage can be taken to educate people about the basic concept of IT and its central role as a communication technology and how it could be used as a tool to transform the way people live, work and play in the national development process using special programmes or even advertisements. While 62.7 per cent of those surveyed in 2004 indicated that they were very interested in the use of computer technology, they perceived that their knowledge in the use of computers was below average (MASTIC 2005).

Nevertheless, 60.1 per cent understood the concept underlying e-commerce and this is necessary for various applications offered by the government services.

While ICT is the cause of the digital rift, it is also purported to be the panacea to resolving the issue and there is an expanding literature (see World Bank 1998; Quibria and Tschang 2001; Mathison 2003) on how ICT can help reduce poverty. It is believed that ICT can reduce poverty indirectly by contributing towards broad-based growth in income and employment, and these benefits reach the poor through the trickle down effect. At the same time, ICT can potentially enhance the welfare of the poor directly in the following ways as summarised in Table 5.14:

- Information about markets and opportunities – information is critical to any well functioning market and the internet is being used to assist in the collection, and delivery and use of such information.
- Employment – ICT is being used to provide information on new employment opportunities as well as becoming a source of new employment opportunities.
- Skills and education – new and innovative experiments exist with respect to the provision of both formal (curricula-based or certifiable) and informal education through the ICT.
- Health care – innovations are being made to deliver health care to the poor through effective utilisation of ICT.
- Delivery of government services – new forms of ICT are used to enhance the efficiency of governments and reduce corruption.
- Empowerment – ICT is being utilised to improve communications between the government and the governed, thus allowing the poor new avenues to air their grievances.

However, before ICT can reduce poverty, it requires the poor to be wired in the first place or have access to a computer in their environment. To address this issue, as at August 2005, 42 *Internet Desa*, 38 *Infodesa* centres and 58 community access centres have been established nationwide but this is not enough to reach the rural communities. Apart from providing internet access at strategic locations in villages and community centres, these centres also train the local communities, develop content application and are one-stop centres for information. These projects are aimed at enabling the usage of ICT to enhance economic value and living skills, transforming participants into knowledge citizens and bringing the underdeserved group into the mainstream of society. At this stage, it is too early to tell how effective or sufficient a connectivity programme this is but it needs to be monitored closely and improved with time.

Table 5.14   Poverty and types of ICT intervention

Correlates of poverty	What ICT can do	Category of poor that benefits	Comparative advantage of ICT over traditional tools
Lack of sufficient nutrition, health, water and sanitation	Information improves delivery of health services. ICT can do little or nothing for nutrition, water and sanitation	Does not help the poor significantly	ICTs cannot provide basic infrastructure and services, but information can improve them, e.g., medical information
Lack of skills or education	Distance education or learning-assisted ICT	Potentially all can benefit, but the poorest segment is likely to be excluded. However, some lower income individuals, not necessarily the poor, might be able to take advantage	ICT can complement traditional teaching resources
Lack of employment or income earning opportunities	Employment in ICT professions such as mobile phone operators, IT industry work	May benefit the lower rungs of income distribution but not necessarily the poor	ICT can help in disseminating employment information
Lack of information and social capital	Market information on agriculture and cottage industry produce, labour market conditions and other income earning opportunities	May benefit the lower rungs of income distribution but not necessarily the poor	ICT can be used in complementary fashion or integrated with traditional media, e.g., radio broadcasting, internet information
Lack of voice and participation	E-mail access to decision makers, participation in news, discussion forum, etc.	Potentially all segments of society, including the poor, can benefit	ICT can be used to complement traditional avenues such as newspapers and other media

Source: Adapted from Quibria and Tschang (2001).

In a 2003 study of the urban population, Faziharudean and Mitomo report that while only 2 per cent of the urban respondents were ICT-illiterate, there is however a 'second level digital divide' where the digital gap is based on the differences in the skill level of the population which can in turn affect incomes earned. This will be a serious issue if life-long learning does not take place to enable Malaysians to participate in the expanding and rapidly changing knowledge economy. The World Bank (2005) notes that 36 per cent of the workers are not equipped to adapt to labour market changes and one important change is the move towards obtaining knowledge skills. As work becomes more knowledge-intensive, multidisciplinary and collaborative, education and training must foster a range of new skills – how to find information, think critically, communicate effectively, work in teams and manage projects, and at the same time be versatile and able to cope with continuing technological changes. For many enterprises and workers, this would be a departure from well entrenched work and management practices and thus require a change in the mindset on the part of those involved.

When workers were asked if they knew where they could acquire these skills, only 17 per cent gave a positive answer while 5 per cent interviewed were currently enrolled in an after work learning programme (World Bank 2005). Thus, lifelong learning is not yet a reality. On the other hand, the National Dual Training Scheme provided by the government is specialized to produce knowledge workers that match industry needs. The programme is two years long and was launched in July 2005. It consists of 20–30 per cent theory and the rest in the form of practical training in various companies, government-linked companies and MNCs. At the end of the training, the companies can choose to absorb the trainees into their workforce.

The total ICT workforce in 2005 was 183 204 and this is expected to increase at a rate of 10.4 per cent per year to 300 000 by 2010 (EPU 2006). The World Bank (2005) reports that firms surveyed indicated that IT skills was the second most needed skill next to English proficiency. The Multimedia University has been in operation since 1998 to offer courses in IT and creative technology to train people to fill in the much-needed positions. After a four-year undergraduate degree, the first batch of 100 students started working in 2003 followed by a second batch of 400 and a third batch of 1000, but this is not enough. It is not just the quality and quantity of workers that matter, as aptly indicated by Abdullah Badawi, the current Prime Minister,[16]

'Institutional structures are powerful determinants of individual and group behaviours. Structures that were appropriate for the agricultural and industrial era are unsuitable for the information or digital era. Instead of rigid and bureaucratic institutional or organizational structures, we need to have more agile and fluid structures like networks or self-directed teams which foster better relationships that enhance creativity, innovativeness, and sharing of knowledge.'

The Malaysian society which is structured around a rigid, submissive, and spoon-fed system is not sufficiently suitable for progress towards an effective K-economy. A dynamic and inquisitive structure should be built to encourage creativity, and nurture differences and diversity. This needs to be stressed early in the education and learning process, which needs to be more open and allow students to make mistakes, encouraging differences and diversity, independent critical thinking and analytical skills.

Without the readiness of the people in the society and economy to use the technology for their use and to create value and wealth from it, the ultimate purpose of being a knowledge economy is defeated. A digital economy is not a physical concept but a socio-economic concept. Inducing ICT use by agents requires a fundamental change in the general public's mentality and mind set. For example, the public must be convinced that a digital signature is just as valid and safe as a written signature. Thus a qualitative transformation of society and nation is required. Nationwide information literacy must be cultivated and people must be prepared to learn, unlearn and relearn.

However, it remains unclear whether the extent of IT use is a reflection of a market failure justifying government intervention. In addition, informatisation affects social interactions as information should be freely generated, transmitted and shared. As information is power, it is a source of control, and sometimes it is necessary for a careful checks-and-balances system to be maintained by the government. Progress in ICT-related sectors will depend on better legal frameworks and enforcement related to the protection of intellectual property rights, the security of commercial information, and privacy safeguards for consumers and companies. Thus, appropriate government intervention is required to support knowledge-based activities. However, a crucial element that was found to be missing or under-emphasised is the immense potential to utilise IT for the purpose of promoting a more transparent and accountable government that would improve Malaysia's democratic system and build a thriving civil society – as foreseen in Vision 2020 (Wahab 2003). It was further explained that although IT had been embraced for the so-called development of the country, vested economic and political interests continue to reinforce the existing government structure strategy, irrespective of whether they fulfil the needs of particular groups, and further marginalise the powerless and the disenfranchised rather than empowering them.

5.5 CONCLUSION

At this stage, it is self evident that encouraging the growth of ICT is imperative and not an option. In 1996, Malaysia had less than 300 ICT companies, and by 2005 that number had reached 3400.[17] It is also likely that the nature and focus of ICT industries will change in the future as newer sources of ICT such as digital content development, e-commerce, shared services and outsourcing, and bioinformatics (the convergence of biotechnology and ICT) emerge to be more popular. Bioinformatics has been targeted as a new growth area for Malaysia to build upon, taking into account the country's strong ICT foundation. The global bioinformatics market which is estimated at US$1.4 billion, is expected to grow at an average annual rate of 15.8 per cent to reach nearly US$3 billion by 2010, reflecting the immense potential of bioinformatics (ninth MP). To harness this wave of technology, the support system in terms of adequate manpower and infrastructure is still lacking.

At the moment, Malaysia is still finding its way with the MSC project and changing focus within the MSC to spearhead Malaysia's foray into the digital era. Thus, to leapfrog into another (although related) area such as biotechnology without sufficient gear in place may not be advisable. First, the rest of the country needs to be 'connected' to harvest the fruits of a knowledge-rich society. ICT development is not simply a matter of giving everyone a computer. Access and equity need to go further in the provision of formal and informal education in terms of literacy, knowledge of English and the ability process information effectively, which remain critical to using ICT productively to accelerate growth and development. Currently, the MSC is fundamentally premised on economic imperatives but ensuring the economic transition from a production-based economy to a knowledge-based economy would not consequently and sequentially enable the necessary social and political changes required to support the system. This means all organisations (public, private and the community) need to change their mindset, approaches and systems in order to optimise the value of their knowledge capital, and to manage that transition effectively a coherent and integrated policy framework to set up an enabling environment must be in place. This also involves protecting intellectual property or enforcing anti-trust laws in the K-economy.

Also of valid concern is the issue of the digital divide, and while efforts targeted at narrowing this gap are being undertaken, they appear limited in scope and reach. Thus, there must be adequate preparation in all related areas with mutual adjustment and sense-making on the part of individuals, firms and institutions within an evolving system to ensure that leapfrogging from an industrial society into a knowledge society does not fall short of its expected success.

NOTES

[1] The MDC has been renamed MDeC.
[2] See details at http://www.mdc.com.my
[3] By 2003, nine cyber laws had been enacted.
[4] Of which 1033 were majority Malaysian-owned, 349 majority foreign-owned and 39 with equal ownership.

[5] This is based on extensive interviews with senior management in institutions and a substantial number of firms in Cyberjaya.

[6] For instance, there is a dialogue session held every month for MSC companies usually between 9.30 am and 12.30 pm where MDC invites speakers either local of foreign and there is a question and answer session but no real dialogue on the affairs of the MSC firms, or worse still with other non-MSC companies.

[7] See *The New Straits Times* 19 February 2005.

[8] See *The New Straits Times* 13 April 2006.

[9] See *The New Straits Times* 19 February 2005.

[10] See *The Star* 17 February 2005.

[11] See *The New Straits Times* 18 January 2004.

[12] This section draws from the published study of the EPU (2005) based on the MyKe survey.

[13] The average for each category of knowledge is based on the performance levels of all industries in that category.

[14] Key note address delivered by Abdullah Badawai as Deputy Prime Minister on 2 September 2003 at the MSC ICT Policy Summit, Seri Kembangan, Selangor.

[15] See http://www.atkearney.com

[16] Keynote address at the 2002 Sixth National Civil Service Conference on 'K-Based Economy: Forging Ahead for National Transformation', Kuala Lumpur, Malaysia.

[17] See *The Star* 8 April 2006.

Appendix 5.1 INFORMATION AND KNOWLEDGE SOCIETY IN MALAYSIAN CONTEXT

Information Society is defined as a society comprised of individuals and organisations (including public, private and non-profit sectors) with the following characteristics:

- Possessing connectivity of networks – human, infrastructure and virtual;
- Using on-line connectivity and real-time interactivity products and services for information;
- Exercising a culture of learning;
- Having equitable access to information – within and across geographical boundaries;
- Possessing ICT literacy;
- Having information literacy;
- Able to use a database to accomplish a specific task.

Knowledge Society is defined as a society comprised of individuals and organisations with the following characteristics:

- Possessing all the characteristics of information society – information society is a prerequisite step towards formation of knowledge society;
- Having the ability to convert or manipulate data and information to knowledge;
- Treating data, information and knowledge as a commodity or as one of the factors of production besides using land, labour, capital and technology;
- Being creative and innovative in adding values to existing products and services by utilising created knowledge;
- Being creative and innovative in inventing new knowledge products and services;
- Being an inclusive society;
- Being socially and economically empowered;
- Being self-regulated and self-controlled.

Source: National Information Technology Council (2000).

6.   Poverty and Income Inequality

6.1 INTRODUCTION

In 1970, Malaysia had sharp spatial and ethnic disparities in income and social well-being, with half its population of all households classified as poor. Nevertheless, the Millennium Development Goal target to reduce the proportion of people living below the poverty line by 2015, was achieved well ahead of that, in 1999. By 2002, only about 5 per cent of households were poor. Malaysia's experience in poverty reduction is of particular interest because it has been achieved in a multi-ethnic and culturally diverse setting. Furthermore, its economic growth strategy has integrated commitments to poverty elimination and restructuring of society as central objectives in its development vision. Thus, it was not a coincidence that growth, poverty alleviation and income redistribution in Malaysia from 1970 to 1990 were achieved under circumstances of both interventionist policies as well as market coordination.

The NEP which was implemented between 1971 and 1990 had 'redistribution through growth' as one of the main instruments for achieving its overriding objective of promoting national unity. The NEP was then succeeded by the National Development Policy in 1991 which retained NEP's basic strategy of growth with equity. From 2001 to 2010, Malaysia is to be spearheaded by the NVP which emphasises a more balanced and equitable participation among bumiputeras and non-bumiputeras.

The interventionist state strategy of Malaysia was to help raise the living standards of Malays, also known as bumiputeras among the Malaysians. The proportion of Malays which was about 55 per cent in the 1960s, has risen to 65.9 per cent while the Chinese and Indians made up 25.3 per cent and 7.5 per cent respectively of the total population in 2005. By ethnicity, the poverty incidence in Peninsular Malaysia was also highest for the bumiputeras at 65 per cent in 1970. While this was successfully brought down to 20.8 per cent by 1990, that for the Chinese decreased from 26 per cent to 5.7 per cent, and that of Indians declined from 39.0 per cent to 18 per cent over the same period. The rural-urban divide is also reflective of the income disparity between non-bumiputeras and bumiputeras as the latter form the majority of those who live in rural areas. The bumiputeras accounted for 80.73 per cent and 73.12 per cent of the population in Sabah and Sarawak respectively in 2005.

131

The ethnic groups in Peninsular Malaysia were sharply differentiated in terms of economic activity in 1970. This is partly due to the colonial heritage which included a multi-ethnic and multi-cultural society, resulting from a flow of Chinese over a long period to Peninsular Malaysia and East Malaysia and a more targeted inflow of Indians to Peninsular Malaysia as rubber estate workers. The bumiputeras were concentrated in rural areas in smallholder agriculture, but were also represented in government, the police and the armed forces; the Indians were heavily concentrated in the plantation sector, as well as in railways and government utilities; while the Chinese dominated trade and commerce. Implicit in the ruling coalition in post-colonial Malaya was the understanding that the Chinese and Indians did not interfere in the Malay-dominated state apparatus of the primacy of Malay political rule and special rights and privileges in return for full citizenship rights, a voice in the government represented by the Malayan Chinese Association and Malayan Indian Congress. But the harmony that prevailed since independence in 1957 was disrupted by the worst racial riots on 13 May 1969 which brought to attention the urgency of the Malaysian poverty and inequality problem. This saw a fundamental shift in public policies towards addressing these issues.

Organisation of the Chapter

In this chapter, we first look at poverty and then move on to discuss the income inequality situation in Malaysia. The section on poverty is organised as follows. First, the definition of poverty as defined by the poverty income line is discussed followed by the trend in poverty using various strata. The next section reviews the shifting focus of poverty alleviation in the light of the emerging trends of new forms of poverty in Malaysia with the advent of globalisation and rapid economic growth.

The last section provides empirical evidence that Malaysia's poverty reduction is a result of rapid growth and explains why this strategy is unsustainable in the long run in the absence of significant improvements in income distribution. This leads to the urgent need for Malaysia to move away from the current absolute measure of poverty and adopt the more appropriate relative poverty as the new poverty indicator. These have implications for future policy as policy development is shown to be a more difficult balancing of growth and equity than in the past.

The section on income inequality, on the other hand, is set out in the following way. First, trends in overall income inequality as well as inter-racial and inter-regional income inequality are reviewed. This is followed by an analysis of the effect of redistributive policies on income inequality and an attempt to look at where Malaysian inequality may be heading.

6.2 DEFINITION OF POVERTY

In Malaysia, the incidence of poverty has traditionally been determined by reference to a threshold poverty income line (PLI). The PLI is based on what is considered to be the minimum consumption requirements of a household for food, clothing, and other non-food items such as rent, fuel, furniture and household equipment, medical and health expenses, transport and communication, recreation, education and other services. For the food component, the minimum expenditure was based on a daily requirement of 9910 calories for a family of five persons comprising an adult male, an adult female and three children of either sex between 1–3, 4–6 and 7–9 years of age. The minimum requirements for clothing and footwear were based on standards set by the Department of Social Welfare for the requirements of inmates in welfare homes. The other non-food items are based on the level of expenditure of the lower income households as reported in the Household Expenditure Survey.

The PLI is updated periodically to reflect changes in the levels of prices by taking into account changes in the Consumer Price Indices, and is calculated to reflect differences in prices and household size in Peninsular Malaysia, Sabah and Sarawak (see Table 6.1). The proportion of all households living below the PLI is the proportion living in poverty and this is monitored through the Malaysian Household Income Survey which is conducted once in every two to three years. Poverty rates as measured using Malaysia's PLI differ from those implied by the one US dollar a day (purchasing power parity[1]) poverty line used by international organisations.

Table 6.1   Poverty line incomes (RM$ per month per household)

	1979	1984	1990	1995	1999	2002	2004
Peninsular	274	349	370	425	510	529	543
Malaysia	(5.4)	(5.1)	(5.1)				
Sabah	410	540	544	601	685	690	704
	(5.4)	(5.4)	(5.4)				
Sarawak	347	428	452	516	584	600	603
	(5.6)	(5.2)	(5.2)				

Note: Numbers in parenthesis indicate the household size. Since 1995, PLIs are adjusted based on an average household size of 4.6 in Peninsular Malaysia, 4.9 in Sabah and 4.8 in Sarawak.

Source: Five-Year Malaysia Plans, EPU.

The usual practice of updating PLI based on CPI was not considered sufficient as the basket of goods included in the expenditure component of PLI should be reviewed to consider changes in taste and consumer demand.

What is considered as the minimum requirement for sustenance of life is also expected to change over time given the activities and lifestyle of people. Thus a revised methodology was used in 2005 to reflect the difference in the cost of living between urban and rural areas, between states, as well as in the demographic pattern of each household (see EPU 2006 for more details). Table 6.2 provides a comparison of PLIs using the previous methodology and the revised methodology of 2005. It can be seen that the revised method provides higher PLIs than the previous method. In particular, the PLI is higher in rural areas and this was attributed to the higher cost of living in rural Sabah as rent and transportation may be more expensive in rural areas because of distribution costs while hypermarkets offer much cheaper goods than small shops in rural areas.[2]

Table 6.2   Comparison of PLIs for 2004

Region	Previous method	2005 Method		
		Urban	Rural	Overall
Peninsular Malaysia	543	663	657	661
Sabah	704	881	897	888
Sarawak	608	777	753	765
Malaysia	588	687	698	691

Source: Malaysia (2006).

6.3   STRUCTURE OF POVERTY INCIDENCE

Here, the trends for poverty incidence for various groups are examined. Table 6.3 shows the difference in poverty levels in rural and urban areas in Malaysia and Peninsular Malaysia. The proportion of urban population in Malaysia rose from 34.2 per cent in 1980 to 62.8 per cent in twenty-five years. As expected, Peninsular Malaysia's poverty rates in the rural areas are lower than Malaysia which includes the less developed states of Sabah and Sarawak. The table also shows that the aggregate poverty incidence has declined uninterruptedly in the period of 1970–97. In fact, the reduction in the poverty incidence to 15 per cent in Peninsular Malaysia by the end of 1990 exceeded the target of 16.7 per cent when the NEP was initiated.[3] The separate targets for the urban and rural groups in Peninsular Malaysia were also achieved by then. The number of poor households has consistently decreased from 1 million in 1970 to 267 900 in 2002, with the largest decline from 1976 to 1984 showing the first signs of success of the NEP initiatives.

There has however been a slight increase in the proportion of households below the poverty line for Malaysia from 6.1 per cent to 7.5 per cent over 1997–99 due to the financial crisis. The risk of becoming poor after the financial crisis is expected to be higher for households in urban areas as the rural poor are largely not employed in the crisis-affected sectors of the economy. The target of the seventh MP to reduce poverty in Malaysia to 5.5 per cent by 2000 has been met but the target of the eighth MP to reduce this further to 0.5 per cent by 2005 was not met. The reduction in overall poverty from 2002 to 2004 came entirely from the fall in rural poverty as urban poverty did not change during this period. Using the revised PLI, the figures also show a decline from 1999 to 2004.[4]

Table 6.3   Incidence of poverty by rural–urban strata (%)

	Peninsular Malaysia				Malaysia			
	Overall	Rural	Urban	No. of poor house-holds (000)	Overall	Rural	Urban	No. of Poor house-holds (000)
1970	49.3	58.7	21.3	791.8	52.4	n.a.	n.a.	1000
1976	39.4	47.8	17.9	764.4	42.4	50.9	18.7	975.8
1984	18.4	24.7	8.2	483.3	20.7	27.3	8.5	649.4
1990	15.0	19.3	7.3	448.9	16.5	21.8	7.5	619.4
1993	10.5	14.9	4.4	325.3	12.4	18.6	5.3	517.2
1995	9.1	14.1	4.1	329.5	8.7	14.9	3.6	417.2
1997	n.a.	n.a.	n.a.	n.a.	6.1	10.9	2.1	332.4
1999	n.a.	n.a.	n.a.	n.a.	7.5	12.4	3.4	409.3
					(8.5)	(14.8)	(3.3)	(409.3)
2000	n.a.	n.a.	n.a.	n.a.	5.5	10.3	2.2	253.4
2001	n.a.	n.a.	n.a.	n.a.	5.3	n.a.	n.a.	n.a.
2002	n.a.	n.a.	n.a.	n.a.	5.1	11.4	2.0	267.9
2004	n.a.	n.a.	n.a.	n.a.	4.3	9.6	2.0	
					(5.7)	(11.9)	(2.5)	(311.3)

Notes: n.a. means not available. The values in parenthesis refer to the revised PLI.

Source: Malaysia Five-Year Development Plans, EPU. *Economic Report 2005/06*, Ministry of Finance.

In general, improvement has been evident across an impressive array of other poverty-related indicators in Malaysia in recent decades. The human poverty index has improved to the point where Malaysia can now claim a rank as high as 16 out of 177 rich and poor countries. The country's human development index, which includes measures of life expectancy, educational attainment and income per head, has also improved, with Malaysia attaining a rank of 61 (Human Development Report 2005). Various social indicators tell a similar story. The proportion of the population with access to safe drinking water rose from 62 per cent to 95 per cent in the thirty years after 1975, and by 2002, 92 per cent of the population had access to health services. The adult literacy rate also rose from 60 per cent in 1970 to 95.1 per cent in 2004.

Although the incidence of poverty has decreased over time, rural poverty remains very much higher than its urban equivalent. Unlike the urban areas where occupational employment is wide ranging in various sectors and hence income earned can vary substantially, the rural sector is mainly agricultural in nature. In general, urban poverty decreased more rapidly than rural poverty and this contributed more to a fall in overall poverty.

The urban poverty reduction was matched in the rural areas as the rural poverty rate in 1970 was halved by 1984 and that of the rate in 1990 was halved again by 2002. In 1979, the rural population in Malaysia made up 62.3 per cent of the total population and 80 per cent of the poor lived in rural areas. In 2003, the rural population proportion declined to 37.5 per cent. Rural poverty incidence was highest among the agricultural, hunting and forestry workers at 11.45 per cent. Rural households headed by the elderly (65 years and above) and female-headed households registered high incidence of poverty at 28.6 per cent and 25.7 per cent respectively in 2002 (EPU 2003).

In terms of within and across ethnic disparities, there has been a consistent improvement in the incidence of poverty, shown in Table 6.4. As discussed earlier, the groups are separated both geographically and occupationally, reflecting their differing settlement patterns. Not unexpectedly, in 1970, poverty was markedly higher among the bumiputeras than the other communities and approximately two-thirds of bumiputera households lived below the poverty line. While ethnic income differentials narrowed over the period of 1970–2002, the Chinese mean household income averaged 1.78 times higher than bumiputeras and the average Indian earned 1.33 times more than the average bumiputera over 1990–2002. Using the revised PLI method, the decline in poverty is seen to continue for all ethnic groups.

Table 6.4   Incidence of poverty by ethnicity (%)

	Bumiputeras	Chinese	Indians
1970	65.0	26.0	39.2
1985	38.0	15.0	24.0
1990	20.8	5.7	18.0
1999	10.2 (12.4)	2.6 (1.2)	1.9 (3.5)
2002	7.3	1.5	1.9
2004	(8.3)	(0.6)	(2.9)

Note: The values in parenthesis refer to the revised PLI.

Source: Five-Year Malaysia Plans, EPU

However, concerns have been raised on the increasing difference in intra-ethnic disparities as opposed to inter-ethnic income differences (Hashim 1998). For example, in 1997, 70.2 per cent of households in the bottom 40 per cent income group were bumiputeras while 62.7 per cent of households in the top 20 per cent bracket were non-bumiputeras. Thus there has been a shift in objective from reducing gaps between ethnic groups in NEP days to that of reducing gaps amongst the ethnic groups under NDP. This change of emphasis in policy may now be more appropriate given the current relatively low levels of absolute poverty. There is now a need to ensure equal economic opportunities for all Malaysians irrespective of ethnic origins and status as the exclusion of individual and groups from the process of development can lead to feelings of frustration and the creation of an underclass, marginalised from the mainstream.

Table 6.5 shows the spatial distribution of poverty that is closely related to Malaysia's pattern of development which in turn is linked to ethnic settlement patterns and industrial structures. Historically, the bumiputera community lived in settlements along the coasts and riverbanks. Chinese and Indian migrants settled along the western coastal plains around the tin mines, agricultural estates and urban centres. Relatively few of these communities settled in the east coast states especially in Kelantan and Terengganu while the west coast of Peninsular Malaysia rapidly developed and attracted significant amounts of FDI. How have the Malaysian states fared in terms of the poverty targets set under the NDP and NVP? The states have been categorised as more and less developed based on the GDP per capita by state in Table 6.5.

Generally, with the exception of 1999 which captured the impact of the financial crisis of 1997/98, poverty incidence for both urban and rural areas in every state have exhibited falling trends. Every state also exhibits a higher incidence of rural compared to urban poverty except for the Federal Territory of Kuala Lumpur which is completely urban. It can be seen that poverty incidences are not evenly distributed. Among the more developed states, Perak has the highest poverty incidences, followed by Melaka, for all years except for 1997. Perak also tends to register the highest incidence of urban poverty. Except for the adverse impact of the 1997/98 financial crisis, Kuala Lumpur has always had the lowest incidence. Poverty incidences in the less developed states are higher with Kedah, Kelantan, Perlis, Sabah and Terengganu registering exceptionally high figures. Urban poverty incidence is also considerably higher in these states and in 2002, urban poverty incidence in all these states except for Kedah, exceeded that of the national average. Using the revised 2005 method, there was also a decline in poverty from 1999 to 2004 for all states.

Table 6.5   Incidence of poverty by state and stratum

	1990			1995			2002		
State	Total	Urban	Rural	Total	Urban	Rural	Total (2004)	Urban	Rural
More Developed									
Johor	9.8	5.8	11.5	3.1	1.6	4.8	1.8 (2.0)	0.8	3.9
Melaka	12.4	4.6	14.2	5.3	1.2	8.3	2.7 (1.8)	1.3	6.0
Negeri Sembilan	9.1	3.5	11.9	4.9	2.1	7.2	2.2 (1.4)	0.8	3.8
Perak	19.2	8.8	24.4	9.1	4.0	15.5	7.9 (4.9)	4.0	15.3
Penang	8.7	4.8	11.4	4.0	3.5	5.6	1.4 (0.3)	1.1	3.0
Selangor	7.6	4.7	9.2	2.2	1.3	5.1	1.1 (1.0)	0.9	3.3
Kuala Lumpur	3.7	3.7	-	0.5	0.5	-	0.5 (1.5)	0.5	-
Less Developed									
Kedah	29.9	14.9	32.1	12.2	5.5	16.1	10.7 (7.0)	3.4	15.7
Kelantan	29.6	19.7	33.3	22.9	18.3	25.3	12.4 (10.6)	6.5	15.2
Pahang	10.0	6.4	11.2	6.8	2.0	9.4	3.8 (4.0)	1.5	5.9
Perlis	17.4	2.8	18.5	11.8	8.6	13.0	10.1 (6.3)	6.9	11.9
Sabah	29.7	8.7	34.9	22.4	10.3	28.8	16.0 (23.0)	8.5	24.5
Sarawak	21.0	4.9	24.7	10.0	2.8	15.7	5.8 (7.5)	1.7	10.0
Terengganu	31.3	19.2	39.1	23.4	13.3	31.8	10.7 (15.4)	5.6	15.6
Malaysia	**16.5**	**7.1**	**21.1**	**8.7**	**3.6**	**14.9**	**5.1 (5.7)**	**2.0**	**11.4**

Note: The values in parenthesis refer to the revised PLI.

Source: Ragayah (2005) and EPU (2006).

Hard Core Poverty

As the PLI does not reflect the intensity and severity of the poverty problem, the government attempted to overcome that with the use of a hard core poverty measure in 1989. This measure was defined to include those poor households whose income is less than half of the PLI but this was the definition before the revised 2005 method of computing PLI. With the latter method, as food requirement is based on a nutritionally adequate diet, the hard core poverty threshold income is much higher than the old definition of half the PLI. Thus the new definition of hard core poverty based on the revised PLI is defined to include those poor households whose income is less than half of the food PLI.

Data on hard core poverty has been available since 1990 and is shown in Table 6.6. The incidence of hard core poverty among Malaysian citizens has declined from 3.9 per cent in 1990 to 0.7 per cent in 2004. The decline in the number of hard core poor households is also seen using the revised PLI. Rapid declines in hard core poverty have occurred in both rural and urban areas, especially in the mid 1990s. As a result of the financial crisis, there was a one off increase in the incidence of urban hard core poverty to 0.5 per cent (13 900 households) in 1999 but this declined to 12 600 households in 2002.

Table 6.6   Hardcore poverty by rural-urban strata

	Incidence of hard core poverty (%)			Number of hard core poor households (000)		
	Overall	Rural	Urban	Total	Rural	Urban
1990	3.9	5.2	2.9	137.1	121.6	15.5
1995	2.1	3.6	0.9	94.0	72.2	21.8
1997	1.4	2.5	0.4	67.5	55.3	12.2
1999	1.4	2.4	0.5	66.0	52.1	13.9
				(91.7)	(79.8)	(11.9)
2002	1.0	2.3	0.4	52.9	40.3	12.6
2004	0.7	1.5	0.2	(67.3)	(53.2)	(14.1)

Notes: n.a. means not available. The values in parenthesis refer to the revised PLI.

Source: Five-Year Malaysia Plans, EPU. *Economic Report 2005/06*, Ministry of Finance.

When non-Malaysian citizens in the country were included, the number of hard core poverty households increased by at least 5000. Thus Malaysia cannot afford to ignore the depth and severity of hard core poverty made worse by its migrant workers who are in direct competition with its citizens for the provision of services. The target of the National Development Policy 1991–2000 to reduce hardcore poverty to 0.5 per cent by 2000 was unsuccessful. Nevertheless hard core poverty is to be eradicated by 2010 (EPU 2006).

Table 6.7 was compiled to unmask the hard core poverty status in the different states which are shown to vary significantly in terms of their urbanisation rate and GDP per capita.

Table 6.7   Hard core poverty by states

State	Urbanisation rate in 2000 (%)	GDP per capita in 2000 (RM$)	1990	1995	2002
More developed					
Johor	63.9	14 058	1.5	0.5	0.2
Melaka	67.3	15 244	3.8	1.6	0.1
Negeri Sembilan	55.0	13 574	2.2	1.0	0.3
Perak	59.5	11 826	4.9	1.9	1.3
Penang	79.5	20 894	2.1	0.7	0.3
Selangor	88.3	18 157	1.1	0.5	0.2
Kuala Lumpur	100.0	29 919	0.5	0	0
Less developed					
Kedah	38.7	8 754	8.4	3.7	3.0
Kelantan	33.5	6 137	7.2	7.4	3.6
Pahang	42.1	9 855	2.1	1.2	0.1
Perlis	33.8	9 739	3.2	2.7	1.8
Sabah	49.1	9 560	9.3	4.9	3.1
Sarawak	47.9	13 248	3.3	1.3	0.6
Terengganu	49.4	22 514	10.4	7.5	2.8

Note: Data for 2004 were not reported as they were only available using the 2005 revised PLI.

Source: EPU (2001a) and *The Malaysian Quality of Life 2004 Report.*

It can be seen that Perak is quite an exception to the group of more developed states, having a relatively high hard core poverty incidence in 2002, but it did have the highest hard core poverty incidence to start off with. Among the less developed states, Pahang's hard core poverty rate is one of the lowest while Kedah, Sabah and Terengganu clearly have deep rooted problems that need attention. Hard core poverty does not appear to have a clear relationship with economic development as it stems from a specific group in somewhat persistent poverty. This includes the indigenous people or *Orang Asli* who have been victims of rapid expansion of development projects such as infrastructure, and this has had an impact on their material and ritual culture which is linked to the forest and ancestral land. Other groups who form the hard core poor are households headed by the elderly and single females who registered an incidence of hard core poverty of 4.9 per cent and 9.4 per cent respectively in 2002. Using the revised 2005 method of PLI, there is also a fall in hard core poverty from 1999 to 2004 for all states.

6.4 CHANGING FORMS OF POVERTY

As a result of Malaysia's economic growth and related social and demographic changes, rural–urban poverty disparity is somewhat less of a problem at present than in the past. Today, new types of poverty are emerging. Within the rural group, there are the hard core poor made up of the *Orang Asli*, single female-headed households and elderly, especially those not covered by pension schemes and who are mainly living in rural areas away from their families. The out-migration of the better educated youth from the rural and agricultural sector also has important implications for the quality of the remaining rural labour in terms of an ageing and less educated force. This has a bearing on adoption of technology transfer, productivity levels and risk taking amongst the remaining labour force. This can result in an exacerbation of the poverty problems of the smallholding sectors and farmers for poverty eradication in terms of its costs and effectiveness.

Within the urban group the poor consists of migrant workers, the urban unemployed and the low-skilled workers. While the rural–urban poverty disparity has not completely disappeared, it has taken on a new form – the digital divide, that is, the gap between the information- and knowledge-rich and the information- and knowledge-poor. This is discussed in detail in Chapter 5.

First, let us consider urban poverty which has become critical with rapid urbanisation and rural–urban migration. The trend of urbanisation in Malaysia was characterised by the increase in urban centres, the extension of administrative urban boundaries, and increase in the concentration of people in the metropolitan and large urban areas (EPU 2003). By 2003, the urbanised population share had gone up to 62.5 per cent. The redefinition of urban areas in 1991, whereby about 6 per cent of the total poor in built-up areas that were previously defined as rural were classified as urban, also contributed to the rise in urban poor. As such, the number of poor households in urban areas in Malaysia rose significantly from 77 900 in 1993 to 99 300 in 1995 primarily due to this redefinition. Regardless of this, the share of poor urban households has been rising, from 14.3 per cent in 1985 to 23.7 per cent in 1995, and 26.0 per cent in 2002.

Ragayah (2003) indicates that internal migration flows among two of the lowest-skilled occupational categories, the production and related workers, and transport equipment operators and labourers, indicates that the percentage of rural–urban migration exceeded the percentage of urban-rural migration for all the years except for 1997. This means that there are net inflows of these low-income groups into the urban areas, contributing to the rise in urban poverty. Thus policies to reduce urban poverty must include productive employment creation in the rural areas to deter the rural poor from seeking jobs in the cities.

There is also international migration into Malaysia that contributes to the urban poverty problem by increasing the share of non-citizens among the poor in the Malaysian poverty landscape. In 1990, the non-citizens constituted about 7.0 per cent but their share rose to 12.6 per cent and 17.5 per cent of the total poor in 1995 and 1997, respectively. Most of these people are in the urban areas where there are relatively more job opportunities, both in the formal and informal sectors. However, since many foreigners were repatriated back to their respective countries during the crisis, their share in the Malaysian poverty incidence moderated to 14.2 per cent in 1999. Foreign workers in Malaysia account for about 20 per cent of the workforce and the majority of them are unskilled. While this group of workers has played a key role in reducing the labour shortage problem, they come at a cost.

Excessive urban growth is said not only to increase urban diseconomies and escalate social costs but also result in uneven distribution of development benefits between urban centres and between rural–urban areas. The presence of foreign workers in large numbers in the urban areas stretched the amenities, particularly housing, to the limit (EPU 2003). Siwar and Kasim (1997) provide evidence that a majority of the urban poor lived in squatters and some 20 per cent were waiting for relocation into permanent houses which for some take more than 20 years before actual relocation takes place. Unless urban problems such as congestion, inadequate amenities, pollution, shortage of housing, etc. are given sufficient attention, the quality of urban life will deteriorate. To this end, although the Malaysian Quality of Life Index 2004 Report[5] shows that there has been an increase in the index of 9.8 per cent in 2002 since 1990, there are no data to show the case for rural and urban areas.[6]

Several survey studies on urban poverty[7] point to the following characteristics of urban poverty. They have low levels of education, face a lack of job opportunities, come from a large family size and lack access to social facilities and public utilities. Thus the causes of urban poverty are multidimensional and include structural, institutional and cultural factors.

Given the emerging new forms of poverty in Malaysia, it is now necessary to conceive of poverty as a process, and the factors that contribute to or prevent individuals and groups moving in and out of poverty may be changing and have to be carefully scrutinised to implement more effective policies to reduce poverty. In addition to identifying those who are poor and undertaking targeted and participatory approaches to address the pockets of poverty in both rural and urban areas, there is an urgency to realistically revise the poverty line. What constitutes poverty in society at a given time can be quite different from the notion of poverty in the same society at a different time.

6.5 DECOMPOSITION OF THE POVERTY INDEX

Reductions in the poverty level can be attributed to two factors. Firstly, a rise in mean income will always reduce the absolute poverty rate if the distribution of relative incomes is unchanged. If economic growth raises the income of all households, that is, shifts the entire income distribution to the right, then the proportion of households below an absolute poverty line will inevitably fall. Secondly, poverty rates will fall if there is a favourable change in relative household income distribution, even if the mean income level is unchanged.

Kakwani and Pernia (2000) argue that to understand the impact of economic growth on absolute poverty we need to distinguish between the effect of changes in mean income and the effect of the change in income distribution that accompanies economic growth. This involves decomposing the observed elasticity of poverty reduction with respect to income growth into a pure growth effect and an inequality effect such that

$$\eta = \eta_g + \eta_I, \tag{6.1}$$

where η is the proportional change in poverty associated with a 1 per cent increase in mean income, η_g is the change in poverty that occurs when income increases but the distribution of income does not change, and η_I is the change in poverty when inequality changes but mean income remains constant. The pure growth effect is always negative because an increase in mean income will always reduce poverty if distribution is unchanged, while the inequality effect can be either positive or negative depending on whether growth is accompanied by improving or worsening inequality.

An index of the degree of pro-poor growth is derived by dividing the proportional change in poverty with respect to growth η by the pure growth effect η_g. The value of this index is greater than 1 when the inequality effect reinforces the pure growth effect (that is, when η_I is negative). In this case the poor benefit proportionally more than the rich and growth can be regarded as being strictly pro-poor. When redistribution against the poor weakens but does not reverse the poverty-reducing effect of growth, the value of the index lies between 0 and 1. A negative value of the index means that adverse distributional changes outweigh the pure growth effect with the result that growth actually brings an increase in poverty.

Using data on income classes and the household distribution of income as well as the percentage of households below the poverty line income in 1970, 1987 and 2002,[8] the Kakwani and Pernia (2001) pro-poor growth index was computed. It is useful to divide the period in 1987 because of the detailed income distribution data we have for that year and because 1987 also roughly coincides with a break in trend in overall equality.

In Malaysia, overall income inequality was lower in 1987 than it had been in 1970, which would lead us to expect that the inequality effect had reinforced the pure growth effect during the intervening period. This expectation is confirmed by the estimates in Table 6.8 Both η_g and η_I are negative for the period 1970–87, and the value of 1.18 for η_g/η_I shows that growth was strongly pro-poor during this early phase of Malaysia's economic transformation. Similarly, the stabilisation in the Gini coefficient after 1987 would suggest that poverty alleviation has now come to depend almost entirely upon the pure growth effect. Again, this expectation is confirmed by the estimates in Table 6.8, which show an inequality effect close to zero for the period 1987–2002.

From this, it is clear that the index of pro–poor growth proposed by Kakwani and Pernia provides a concise way of summarising the extent to which distributional changes augment or diminish the poverty-reducing effect of sustained economic growth. Aspects of the index nonetheless have the capacity to mislead the casual observer. In the Malaysian case, the increase in the overall elasticity of poverty reduction with respect to growth and the increase in the pure growth effect after 1987 might easily create the impression that the poverty-reducing power of growth has been increasing, when the reverse has in fact been the case. The difficulty is that elasticity measures are insensitive to changes in scale, since they treat a reduction in the poverty rate from 50 to 40 per cent as being the exact equivalent of a reduction from, say, 5 per cent to 4 per cent. The calculations underlying Table 6.8 actually imply that the pure growth effect, for example, was responsible for a reduction in absolute poverty of 29 percentage points between 1970 and 1987, compared with a reduction of only 14 percentage points between 1987 and 2002, even though η_g was higher in the later period and the annual rate of growth in mean household income was much the same in both periods. The rise in η_g after 1987 means only that the proportional reduction in poverty associated with a given rate of economic growth was greater than in earlier years, which is of little consequence for policy given the diminution in the base to which this proportional reduction refers.

Table 6.8   Growth and inequality effects on poverty headcount ratio

	Poverty elasticity	Pure growth effect	Inequality effect	Pro-poor growth index
1970–1987	–1.53	–1.29	–0.23	1.18
1987–2002	–2.11	–2.06	–0.05	1.02

6.6 MALAYSIA'S POVERTY TRANSITION

Malaysia's policymakers are understandably proud both of their country's success in the war against poverty and of the fact that the rapid economic growth of recent decades has been accompanied by a fall in the overall level of economic inequality. But the reductions in poverty and overall inequality, though broadly contemporaneous, have not simply been two sides of the same equity coin, as much of the policy discussion appears to assume. When poverty is measured in absolute terms, as is still the case in Malaysia, there is no necessary connection between changes in poverty and changes in equality, since equality is inherently a relative term while absolute poverty is not. Absolute poverty and relative equality can therefore move in opposite directions, and they have done so more than once in Malaysia's history. Similarly, absolute and relative poverty, being different concepts, can also move independently of one another.

This section dwells on the distinction between absolute and relative poverty, but is not concerned with the shorter-run movements that are so prominent in the literature. Rather, it develops two longer-run arguments. The first is that Malaysia's success in reducing the incidence of absolute poverty since 1970 has owed little to income redistribution and much to the achievement of rapid and sustained economic growth. While this has been shown in the decomposition of the poverty index above, here, a different and more general approach is undertaken. In essence, poverty-alleviation policies have worked because they have been growth policies directed at raising the productive potential of both the rich and the poor. The second argument is that the success of sustained growth in reducing absolute poverty has itself made the current poverty standard less central than it once was. Malaysia is literally outgrowing its thirty-year-old poverty line and consequently, different ways of measuring poverty are now required. These arguments are pursued in the next two sections of the chapter, which develop the notion of a poverty transition that is characteristic of initially poor countries that succeed in reducing the level of absolute poverty through the pursuit of economic growth. A third section takes the first steps in the direction of developing a poverty indicator that is more relevant to the current circumstances of the Malaysian economy, and the chapter ends with a discussion of the consequent reshaping of poverty policy that will be required.

6.6.1 Poverty, Inequality and Growth

The decomposition done earlier showed that the incidence of poverty fell essentially because average real income was growing strongly. The point is that Malaysian poverty is defined with reference to an unchanging absolute standard, and that a sufficiently high rate of growth thus has the power to reduce the number of households in absolute poverty even when the share of the poor in total income is falling. The empirical evidence of the strong poverty-reducing effect of economic growth and the minor role of the reduction in income inequality in poverty reduction is now illustrated using a more general approach. This approach is rather powerful as it illustrates the relationship between relative and absolute poverty and enables the discussion on the concept pf poverty transition.

The two counterfactual cumulative income distributions for 2002 in Figure 6.1 show why this has been so. Counterfactual A_{02} combines the distribution of income in 2002 with the monthly mean level of income per household in 1970. Arithmetically, this counterfactual is derived by multiplying the boundaries of each income class in the 2002 distribution by Y_{70}/Y_{02}, where Y_t is mean household income in current prices. The counterfactual thus shows the cumulative distribution of income that would have prevailed in 2002 had Malaysia achieved the reduction in income inequality that took place between 1970 and 2002 without also managing to secure any increase in average income over this period. The calculations ignore the fact that the 2002 distribution refers to the country as a whole while the distribution for 1970 was derived from a sample of households drawn from Peninsular Malaysia alone, since any loss of accuracy on this account is trivial in the present context.

Counterfactual B_{02} is the distribution of income that results when the boundaries of each income class in the 1970 distribution are multiplied by y_{02}/y_{70}, where y is mean household income in 1970 prices. This counterfactual thus incorporates the growth in average real income that actually took place over the period 1970–2002 while at the same time preserving the initial distribution of income between households.

The Malaysian authorities regard a household as being poor if its monthly income is below a real PLI that was established in the 1970s. The PLI shown in Figure 6.1 is positioned at the intersection of the 1970 household income distribution with the horizontal line showing the official poverty rate of 52 per cent for that year. The PLI in the figure thus refers to the household income that reconciles the distribution reported in the 1970 income survey with the official estimate of the percentage of households in poverty. In this sense it is the average PLI for 1970, and it is standardised on that year's household characteristics. To the extent that household characteristics varied with income in 1970, and to the extent that the relevant characteristics have since changed, points on the line elsewhere than at its intersection with the 1970 distribution would lie a little to the right or left of the perpendicular in the figure, depending on the exact combination of changes involved. The PLI has nonetheless been drawn as a perpendicular because refinements of this kind have no significant effect on the broad magnitudes that the figure is designed to illustrate.

Counterfactual A_{02} intersects the PLI at 48 per cent. If this counterfactual had eventuated – that is, had there been a fall in the level of inequality on the scale that actually took place but no accompanying growth in real household income – then nearly half of Malaysia's households would still be in poverty. In contrast, only 10 per cent of households fall below the intersection of counterfactual B_{02} with the poverty line. This is the level of poverty that would have been seen in 2002 if there had been no distributional change after 1970, and if average real household income had grown as it did in the intervening period. Since absolute poverty fell from 52 per cent to 5 per cent between 1970 and 2002, we can infer that almost 90 per cent of the reduction in poverty in this period can be attributed directly to the growth in average income.

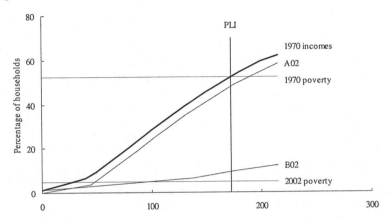

Figure 6.1   Cumulative percentages of households by monthly income

That is, very little of the long-run reduction in poverty can have been a reflection of changes in income distribution as such. This is not to say that redistribution was unimportant in Malaysia. On the contrary, the reduction in the Gini ratio has been a notable achievement, particularly as the general expectation in 1970 must have been that future growth, if achieved, would be likely to have involved a Kuznetsian rise in inequality in the absence of explicit counter-measures. But this reduction in overall inequality, important as it has undoubtedly been in other contexts, turns out to have had little long-run impact on the extent of absolute poverty, because most of the change in the overall income distribution since 1970 has reflected changes among the 95 per cent of the population who were not in any case poor by the end of the period, rather than a redistribution between this 95 per cent and the remaining 5 per cent who now constitute the poor.

While the particulars of Figure 6.1 relate specifically to Malaysia, the conclusions apply to any country with a high initial level of absolute poverty. Because much of the population is poor, redistribution in the absence of growth has a very limited capacity to reduce the number of poor households. Growth on a sufficiently large scale, on the other hand, will pull many households out of poverty in the long run, even if it is not accompanied by any significant reduction in overall inequality.

At one level, this is nothing more than arithmetic. But arithmetic imposes its discipline unremittingly, and an important economic point is also involved. When many in the population are poor, as they were in Malaysia in 1970, economic growth that leaves income distribution unchanged is necessarily growth that involves the poor. Poverty alleviation policies thus merge with growth policy, and where they are successful, economic growth will occur in ways that multiply the opportunities for self-advancement for rich and poor alike.

This aspect of poverty alleviation has been understood from the earliest days of the Malayan federation and it formed an integral part of the NEP implemented in Malaysia after 1970. The second MP, written in the aftermath of the 1969 riots, naturally gave much attention to the question of racial economic balance and hence to measures designed to increase the participation of Malays and other indigenous groups in the modern sector. The Plan insisted, however, that these goals were to be pursued in the context of a 'rapidly expanding economy' that offered 'increasing opportunities for all'. No particular group was to 'experience any loss or feel any sense of deprivation', an outcome that was obviously predicated on the achievement of successful economic growth (EPU 1971). These sentiments were echoed in the Plan's mid-term review, which could hardly have been more explicit about the importance of growth as a weapon against poverty. The eradication of poverty would be achieved by 'raising income levels and increasing employment opportunities for all Malaysians', which would depend in turn upon 'raising the productivity and income of those in low productivity occupations' and the 'expansion of opportunities for inter-sectoral movements from low productivity to higher productivity activities' (EPU 1973). The strategy was clear: poverty was to be conquered by making the poor more productive, both by increasing the productivity of the traditional sector and by encouraging the movement of the poor into an expanding modern sector.

6.6.2   The Poverty Transition

This strategy, while it sought to reduce the proportion of households in absolute poverty, had no necessary implications for the incidence of relative poverty. An absolute concept of poverty is one that is fixed in terms of some standard. If the standard is real income (as it usually is), a household is counted as being poor if its income is less than some benchmark level, and the real income benchmark remains the same even if a population's economic circumstances subsequently change. A relative notion of poverty, in contrast, is one that allows the benchmark for identifying poor households to change with relevant economic circumstances, the usual practice being to define a poverty line that is a certain proportion of the relevant population's mean or median income. With relative poverty, therefore, the benchmark real income will rise when average real income rises (Jantti and Danziger 2000).

Malaysian policy has consistently taken an absolute view of poverty. The real-income benchmark for identifying the poor thus remains the same as that used when the PLI was first introduced. Moreover, policymakers have been reluctant to accept suggestions that the benchmark be updated, or that poverty might also be defined in relative terms. The official rejection of a relative concept of poverty seems at times to rest on an inadequate understanding of what the term implies. Thus the fifth MP, for example, describes the proportion of households with less than half the median income as 'more a measure of income inequality than a poverty measure', which it plainly is not. The Plan then goes on to note the fact that this measurement leaves poverty unchanged when each household's income increases by the same percentage, describing this as a 'shortcoming' when the measure is of course designed to produce precisely this result (EPU 1986).

So ingrained is the absolutist view that official publications tend to frame even purely distributional questions in absolute terms. Thus the recent mid-term review of the eighth MP argues that the 'overall income distribution among households improved during the review period', citing as evidence a decrease in lower-income households and an increase in middle-income households as a share of the total between 1999 and 2002. But the review defines these income groups in reference to fixed income classes (a gross monthly income of under RM1200 for lower-income households, and from RM1200 to RM3499 for middle-income households). The 'distribution' that is being discussed is thus the distribution of households among income classes, not that of income among households. The income classes themselves are fixed in absolute (and apparently current-price) terms, a device that allows the review to proclaim an 'overall improvement in income distribution' during a period in which the Gini coefficient based on exactly the same data increased from 0.44 to 0.46 (EPU 2003).

A preoccupation with absolute poverty is of course entirely appropriate in a poor country, where many in the population are neither fed nor housed to a minimally acceptable physical standard. In these circumstances, defining poverty by reference to a minimum standard of food intake and shelter gives policymakers a tolerably clear and unambiguous target. A poverty line based on the money income that is required to purchase the bundle of goods delivering the minimum standard is not difficult to determine, and its real content can be preserved by use of an appropriate price index.

But there is usually a social element even in poverty lines that are derived in this way, since a society's notion of what constitutes an acceptable minimum will itself vary with circumstances. Thus the Malaysian poverty line was clearly influenced by the economic conditions of the 1970s when the PLI was being calculated. The benchmark income allowed for a significant margin above bare subsistence, and this in turn reflected the fact that average real income in Malaysia was at that time already well above the level to be found in most poor countries. In 1973, GDP per head in 1990 international dollars was the fifth highest in East Asia and more than 50 per cent above the average for the region as a whole (Maddison 2001). The energy content of the food budget was accordingly set as high as 2530 calories per adult per day compared with the 2100 calories adopted as a minimum standard by the World Bank, while the non-food component of the budget was a generous one that included 'items of expenditure which might be considered nonessential for subsistence, in particular, expenditure on recreation, education, and cultural services' (Perumal 1992).

A poverty line defined in this manner contains both relative and absolute elements in that it takes account of cross-sectional differences in income levels between Malaysia and other poor countries but is insensitive to subsequent changes in income within Malaysia itself. This adherence to a high but fixed standard left the country in a rather curious position with respect to the then emerging consensus that poverty should be measured in relative terms in rich countries but absolute terms in poor ones. Within this framework the country was clearly poor enough for an absolute standard to be appropriate because a significant fraction of the population was still poor by the minimum standards applicable to poor countries. At the same time, however, average income was high enough to justify the setting of this absolute standard at a relatively high level.

The Malaysian authorities do not appear to have fully appreciated that the combination of circumstances in which the PLI had been set would be no more than a passing phase if the country's growth policies turned out to be successful. At some point, prolonged economic growth will cause any given absolute standard to lose relevance. Figure 6.2 illustrates the way in which this comes about.

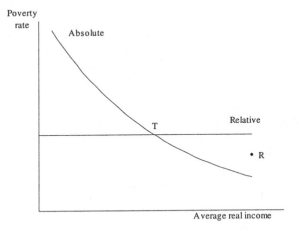

Figure 6.2   The poverty transition

Again, the Malaysian position in 1970 is used as a starting point. With the initial distribution of income and household characteristics held constant, absolute poverty declines with the growth in average income at a rate that is determined by the shape of the lower tail of the income distribution, while relative poverty obviously remains unaffected in the absence of changes in the distribution of income and the composition of households. The curve showing the course of absolute poverty in Figure 6.2 traces out the points of intersection of a series of counterfactuals B_t with the PLI that featured in Figure 6.2, with each counterfactual now incorporating successively higher values of y_t/y_{70}. The level of absolute poverty shown at the lowest point on the curve in Figure 6.2 is that implied by counterfactual B_{02} from Figure 6.1. The line depicting relative poverty is of course horizontal, and it takes as its starting point the percentage of households in the 1970 survey with less than half the median household income. The basic point made by the figure does not depend however upon this particular definition of relative poverty since it also holds if mean income is used in place of the median or if other proportions (such as a third or two-thirds of the median or the mean) are applied instead of a half.

The figure brings out the crucial fact that households in relative poverty in a poor country are a subset of those that are absolutely poor, a fact that underlies and justifies the initial focus on policies aimed at a reduction in the incidence of absolute poverty. As income grows, however, and in the absence of distributional change, the gap between the absolute and relative poverty levels diminishes. At the transition point T this gap disappears altogether, and thereafter the initial relationship between absolute and relative poverty is reversed. Absolute poverty is now a subset of relative poverty, and the gap between the two measures of poverty widens with each subsequent increment to average income.

A focus on absolute poverty thus misses little that is essential in the initial phases of income growth in a poor country. But once the transition point is passed an index of absolute poverty becomes increasingly unsatisfactory as a representation of the poverty level, and an exclusive policy focus on the now outdated poverty line becomes increasingly out of place.

A transition point of the kind illustrated in Figure 6.2 is reached sooner or later in every country that successfully frees the bulk of its people from absolute want. Every rich country was once poor by modern standards, and every rich country that now defines poverty in relative terms once took an absolute view of poverty. But economic growth in these countries eventually raised mean income to a significantly large multiple of that necessary to sustain a minimally acceptable physical standard of living, and the proportion of households below the old poverty line dwindled. Rich countries nonetheless came to accept that the problem of poverty had not been solved by economic growth, in spite of the near elimination of absolute poverty. Rather, it became clear that a household might have an income that was sufficient to finance an acceptable level of food, clothing and shelter and yet fall short of the levels of consumption, comfort and amenity taken for granted by most of the country's population. A household at R in Figure 6.2, for example, suffers from what has come to be called relative deprivation even though it is far from being poor by the old absolute standard. Households in this position are regarded as being poor because they lack the resources to 'participate in the activities and have the living conditions and amenities which are customary, or at least widely encouraged or approved, in the society to which they belong' and are thereby effectively excluded from that society's 'ordinary living patterns, customs and activities' (Townsend 1979).

In a brief but influential contribution, Fuchs (1969) outlined the importance of relative deprivation in a country such as the United States in the 1960s, where poverty was 'largely a matter of economic *distance*'. When most Americans had 'a great deal', Fuchs argued, those with 'much less' were poor 'regardless of their absolute level of income', and with continuing economic growth a population's standards 'must change'. What was needed therefore was a definition of poverty that kept 'pace with changes in the society'. A definition that regarded as poor any family with an income less than some specified fraction of the median, for example, would acknowledge that 'all so-called "minimum" or "subsistence" budgets are based on contemporary standards and political realities and have no intrinsic or scientific basis', as well as providing 'a more realistic basis for appraising the success or failure of antipoverty programs' (ibid).

Fuchs was particularly impressed by the change in perspective that such a relative measure of poverty would bring to policy analysis. With a fixed standard, the percentage of families defined as poor in the United States had been cut almost in half in the preceding twenty years, but there had been no corresponding reduction in the percentage of families with less than half the median income during the same period. Figure 6.3 graphs the estimates presented by Fuchs (1969), using $US3000 (in 1965 prices) as the benchmark income for identifying families in absolute poverty.

To Fuchs, the pattern evident in Figure 6.3 was 'a sobering reminder' that when poverty is defined in relation to contemporary standards there had not been 'any decrease in the entire postwar period' (Fuchs 1969). In the context of the present discussion, a striking aspect of the figure is the close resemblance that it bears to Figure 6.2, which draws on the same definition of relative poverty that Fuchs used for the United States but applies it to the Malaysian experience. The benchmark incomes for identifying families or households in absolute poverty are of course very different in the two diagrams but each is held constant at its initial level, and each eventually becomes unsatisfactory as growth proceeds.

Given the great increase in Malaysian real income per head since 1970, there would thus seem to be strong grounds for raising the country's PLI to reflect the increased standards of the general population. But the authorities have shown no inclination to move in this direction. If anything, the movement is the other way, judging by the priority now given to the eradication of hard core poverty, which is defined by reference to a benchmark income that is half the long-established poverty line income. This is not to say that hard core poverty should be neglected. Obviously, the poorest of the poor need special attention. But this should not blind policymakers to the fact that economic growth has made the old poverty line income unsatisfactorily low as a basis for identifying the general incidence of poverty. Mean household real income is now over three times the level prevailing when the PLI was first determined.

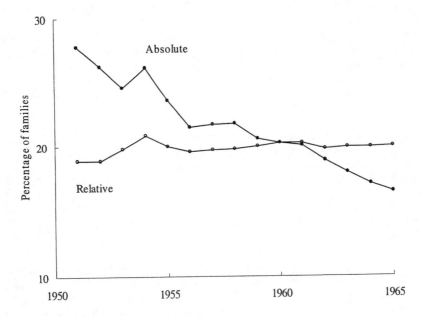

Source: Drawn using data from Fuch (1969).

Figure 6.3   Absolute and relative poverty in the United States, 1951–65

The pattern in Figure 6.2 would therefore seem to imply that households in absolute poverty have for some time been outnumbered by ones that are relatively poor. But the curves in the figure are counterfactuals designed to bring out the *ceteris paribus* effect of growth on the incidence of absolute and relative poverty, and they hold constant potentially important factors that have in fact changed. In particular, an allowance has to be made for the changes in overall inequality outlined earlier in the chapter. It is true that these changes have been modest in extent and might therefore be expected to have had little material impact on the broad magnitudes shown in the figure. But the only way to be sure of this is to do the necessary calculations, and this is the principal task of the next section.

6.6.3   Sketching the Course of Relative Poverty

First, however, a possible source of confusion needs to be cleared away. While the Malaysian authorities have resisted the notion of relative poverty as that term is generally understood in rich countries, they have adopted the same words to describe something that is very different. The sixth MP introduced the term as a shorthand expression for income disparity ratios, which are widely used in the Malaysian literature to compare the mean incomes of various groups in the population. In particular, the Plan spoke of achieving a reduction in 'relative poverty' through the reduction in 'income gaps, especially between the top 20% and the bottom 40%' of households (EPU 1991a). This terminology remains current in official publications, with a recent policy document drawing attention to 'relative poverty' as a means of assessing 'income disparities between income groups'. Again, the principal disparity envisaged is that between the top 20 per cent and the bottom 40 per cent of households (EPU 2005b).

The income disparity between groups however is not a measure of the incidence of poverty but an aspect of inequality, even when one of the groups being compared is at the bottom of the income distribution. Using the ratio of mean incomes of two groups that are defined as fixed percentages of the whole population of households to measure relative poverty, as the Malaysian authorities now do, is effectively to regard the poor as a fixed proportion of the population. In this approach poor households are always 40 per cent of the total, and the incidence of poverty is measured by the disparity between the incomes of these supposedly poor households and the incomes of the top 20 per cent.

But defining a household on the fortieth percentile of the income distribution as poor makes little sense in countries that already lie some way to the right of the transition point T in Figure 6.2. In these countries the more general practice is to take the percentage of households with incomes below some critical but changing level as a measure of the incidence of relative poverty. This income level, moreover, is not usually defined by reference to the richest groups in a society, since the poor are not the only ones excluded from the 'ordinary living patterns, customs and activities' of the very rich. Rather, the appropriate point of reference is one to which the poor themselves can be expected to relate, and this normally involves a comparison with the standards that are enjoyed by the bulk of the general population.

A simple and widely used way of achieving this comparison is to define a relative poverty line income that is some fixed proportion of the median or the mean. The proportion chosen is generally a half, and outside the European Community (which uses the mean) the usual reference point is median income. A relative poverty line set at one half of median income is of course the standard already applied in the counterfactuals employed in Figure 6.2 and in the analysis of the poverty transition in the United States in Figure 6.3. Figure 6.4 shows that applying the same definition of relative poverty to the income distribution data for Malaysia since 1970 produces yet again the long-run pattern that is evident in both Figures 6.1 and 6.2.

The estimates of absolute poverty in Figure 6.4 are taken directly from the various Malaysian Development Plans. The calculations underlying the estimates of relative poverty in the figure are also very preliminary since only broad orders of magnitude are necessary to make the essential point. The proportion of households with less than half the median income in 1970, 1987 and 2002 is estimated by linear interpolation within the income class that brackets this income in the relevant year. The 1970 calculations use the 32 income classes from the post-enumeration survey that are reported in Anand (1983), and the 1987 calculations use a distribution into 22 income classes from the household income survey for that year. The estimated proportion of households with less than half the median income in each of these two years (21.8 per cent in 1970 and 19.0 per cent in 1987) is therefore likely to be fairly accurate, in spite of the simplicity of the procedure used. For 2002, we are limited to the summary distribution published in the mid-term review of the eighth MP (EPU 2003), which has only eleven income classes. Even so the estimate for this year (19.8 per cent) is also likely to be fairly close because the relative poverty line of RM1025 happens to lie close to the lower boundary of the RM1000 to RM1199 income class.

No adjustments have been made for household composition, regional or urban location. These and other refinements will of course be desirable when the authorities eventually face up to the need to develop a measure of relative poverty that is appropriate to a country where the old standard of absolute poverty is no longer relevant. But no amount of refinement along these lines has the potential to undermine the two main lessons to be drawn from Figure 6.4. The first lesson is that economic growth carried Malaysia past the transition point identified in Figure 6.2 at some time in the 1980s. Malaysia's poverty transition is now well and truly complete. Households in absolute poverty, as defined in the official figures, have thus been a rapidly shrinking subset of those in relative poverty for the past twenty years. This confirms the power of the counterfactual analysis in Figure 6.2, and it also highlights the essential similarity of the evolution of the relationship between economic growth and absolute and relative poverty in economies as different as those of Malaysia and the United States.

The second lesson of Figure 6.4 is that the incidence of relative poverty has changed very little since 1970, as the modest changes in overall inequality might have led us to expect. The successful assault on absolute poverty has thus left relative poverty much as it was in 1970, a fact that has important implications for future policy. While a preoccupation with the more immediate problem of absolute poverty was entirely appropriate in the early stages of economic growth this focus is now patently too narrow. The completion of the poverty transition has been a major policy achievement but it has brought new challenges that call for a refocusing of Malaysia's approach to the problem of poverty in ways that are discussed in the following and final section of the chapter.

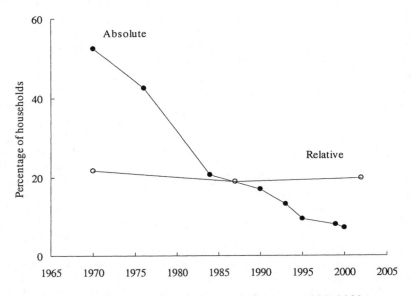

Figure 6.4   Absolute and relative poverty in Malaysia, 1970–2002

6.6.4   The Changing Focus of Malaysian Poverty Policy

The logic of the poverty transition suggests that the focus of policy can be expected to change in predictable ways in an initially poor country that manages to achieve rapid and sustained economic growth. In the early stages of this growth, absolute poverty levels can be expected to fall quickly, as Figure 6.2 has made clear. Poverty policy during this early period is essentially a matter of raising the productivity of the mass of the population, and the success of this strategy in Malaysia's case is readily apparent in the reduction in the incidence of absolute poverty that took place after 1970. But the characteristic shape of the lower tail of the income distribution ensures that as growth continues, its power to bring further reductions in absolute poverty eventually diminishes. One aspect of this diminished power is implicit in the notion of there being a constant elasticity of poverty reduction with respect to increases in mean income. This can be illustrated using the World Bank's suggested rule of thumb that a 1 per cent increase in mean real income can be expected to reduce absolute poverty by 2 per cent (World Bank 2000). When half the population is below the poverty line, and in the absence of distributional change, this elasticity implies that sustained growth at 4 per cent a year will reduce the poverty level by 20 percentage points in six years. But when the absolute poverty rate has already fallen to five percent, as is now the case in Malaysia, continued growth at the same rate brings a fall of only 2 percentage points in six years, and a further reduction of 2 percentage points beyond this requires another 15 years of growth in mean income at the same rate.

Even this, however, exaggerates the power of economic growth to bring further falls in absolute poverty once the latter has been reduced to the current Malaysian level. A relatively constant elasticity of poverty reduction with respect to income growth can only be expected to hold during the period in which many able-bodied and economically active households remain poor because productivity is low in the economy as a whole. With the economic transformation that growth brings, these households have a greater opportunity to become more productive and are therefore increasingly capable of supporting a standard of living above the absolute poverty line through their own efforts. There is, however, a residual group of households that will be unable to support themselves at this level from their own resources no matter how fast the economy grows, since illness, disability, or other disadvantages beyond their individual power to control mean that such households will never have a realistic prospect of participating fully in productive activity. Growth in average income thus affords these disadvantaged or incapacitated households little or no opportunity to raise themselves above the poverty line.

As growth continues, and as large numbers of initially poor but able bodied and economically active households work their way out of poverty, the relative importance of this incapacitated group among the remaining poor can be expected to increase. Eventually these residual households will come to make up the bulk of those in absolute poverty. Policy must therefore evolve to reflect this change in the composition of the poor. In Malaysia's case, the accompanying policy evolution has involved the development in the past 10 to 15 years of an explicit focus on hard core poverty, together with a greater emphasis on transfers and safety nets, a tighter targeting of poverty programmes, and a greater concern with defining the benchmark poverty line income in ways that reflect variations in local circumstances. Economic growth has thus become less central to poverty policy than in the past. Growth is also less prominent in the academic literature on Malaysian poverty than it once was. Ragayah's (2005) analysis of urban poverty, for example, mentions growth only in passing, and policy measures that are designed to raise the productivity of poor households form only a minor part of the recommendations made in the paper. Rather, Ragayah places emphasis on the need to improve social security and social safety nets, on the need for more low-cost housing, and on the desirability of targeting the poor more effectively by revising the poverty line to take account of differences in living costs, consumption patterns, and family size between urban and rural households.

The development of poverty policy along these lines is entirely natural in a country that has moved well past T in Figure 6.2. But a second path of policy evolution that is implicit in the poverty transition is yet to be considered. By definition, growth without distributional change leaves relative poverty untouched. And, as Figure 6.2 has made abundantly clear, the trend fall in absolute poverty that is brought about by economic growth can be expected to bring this unchanged level of relative poverty to the fore. The exact location of the transition point after which households in relative poverty come to outnumber those in absolute poverty depends of course upon the particular poverty line income that is adopted and the particular definition of relative poverty that is used, and these naturally vary in detail from country to country. But upon any defensible set of poverty definitions successful economic growth will eventually take a country past this transition point, and thereafter questions of relative poverty become increasingly difficult to set to one side.

That is, once the transition point has been left behind, a country's poverty policy must address the trend in both absolute and relative poverty. These two aspects of poverty, moreover, require increasingly different policy approaches. The further a country is to the right of the transition point, the more is absolute poverty policy likely to be a matter of transfers and safety nets rather than of economic growth. Well designed transfers and safety nets can alleviate absolute poverty in countries where households in absolute poverty have already been reduced to a small fraction of the population, partly because the scale of expenditure involved of these poverty-reducing programmes is small relative to the potential tax base, and partly because the absolute poverty line is so far below average living standards that few households capable of ordinary economic activity are tempted to rely on government welfare programmes directed at the absolute poor.

In contrast, the size of the transfer that would be required to raise a significant fraction of the households in relative poverty to half the median income is unmanageably large. Even reducing relative poverty to, say, 15 per cent would involve transfers on a daunting scale. Households on the fifteenth percentile would require transfers equal to one-third of their current income, and a policy that did not also raise the income of still-poorer households by at least this much would be very difficult to justify. Nor is this the end of the extra expenditure that would be required, since the administrative costs of implementing transfers to about one-fifth[9] of the whole population would dwarf those involved in administering the current programmes against absolute poverty.

Taxation on the scale necessary to fund such a programme is beyond the bounds of political possibility in Malaysia today. The sheer magnitude of the budgetary costs involved would therefore rule out the tackling of relative poverty through taxes and transfers even if it were not for the still larger potential cost of such a policy flowing from its effect on incentives. With such a programme in place, many households that currently work hard to achieve incomes that are not far above the relative poverty line might ask themselves whether this continued effort is worthwhile. The difficulty of counteracting this adverse incentive effect has of course long been a recurring feature of policy experience in countries that have turned to welfare programmes as a remedy for relative poverty, and the potential for these programmes to undermine economic growth has been an enduring policy concern.

Malaysia, though no longer poor by the standards of poor countries, is far from being in a position where a percentage point or two of growth can comfortably be sacrificed in the cause of alleviating relative poverty. One implication is that for the immediate future a reduction in relative poverty will require policies that not only maintain the overall pace of growth but also increase the productivity of the bottom fifth of the population relative to the average for the economy as a whole. Policy is thus likely to become more difficult than it has been in the past. Any potential trade-off between growth and equity could operate at the outer margins of policy in 1970, in spite of the prominence of 'growth with equity' in the policy discussions of the time. With half the population in absolute poverty, successful economic growth would have been sufficient to reduce the number of poor households almost irrespective of the trend in inequality. Because growth could bring absolute poverty tumbling down, an equity improvement could rightly be claimed even if the relative position of the poor remained unchanged. But the poverty transition relegates this achievement, considerable though it is, to history.

The very success of economic growth in the battle against absolute poverty brings the relative position of the poor in from the margins of policy discussion, and a more challenging balance of growth and equity objectives then becomes necessary. With the eradication of absolute poverty now in sight, Malaysia has clearly reached the point where the question of relative poverty needs to be taken seriously, as it generally is other countries that lie to the far right of Figure 6.2. The reframing of poverty policy in relative terms would be an acknowledgment of the fact that in this respect the country is no longer to be numbered among the world's poor and that Malaysia now stands ready to accept the new policy challenges arising from the country's successful completion of the poverty transition.

6.7 INCOME INEQUALITY TRENDS

Although the relevant data for studying income inequality is that of wealth, similar to many other countries, data on wealth is non-existent in Malaysia and hence income is used as a proxy. Furthermore, the inequality data and Gini coefficients for Malaysia are based on income and not expenditure data. Table 6.9 shows that income inequality increased for all categories until 1970 and Table 6.10 shows a decline in the trend of Gini coefficients from 1970 to 1990.

Table 6.9   Gini coefficients 1957/58–1970

	1957/58 (Adjusted)	1967/68 (Ford survey)	1970	1970[1]
Area				
Peninsular Malaysia	0.412	0.444	0.502	0.5129
Rural	0.374	0.399	0.463	0.4689
Urban	0.429	0.447	0.494	0.5073
Race				
Malays	0.342	0.400	0.466	0.4664
Chinese	0.374	0.391	0.455	0.4656
Indians	0.347	0.403	0.463	0.4722

Source: Snodgrass (1980); [1]Anand (1983).

It can be seen in Table 6.10 that although NEP was first implemented in 1971, its impact was not felt in Peninsular Malaysia during the early years and income inequality persisted until the mid 1970s, but undoubtedly there has been a decline since then to 1990. For Malaysia too, there was a fall in the Gini ratio from 1970 to 1990. In general, the Gini coefficients in Peninsular Malaysia can be expected to be higher than that of Malaysia as the less developed states of Sabah and Sarawak have a higher proportion of rural households than urban, and income dispersion in rural areas is more even than in urban areas.

However, no data are available on the income inequality trend in Peninsular Malaysia after 1990 and it is not exactly clear why the Malaysian authorities have since then shifted their focus to Malaysia. One reason could be that the NEP launched in 1971 set targets for only Peninsular Malaysia to be attained by 1990. Thus further reporting on Peninsular Malaysia could have been deemed unnecessary. Another likely reason could be to that the neglect of East Malaysia has been addressed and the growing potential exploited by consciously developing and modernising the states of Sabah and Sarawak.

Interestingly, the reported Gini coefficients since 1990 in Table 6.10 are quite different depending on which official publication is used, but the reported trend can be generalised as indicating an increase from 1990 to 1995, and possibly to 1997 and 1998 due to the crisis, but income inequality decreases in 1999, only to increase in 2002 and 2004. The income share of the bottom 40 per cent of households decreased from 14 per cent in 1999 to 13.5 per cent in 2004 while that of the top 20 per cent of households increased from 50.5 per cent in 1999 to 51.2 per cent in 2004. Consequently, the Gini coefficient worsened from 0.452 in 1999 to 0.462 in 2004 (EPU 2006). It has been targeted in the ninth MP that the Gini coefficient be reduced to 0.35 per cent by 2020.

Table 6.10   Gini Coefficients 1970-2004

	Peninsular Malaysia	Malaysia	
1970	0.513	0.501	
1976	0.529		
1979	0.508	0.493	
1984	0.480		
1987	0.456		
1990	0.445	0.446[1]	0.442[3]
1993		0.459[2]	
1995		0.464[1]	0.456[3]
1997		0.470[2]	
1999		0.452[4]	0.443[3]
2002		0.461[3]	
2004		0.462[4]	

Source: Anand (1983), EPU (1981, 1986, 1991a); [1]EPU (1996); [2]EPU (1999); [3]EPU (2001a, 2001b, 2003); [4]EPU (2006).

The information on income inequality relating to the existing data points does not allow us to establish a direct statistical empirical link between growth and income inequality. Even if there was some trade-off between growth and inequality, this could not have been significant. To date, the trade-off underlying Kuznets' hypothesis for Malaysia has been tested using cross-sectional data by Anand (1983) and Hashim (1997), and time series data by Perumal (1989). While there are mixed conclusions, none of these studies had more than ten degrees of freedom to statistically validate their findings.

The literature on the relationship between income inequality and growth stands divided on both theoretical and empirical grounds. Inequality is generally perceived as a necessary precondition for the eventual improvement of everyone's income and this argument is formalised in the celebrated Kuznets (1955) inverted U-curve hypothesis. The implicit assumption in testing the Kuznets curve is that causality runs from growth to inequality. This assumption has been challenged on the grounds that inequality also affects growth. These views have been questioned further by the notion that there is no trade-off between growth and equity.

Studies by Ram (1988), Anand and Kanbur (1993), and Jha (1996) provide mixed evidence on the existence of a trade-off between economic growth and inequality. Research by Birdsall et. al (1995), Perotti (1996), and Glyfason and Zoega (2001) show that equality is good for growth. On the other hand, Barro's (1999, 2000) empirical evidence suggests that there is a certain threshold of income growth beyond which an economy can be expected to benefit from inequality. Thus the current wave of research on income inequality has failed to definitively confirm or reject the Kuznets hypothesis. These days, the literature is littered with calls for careful reassessment of the relationship between economic growth and inequality to evaluate the specific channels through which the variables may affect one another.

In the case of Malaysia, she has successfully avoided the trade-off between growth and income inequality from 1970 to 1990 but since then, income inequality has been rising. In relation to this, the move from NEP to NDP and then to NVP has already been criticised as being less aggressive in terms of redistributive plans. This shift in policy direction reflects the government's decision to allow market forces to play a greater role so that economic growth is not hampered by unnecessary intervention.

6.7.1   Inter-racial and Inter-regional Income Inequality

Here, a closer look is taken at ethnic inequality as well as rural–urban inequality. Inter-ethnic economic imbalances improved with a fall in the income disparity ratios (which is the ratio of the mean income of one group to the other) between bumiputeras and non-bumiputeras over 1970–87 as seen in Table 6.11.

Table 6.11   Income disparity ratios

Peninsular Malaysia	Bumiputeras–Chinese	Bumiputeras–Indians	Rural– Urban
1970	1 : 2.29	1 : 1.76	1 : 2.14
1976	1 : 2.28	1 : 1.57	1 : 2.12
1979	1 : 1.91	1 : 1.54	1 : 1.90
1984	1 : 1.76	1 : 1.28	1 : 1.87
1987	1 : 1.65	1 : 1.25	1 : 1.72
1990	1 : 1.70	1 : 1.29	1 : 1.73
Malaysia			
1990	1 : 1.74	1 : 1.28	1 : 1.71
1995	1 : 1.80	1 : 1.33	1 : 1.99
1997	1 : 1.83	1 : 1.42	1 : 1.97
1999	1 : 1.74	1 : 1.36	1 : 1.81
2002	1 : 1.80	1 : 1.28	1 : 2.11
2004	1 : 1.64	1 : 1.27	1 : 2.11

Source: Data were obtained from Shari (2000), EPU (1996, 2003, 2006), and Department of Statistics (2002).

Table 6.11 also shows that the mean income is highest for the Chinese followed by the Indians. The increase in inter-ethnic income disparity trends from 1990 to 1995 is not surprising as the inclusion of the states of Sabah and Sarawak can be expected to lower the mean income of bumiputeras far more than the other races. However, it is unclear if the fall in the ratio from 1995 to 1999 shows any real improvement in ethnic imbalances as Malaysia was in the midst of the 1997/98 financial crisis then. Since the decade of the 1990s, Malaysia has been undergoing a period of adjustment and this transition in the form of structural changes in the economy where there is a greater shift towards services and higher value added manufacturing activities may have caused income imbalances favouring some ethnic groups more than others. Thus although all income groups shared in the ample opportunities springing from the rapid annual increase in GDP from 1990 to 1999, they did not do this equally as Chinese and Indian household incomes rose more than those of bumiputeras. In general, there is no clear trend in income disparity ratios since 1990. With the rural–urban income disparity, Table 6.11 shows a fall until 1990, an increase in the early half in the 1990s and a fall in the late 1990s, after which it rose in 2002 and has remained the same in 2004.

Table 6.12 shows that income inequality declined within the three ethnic groups until 1990 in Peninsular Malaysia in line with one of the aims of the NEP. The declines within each ethnic group however varied, and the non-bumiputeras experienced greater reduction in income inequality than the bumiputeras. However, from 1999 to 2004 when East Malaysia is also included, there has been an increase in inequality within all the races. With rural households, income inequality declined faster than urban inequality for Peninsular Malaysia until 1990 and for Malaysia since 1999.

Table 6.12   Inter-racial and inter-regional Gini ratios

Peninsular Malaysia	Bumiputeras	Chinese	Indians	Rural	Urban
1970	0.466	0.466	0.473	0.469	0.503
1976	0.506	0.541	0.509	0.500	0.512
1979	0.488	0.470	0.460	0.482	0.501
1984	0.469	0.452	0.417	0.444	0.466
1987	0.447	0.428	0.402	0.427	0.499
1990	0.428	0.400	0.394	0.409	0.445
Malaysia					
1999	0.433	0.434	0.413	0.421	0.432
2004	0.452	0.466	0.425	0.397	0.444

Note: Data for Peninsular Malaysia are not published after 1990 and that for Malaysia are only available as shown above.

Source: Shari (2000) and EPU (2006).

6.8   EFFECT OF REDISTRIBUTIVE POLICIES ON INCOME INEQUALITY

The Success of the National Economic Policy in 1971–90

The National Economic Policy has been hailed as a successful model for redistributive policies and there is consensus among studies such as Lucas and Verry (1996), Hashim (1997), and Rasiah and Shari (2001) as to why and how income inequality was reduced in this period.

Alongside the implementation of the NEP in 1971, there was a move from import-substitution to export-orientation in Malaysia's economic restructuring efforts. With the establishment of the free trade zones in 1972, the creation of a liberalised foreign investment environment in the form of the Promotion of Investment Act passed in 1986, Malaysia was poised for increased growth. The government took the initiative to lead the economy and state expansion took the form of numerous public enterprises in manufacturing, commerce, and banking. Public sector employment growth was strongest in the 1970–81 period (World Bank 1993). The privatisation policy launched in 1983 also allowed bumiputeras to extend their participation in business. Under the Industrial Co-ordination Act, foreign investors were influenced to comply with NEP employment and ownership targets for bumiputeras by specific fiscal incentives.

The 1980s saw a strengthening of existing bodies and the establishment of new public enterprises and trust agencies which provided a range of financial, educational and training services to bumiputeras. Institutions such as the Majlis Amanah Rakyat, Bank Bumiputera Malaysia Berhad and Perbadanan Nasional were given wider roles and access to capital to raise the position of bumiputeras. While statutory bodies such as the National Corporation and National Equity Corporation were used to implement and promote bumiputera ownership in leading sectors, the Urban Development Authority on a national level dealt with urban sectors ranging from property development to retailing and other services.

There was also direct intervention with the use of employment quotas for getting bumiputeras into non-agricultural jobs whereby written proficiency in Bahasa Melayu[10] was imposed to provide an advantage for the bumiputeras. Targets set for the ethnic composition of employment in each major sector were also successfully met by 1990. In tertiary education, the importance of restructuring has been explicit in the form of a quota which, since the early days of the NEP, reserved 75 per cent of places for bumiputeras, though the quota was later lowered to 55 per cent. This saw the proportion of bumiputera students at public universities increase from 12 per cent in 1970 to about 70 per cent in 1995.[11] There are special Malay-only programmes and education institutions for matriculation to increase Malay intake first into diploma courses and then to transfer them to degree courses.

Obviously, the opportunities that this has afforded initially in public service in industry, have aided those bumiputeras fortunate enough to attend university. In general however, because of rapid growth that made the implementation of NEP economically possible, non-Malays also benefited indirectly (Tori 2003).

The National Development Policy in 1991–2000

The National Development Policy which superceded the NEP in 1991 and carried through until 2000, was seen to be less aggressive in terms of income distribution. Unlike the NEP, no time frame was set for achieving distributive targets in the associated five-year development plans of the NDP. While there was still emphasis on the strategy of growth with equity, the NDP relied on the private sector to be responsive and proactive in attaining these objectives. This is in line with the government's move to ride on the waves of globalisation and liberalisation. While this meant that there would be increased economic opportunities for non-bumiputeras, one cannot rule out the positive outcome of the development of more genuine and capable bumiputera businessmen and entrepreneurs given the environment.

Nevertheless, the privatisation efforts of the government remained an important means of enhancing bumiputera participation in the corporate sector. The Third Outline Perspective Plan 2001–2010 reports that as of April 2000, the government privatised a total of 180 companies of which 109 were managed and controlled by bumiputeras. Also, while the NEP concentrated and succeeded in increasing bumiputera participation in the non-agricultural sectors, under the NDP, emphasis was given towards raising the quality of bumiputera participation in the corporate sector. Table 6.13 shows the employment by ethnic group in various sectors of the economy.

It can be seen that in the agricultural sector, the proportion of bumiputera employed is not seen to decline given that it was 68 per cent in 1970, 76.4 per cent in 1990 and 75 per cent in 2003, and in manufacturing, the increase in bumiputera participation was quite insignificant. While there was some increase in bumiputera participation in the transport, finance, insurance and real estate, as well as the wholesale and retail sectors from 1990 to 2000, Chinese domination in most sectors has declined except in the wholesale and retail sector. The proportion of Indians involved in most of the sectors has also declined over time.

Large imbalances in the racial pattern of occupational employment in the 1970s were first noted by Anand (1983). For 1970, Anand found that bumiputeras constituted 85 per cent of all farmers but only 28 per cent of all sales workers, and in the administrative and managerial, clerical and related, and production worker categories, the bumiputeras accounted for little more than 30 per cent of the workforce. In contrast, the Chinese constituted less than 13 per cent of farmers but some 60 per cent of sales workers, and 57 per cent of production workers, and 46 per cent of the administrative and managerial, clerical and related personnel. However there has been some improvement in all occupational categories over time except in agriculture workers from 1970 to 2000. The most notable increase comes from the teachers and nurses professions as there is more government control in these jobs given the large number of government-owned schools and hospitals in Malaysia. However, the smallest proportion of bumiputeras at 34.7 per cent in 2000 was seen in the administrative and managerial positions which remain dominated by the Chinese. The low make-up of bumiputeras in this category is the least successful aspect of restructuring of the society in the decade of the 1990s (Malaysia 2001a). In 2005, the share of bumiputeras employed in the senior officials and managers category remained low at 37.1 per cent.

Another unsuccessful policy has been the capital and assets accumulation policy of encouraging and regulating the private sector to ensure bumiputeras held at least 30 per cent of the share capital of limited companies. Initiated under the NEP in 1971, this policy was continued under the NDP. While there was a marked increase in the share from 2.4 per cent in 1970 to the highest level of 20.6 per cent in 1995, the target of 30 per cent has yet to be achieved as seen in Table 6.14. In fact, there has been a decline in the bumiputera share since 1995.

The highest proportion of bumiputera equity ownership was found to be 31 per cent in the transportation sector followed by 26 per cent and 16.5 per cent in the construction and agriculture sectors respectively in 1995. In the manufacturing sector, the share was 13 per cent. In 2004, the proportion in manufacturing declined further to 8.1 per cent and that in agriculture rose to 35.2 per cent in 2004. Foreign equity share on the other hand has increased in the 1990s reflecting the significant inflow of FDI. In line with the efforts to revitalise the economy after the 1997/98 crisis, there was a relaxation of regulations on foreign equity ownership, and as a result, foreign equity ownership in the manufacturing sector was highest at 64.7 per cent in 2004.

The National Vision Policy in 2001–2010

The National Vision Policy is similar to the NDP without being less or more aggressive in its redistribution stance. While the strategy of reduced state involvement was adopted under the NDP, with the NVP the government has indicated areas in which it will address possible economic imbalances arising from its market-orientated approach. For instance, the *Third Outline Perspective Plan for 2001–2010* has plans to

- be target-specific in their poverty eradication programmes in remote areas and among bumiputera minorities in Sabah and Sarawak;
- promote a conducive environment for bumiputeras to face the challenges of globalisation by facilitating and assisting in the promotion of their products overseas and enabling bumiputera entrepreneurs to venture into niche international markets;

Table 6.13 Employment by sector and ethnic group (% of total employed)

		Agriculture, forestry and fishing	Mining and quarrying	Manu-facturing	Uti-lities	Construc-tion	Transport and com-munication	Whole-sale and retail	Finance, insurance, real estate	Govern-ment and other services
1970	Bumi	68.0	25.0[1]	29.0	48.0	22.0	43.0	24.0	n.a	n.a
	Chinese	21.0	66.0	65.0	18.0	72.0	40.0	65.0	n.a	n.a
	Indians	10.0	8.0	5.0	33.0	6.0	17.0	11.0	n.a	n.a
1980	Bumi	73.1	34.0	40.9	67.1	39.1	50.6	35.2	36.9	59.4
	Chinese	16.4	54.7	50.4	9.7	53.4	30.2	58.3	55.3	29.2
	Indians	9.7	10.6	8.0	22.6	6.4	13.9	7.4	7.4	10.1
1990	Bumi	76.4	48.8	50.3	69.8	43.0	54.1	38.2	41.1	66.4
	Chinese	16.1	38.9	36.9	12.9	49.9	32.4	54.1	47.4	24.9
	Indians	6.7	10.8	12.2	16.6	6.2	12.8	6.9	10.3	8.1
1995	Bumi	76.1	57.5	49.8	72.1	37.4	53.2	36.5	45.1	64.4
	Chinese	11.7	22.0	30.3	10.4	41.1	29.4	50.0	42.3	21.2
	Indians	6.0	10.6	11.3	11.1	4.7	11.7	6.1	9.3	6.8
	Others	0.8	1.5	0.5	0.2	0.9	0.4	0.9	1.0	1.0
2003	Bumi	74.9	63.3	54.5	72.3	43.9	56.2	40.5	45.8	69.5
	Chinese	13.5	22.8	32.6	11.9	45.7	28.7	51.3	41.7	22.2
	Indians	7.4	11.0	12.4	11.8	5.4	12.1	7.1	10.0	7.3
	Others	4.2	2.9	0.5	4.0	5.0	3.0	1.1	2.5	1.0

Note: Bumi refers to bumiputeras. [1]This figure is only for the mining industry unlike all other years.

Source: Five-Year Malaysia Plans, EPU.

Table 6.14   Corporate equity ownership (%)

	Bumiputeras	Non-bumiputeras	Foreign
1970	2.4	32.3	63.4
1975	9.2	37.5	53.3
1980	12.5	34.3	43.0
1985	19.1	35.9	26.0
1990	20.3	46.2	25.1
1995	20.6	43.3	27.7
1999	19.1	40.3	32.7
2000	18.9	41.3	31.3
2002	18.7	43.2	28.9
2004	18.9	40.6	32.5

Note: The figures do not add to 100 as the information on nominee companies is not included.

Source: Five-Year Malaysia Plans, EPU.

- promote effective participation of bumiputeras and other disadvantaged groups in a knowledge-based economy with a bumiputera Information and Communications Technologies Agenda to obtain recognition as reliable and capable market players;
- retrain (unemployed) social science bumiputera graduates with market-related knowledge and skills to benefit from employment opportunities in other sectors of the economy.

In addition, the NVP states that it would continue achieving bumiputera equity ownership of at least 30 per cent by 2010 without resorting to micro-restructuring of existing ventures. Here, the government is open about its limited intervention in this particular goal, probably realising that this may never happen given that it has been unsuccessful since 1970. There is also continued emphasis on enhancing regional balance through the rapid development of the less developed states. Here, a gradual approach to developing the less developed states should be encouraged as too rapid an increase in the urbanisation rate without appropriate evenness in income dispersion (by means of sustained employment generation) would lead to greater overall income inequality.

Lastly, the NVP intends to have bumiputera participation in leading sectors reflect the ethnic composition of the population. This has an advantage as the racial employment targets would be implemented in relation to flows rather than stocks, because the racial allocation of new labour force entrants would be in proportion to the population ratios of the racial groups. In terms of bumiputera employment in major sectors, Table 6.13 shows that the agriculture and utilities sectors could do with a decrease in bumiputera participation. While some improvement has taken place in bumiputera participation in the manufacturing and non-government services, the racial make-up of 66 per cent bumiputeras (in line with the ethnic composition of the population) has yet to be achieved in these sectors.

However, employment restructuring by sector alone will only help to narrow income differences between the races but not to eliminate them. The occupational structure of employment within each sector too has to be balanced racially so that the income differences between the races will be reduced more effectively. Table 6.13 shows that bumiputera participation improved in all occupational categories but there is a dire lack of bumiputeras in the administrative and managerial category. Production, sales and clerical workers also need an increase in bumiputera participation of about 10 per cent to achieve the 66 per cent target in relation to the population's ethnic composition.

6.9   WHAT NOW FOR MALAYSIAN INCOME INEQUALITY?

Although Malaysia's redistributive policies in the past have been successful, Rasiah and Shari (2001) note that the government could have better managed its ethnic-based redistributive policies as 'access to carrots was hardly countered by the stick of discipline' and if some of 'the promotion of crony interests that sapped the economy of rents' could have been avoided. But this is bound to happen in any society with a government strongly involved in addressing ethnic imbalances. It must however be true in the case of Malaysia, given its record of economic success, that these effects may have been insignificant. Furthermore, the increased role of the market forces underlying the NDP and NVP can be expected to keep a check on such effects in the future.

The market-oriented approach of the NVP is further welcome as redistributive action of any kind, if undertaken at the considerable cost of growth, is unlikely to be sustained and effective. The widening of relative inequalities, if accompanied by rapid economic growth in the expansion of productive capacity and its effective utilisation, need not necessarily have long-lasting adverse effects. As long as economic growth keeps income inequality at a 'tolerable' level it should not cause concern but what this level is is the sixty-four million dollar question. Perhaps a different type of question can throw some light on this issue.

Given Malaysia's developments and achievements so far, how important is ethnic economic imbalance today? It can be argued that a more unequal society of the present is likely to confer more benefits than harm in the long run (Nelson 1993). Also, should there not be a limit to the provision of continued support and opportunities to the disadvantaged ethnic group?

Snodgrass (1980) notes that the responsiveness of the ethnic groups in Malaysia to economic opportunities is (or has been) different and the capacities of different groups to respond may vary systematically given differences in achievement motivation. At the risk of over-simplification, Snodgrass provides evidence of the cultural hypothesis which fundamentally says that, '*something* in Malay culture – or could it be a "culture of poverty" generated by Malay poverty itself? – makes the Malays immobile, irresponsive to economic opportunity and therefore poor, while *something* in Chinese culture – or in a "culture of immigrants" – makes the Chinese mobile, more adept at seizing economic opportunities, thrifty, and therefore relatively prosperous'. Snodgrass explains that such characteristics are inherent, or at least hard to change, and this is a powerful deterrent to direct efforts to ameliorate economic inequality. Thus in the past, while the NEP has been successful in raising the living standards of bumiputeras, what needs to be avoided is for bumiputeras born in the second generation during the NEP period, to consider it their right to be favoured without having to work hard for it.[12]

Studies such as Yusof (2001) and Rasiah and Shari (2001), which have voiced concern over the rising trend of income inequality, point to the possible cause of government policy reversal towards liberalisation, deregulation and privatisation since the late 1980s. But in the era of globalisation, Malaysia has little choice but to allow the more responsive and less bureaucratic private sector to take up the challenges of operating in a more market-friendly and competitive global environment. This is a timely move on the part of the government as income inequality is a less politically sensitive issue than it once was due to the remarkable increase in living standards experienced in the economy.

There have been claims by Ragayah (2000) and Shari (2001) that increases in capital intensity and manufacturing employment resulting in a wide dispersion of wages and salaries, explain the resurgence of income inequality in Malaysia. The increases in capital intensity and manufacturing employment are inevitable for an economy like Malaysia which has been attracting FDI since the 1980s. The development/modernisation hypothesis believes that even if FDI initially stimulates growth in only some leading or favoured sectors, the growth in these sectors could in the long run facilitate more even income distribution via positive spillover effects. While Authukorala and Menon (1997) show how FDI-related export-led industrialisation has generated employment opportunities and reduced income inequality, Mahadevan (2002) notes that FDI in manufacturing is currently at the low level of the technology ladder, and this means that the concern on the wage levels being stretched if demand for skilled workers outpaces the supply may be overstated. Furthermore, FDI inflows into Malaysia have slowed down from an annual increase of 78 per cent in 1988–91, to 20 per cent in 1990–95, and 7 per cent in 1995–2000. This together with the financial crisis of 1997/98 has blurred the effect of FDI on income distribution.

Even if FDI increased income inequality, for Malaysia today FDI is a necessary evil to gain access to better technology and remain competitive in the global market. But if FDI is aimed at the higher value added manufacturing activities, then wage levels can be stretched if human resources development policy does not sufficiently ensure that there are enough high skilled workers and this would widen earnings differential. In order to reduce the earnings differential, the government has to increase its budget allocation for education and training at the macro level while firms should provide both pre-entry and in-service to their workers. Thus, if policies related to human resource development can be devised appropriately and implemented effectively, the purported increase in income inequality due to FDI can be checked on.

However, one view of FDI and international openness is that it benefits most of the domestic residents who are already well off in the sense that rich groups are most able to take advantage of the opportunities offered by trade expansion. While trade liberalisation has distributional consequences, that is, there are 'winners' and 'losers' in the short run, it is also true to say that not all losers may come disproportionately from the disadvantaged group. To the extent that trade openness raises national income, it strengthens the fiscal ability of a society to provide safety nets or consider options to directly help the bumiputeras.

6.10 SOME OBSERVATIONS

While the experience of unequalising consequences of faster growth was not borne out in the Malaysian growth process, it appears that there is no single general trend in the evolution of the distribution of incomes that applies to all countries over the past two centuries. Falling inequality has not been the rule in modern industrial societies, any more than rising inequality is found in all industrialising economies.

To the question of whether the twin objectives of growth and equity can be pursued simultaneously, there is clearly no direct or simple answer. In the field of economics and other social disciplines, growth and equity is often seen as a zero-sum game but this need not be the case as growth is necessary to gain equity (thereby supporting the trickle-down effect) and so is equity necessary for growth (thus a need for redistributive policies). The relevant question is then, how can an appropriate balance of growth and equity be achieved to maximise the benefits from both objectives to improve overall income and welfare? As Fields (1980) concludes, 'Growth itself does not determine a country's inequality course, rather, the decisive factor is the type of economic growth'. This in some sense is a warning against a rapid pace of industrialisation which may promise growth in the short run but the pace may not be right if the economy is ill-equipped to support the growth path in the long run. This would cause a large divergence in the incomes of people and hence an increase in income inequality. The growth–equity relationship is not only complex but is also fragile, as it could become a vicious cycle whereby inequity can prevent growth and poor growth can in turn lead to unrest and lower the chances of improving equity.

More often than not, a revolution or uprising of some sort motivates governments to intervene and prescribe redistributive policies to stabilise the economy. But governments today need only to look around to see that they should not wait before acting. Malaysia was blessed that the May 1969 riots which forced the government to reassess its economic objectives with redistribution as a key thrust, did not turn out to be one of those social revolutions (such as the Chinese and Russian revolutions) which overturned the class structure. Snodgrass (1980) highlights the operation of ethnic policies on behalf of a politically dominant but economically weak community as the motivation behind the riots in Malaysia. The situation is similar to the three coups (since 1987) of Fiji where the indigenous Fijians who are poorer than the Indian Fijians have gained political clout to make their demands on the government. A lesson to be learnt from Malaysia is that the political solution to inter-group conflicts is through some formula of power-sharing that is viable and enduring, that is, the sharing of economic power and wealth if there is to be success.

For economies battling with land tenure issues related to their agricultural activities, much can be learnt from Malaysia which successfully avoided tackling the question of land reform directly and instead developed programmes which have brought about significant redistributive achievements. While Malaysia's initial rural development policies were not as successful as hoped,[13] they nevertheless provide lessons to agricultural-based developing countries to draw up better plans for reallocating resources.

In Malaysia, rapid and sustained economic growth, educational advancements, affirmative action programmes, tolerance or acceptance of government's redistributive policies and luck have all helped contribute to a sunny story on Malaysian equity. While there is no one-size-fits-all approach to improving income inequality, an appropriate institutional prerequisite and commitment on the part of politicians are however essential for successful policy formulation and implementation. Salleh and Meyanathan (1993) explain how political will and institutional strength enabled the Malaysian government to engineer fundamental changes in development strategy with redistribution as one of the objectives. A coalition of ethnic-based political parties, in which the Malay grouping (UMNO) is the dominant partner, has retained power since 1955. The long stay of a single political party in power can be advantageous in implementing policies that have long-term objectives. In Malaysia, political stability is unique as it reflects a social contract between the ethnic groups, allowing Malays to dominate the governance of the country while Chinese business interests remain intact.

In evaluating government actions towards maintaining the balance between growth and equity, the right emphasis is not on a simple, state versus market approach, but on the closeness of fit between strategy, circumstances and institutional capability on one hand, and development goals on the other. It takes time as well as the right group of people to build and cultivate the synergy between these various aspects to ensure that equity co-exists with growth, be it a developing country or a more open economy. For an economy intending to deregulate and become more open, the process towards such a move should be gradual so as to give the economy and its people enough time to cope with the demands and consequences of openness. Importantly, the government needs to ensure that equity issues are not sidelined and redistributive policies go hand in hand with new opportunities arising from globalisation.

NOTES

---

[1] The purchasing power is fixed across countries to facilitate international comparisons more readily.

[2] This explanation was offered by the Prof Ragayah Mat Zin who was one of the technical groups involved in these computations (*The Sun* 24 April 2006).

[3] The NEP was explicit in its concern for Peninsular Malaysia as Sabah and Sarawak's ethnic problems were quite different and less pressing than those of Peninsular Malaysia.

[4] However, it is unclear why 1999 was chosen as a year for comparison using the revised PLI as it would reflect the effects of the financial crisis.

[5] This index is an aggregate measure computed using 42 indicators representing 11 components of life. For details, see *The Malaysian Quality of Life 2004 Report.*

[6] At the state level, this index is only given for five categories such as income distribution, transportation and telecommunications, health, education, and public amenities.

[7] These include Onn (1989), Hassan and Salleh (1991), Siwar and Kasim (1997), and Ragayah (2005).

[8] Data for 2004 were not published for various income classes.

[9] Analysis of the 2002 income distribution implied that 19.8 per cent of the households were in relative poverty.

[10] Bahasa Melayu, which is the mother tongue of the bumiputeras, was adopted as the medium of instruction since the 1970s.

[11] Although the quota system was terminated in January 2002, and replaced with a 'meritocratic'-based admission policy, many critics have pointed out the existence of questionable practices in the new admission policy that essentially disadvantages non-Malay applicants.

[12] Somun (2003) reports Mahathir Mohamad's words on this matter, '... Malays lean on the crutches of Malay privileges in order to protect themselves. Malays consider these crutches as symbols of their superior status in the country. The sad thing is that they are not even using the crutches properly.'

[13] For a detailed analysis, see Snodgrass (1980) and Tan (1982).

7. Conclusion

7.1 INTRODUCTION

Malaysia has pursued industrialisation for more than four decades, and today is one of the rapidly growing middle-income economies aspiring to reach developed country status by 2020. Although since 1995, Malaysia has been underperforming with its annual GDP growth below the target of 7 per cent (mainly due to external shocks), progress on various fronts has been made. In fact, Castells (1998) calls Malaysia 'the fifth tiger' and indeed by some indicators, Malaysia has been at the forefront of the second-tier NIEs in terms of GDP per capita as well as unemployment, inflation and poverty rates.

However, to the extent to which Malaysia is a 'tiger', it is one of a different stripe for two reasons. First, Malaysia is a semi-developing state compared to the first-tier NIEs and thus faces a different set of challenges and prospects in its pursuit of the developed country status. Second, the changing economic landscape within Malaysia and the new global environment necessitates the re-examination of current policy making for sustained growth.

The process of globalisation has been going on for a long time but there are several differences between globalisation today and globalisation in the past. The first obvious difference is in its scale. A second difference is the speed of communication which makes for a much higher degree of integration. The third difference is the process of democratisation. There is much more public scrutiny now of what is going on and that is why there is a stronger debate on globalisation today than in the past.

Perhaps Malaysia's first step towards recognising the benefits of globalisation is seen under the IMP1 with the promotion of the Investment Act in 1986, indicating a permanent move to export-orientation by attracting FDI. By 2005, Malaysia was ranked the 19th world's most globalised nation out of 62 countries by A.T. Kearney, but this is far from signalling Malaysia's full acceptance of globalisation. Rather, Malaysia has been open in its cautious and sceptical attitude towards globalisation as seen by the some of the views held by the heads of state.

> There is no doubt that globalisation is an idea whose time has come ... but the fact that it has come ... does not mean we should sit by and watch as the predators destroy us. (Dr Mahathir bin Mohamad, the then Prime Minister of

Malaysia, in a 1999 keynote speech delivered at the Fourth Langkawi International Dialogue in Langkawi, Malaysia)

We support the process [of globalisation] as long as it results in a fairer and more equitable world. ... participate in globalisation on our own terms so that we can continue to be competitive but at the same time preserve what we value. (Dato Seri Abdullah Ahmad Badawi, then Deputy and now current Prime Minister of Malaysia, in his 2002 key note address at the Seventh National Service Conference in Kuala Lumpur)

But what does globalisation mean for Malaysia? This chapter attempts to answer some key aspects of this question in the context of the national economy, international trade and investment, the role of the government, regionalism, national sovereignty and security, and socio-cultural impacts. The role that these issues play in policy making and the transformation of Malaysia into a developed country in an increasing global environment is also critically assessed.

7.2   REGIONAL GROWTH DEVELOPMENT

Economic development in the long run is seen as a process of structural change that is affected by economic growth. Malaysia is no exception to this but the recent phenomenon of globalisation has accelerated its pace towards industrialisation such that there is regional inequality among the Malaysian states in economic growth and hence income inequality (Hassan 2004). As early as the late 1970s, since the third MP, the need for a balanced regional development was identified but efforts towards this have somewhat been lacking.[1] This in part is due to the diminishing role of agriculture. In fact, total workforce in agriculture will decline by about 200 000 workers from 1995 to 2020 and the GDP share of agriculture is to shrink from 13.5 per cent in 1995 to 7 per cent in 2020 (MITI 2006).

While the renewed role of agriculture is much discussed in Malaysia of late, the emphasis on intensifying agricultural diversification and increasing value added to this sector by further developing and processing agricultural produce will help strengthen the links between the agricultural and manufacturing sector by creating greater employment opportunities. Regional development is also better enabled if such labour-intensive manufacturing activities can be located in East Malaysia because of the availability of cheap labour. This will mean a demand for infrastructural development which will enhance the quality of life in these areas as well. The need for marketing and business services too will be created with these activities, and hence the more skilled labour can be employed in these jobs without moving to the capital cities which are perceived to offer better job prospects. Raising the incomes in the less developed states would create higher domestic demand for more goods and services and stimulate growth.

The move towards agribio is a welcome attempt to boost the agricultural sector except that there will be problems obtaining skilled manpower as has been the case in most other sectors of the economy. The ninth MP has set out plans of developing a palm oil industrial cluster, an integrated halal food hub, and permanent food production parks in various parts of the less developed states. This location factor is important as patterns in regional growth/production inequality studied by Hassan (2004) indicate that in the past, more than half of rubber and oil palm estates located in the more developed states especially in Negri Sembilan, Johor, Selangor and Perak, have had a significant impact on the development of these states. And the economic activities in the less developed states were mainly developed and owned by domestic investors who produced for the domestic market. Thus, there is a move to encourage FDI into these developing states by enhancing infrastructure in the northern, eastern and southern regions.

While it appears that various plans for the development of the agriculture sector are quite concrete, it however remains to be seen how well and quickly they will be implemented to bring forth benefits. The focus on agriculture takes advantage of the natural resource position of Malaysia and can be expected to help mitigate harmful effects (if any) due to the rapid structural transformation towards promoting the manufacturing and services sectors which may be unsustainable if not undertaken carefully. Interestingly, unlike many other resource-rich countries that experience increases in real exchange rates that hamper competitiveness in other industries (the so-called Dutch disease), Malaysia has somehow been lucky not to have faced similar problems.

As a late industrialiser, Malaysia was able to enjoy latecomer advantages in terms of access to technology for labour-intensive manufacturing activities, when there was a big rush by the developed countries to find the right locations to establish their FDI operations. But in this time and age, the latecomer advantages are unclear in high technology areas such as ICT and biotechnology. Incremental learning-by-doing as a cumulative process is necessary to avoid human capital bottlenecks in order for new technologies to be diffused at a faster pace. Efficient adoption of new technologies may also pre-suppose the existence of business infrastructure in the form of hard and soft capital. Thus, while it is possible for new individual firms to overtake established industry leaders, it is more difficult for an entire nation to leapfrog other nations technologically. It is unclear if the rapid market growth and technological opportunities created by new technologies such as ICT will effectively create a digital divide between the developed and late-industrialising countries such as Malaysia.

7.3   THE ECONOMIC ASPECTS OF GLOBALISATION

Being a relatively small and open economy, Malaysia is largely integrated with the global economy through trade and investment flows. This section focuses on FDI and international trade as these are prominent indicators of the economic dimension of globalisation.

7.3.1   Investment

Malaysia's investment regime is very open to both short- and long-term financial flows. Foreign long-term investment generally referred to as FDI, provides a unique combination of long-term finance, technological know-how, marketing and management expertise. Table 7.1 shows that, compared to the other ASEAN countries (with the exception of Singapore), Malaysia has experienced a sustained period of FDI inflows. From being ranked among the top 10 FDI receivers until the mid 1990s, Malaysia fell in ranking every year in the latter part of the decade, reaching 75th place in 2001–03 (UNCTAD 2004–05).

Table 7.1   FDI inflows into selected Asian economies (US$ million)

	1990	1995	2000	2004
Indonesia	1093	1652	−4550	1023
Malaysia	2332	4254	3788	4624
Thailand	2444	1521	2813	1064
Singapore	5575	11 619	16 479	16 060

Source: World Investment Report, various issues.

In terms of FDI stock to GDP, Table 7.2 shows that Malaysia's share has not only decreased since 2000 but lags far behind the first-tier NIEs. Furthermore, the decline in Inward FDI Performance Index (in parenthesis) shows the threat posed by emerging economies such as China and Vietnam. Unlike Malaysia, China, India, Thailand and Singapore were ranked as one of the most attractive global business locations (UNCTAD 2005–06).

As early as the 1980s, the lack of domestic entrepreneurship has led to Malaysia attracting FDI. While it is undeniable that FDI helped increase employment and promote exports and GDP growth, the spillover effects in terms of technology transfer are somewhat unclear. While the World Bank (1997) shows that there have been substantial spillover effects from FDI to the local firms, Narayanan and Wah (2000) provide evidence that technology transfer from MNCs have been limited in the areas related to operations, maintenance, production management and quality control, all of which are aspects of process technology. For example, the MSC Impact Survey 2005 reports that in 2005, 73 per cent of the MSC status companies affirmed that they were involved in process development related to industry applications.

Table 7.2 Percentage of inward FDI stock to GDP

	1980	1990	2000	2004
Malaysia	20.7	23.4 (5)	58.6 (51)	39.3 (56)
Thailand	3.0	9.7 (17)	24.4 (44)	29.7 (106)
Indonesia	13.2	7.7 (57)	16.5 (138)	4.4 (136)
China	3.1	5.8 (46)	17.9 (52)	14.9 (45)
Vietnam	—	25.5 (47)	65.7 (38)	66.3 (50)
Singapore	52.9	83.1 (1)	123.1 (6)	150.2 (8)
Hong Kong	436.2	198.1 (3)	275.4 (2)	277.6 (7)

Note: The figures in parenthesis are rankings of the Inward FDI Performance Index which is calculated as the ratio of a country's share in global FDI inflows to its share in global GDP. It is a three-year moving average ending in the year indicated.

Source: World Investment Report, various issues.

It has also been argued that MNCs have yet to share in the area of R&D expertise such as product or equipment development, and design or moulding, which are important aspects of sustained technology development (ibid.). Similar evidence is provided by Ariffin and Figueiredo (2004) while Giroud (2003), on the other hand, highlights the lack of linkage establishments with local firms in general. But Rasiah (2002, 2003a) argues that technology transfer has taken place in the electronics industry in the Penang region. In the 2005/06 Global Competitiveness Report, among the Asian economies reliant on FDI, Singapore recorded the highest technology transfer index (6.2), followed by Malaysia (5.7), Hong Kong (5.4), Thailand (5.3) and Indonesia (5.0). But unlike Korea and Taiwan, both Malaysia and Singapore have yet to successfully upgrade from original equipment manufacturing to original design and manufacturing, as the latter economies are still very dependent on foreign technology transfer (Lai and Yap 2004).

While the literature argues that FDI can adversely affect domestic entrepreneurship, this is not the case for Malaysia (World Bank 2005) although domestic producers are mainly SMEs, which comprised 89.3 per cent of the total manufacturing companies and contributed 16.3 per cent of total manufacturing output in 2004. The more pressing concern about Malaysia's FDI has been its effect on wide wage dispersion due to demand for skilled labour outpacing the demand for unskilled workers (ILO 1998, and Ragayah 2003).

Another argument on widening income inequality is that FDI and international openness are said to benefit most of the domestic residents who are already well off in the sense that rich groups are most able to take advantage of the opportunities offered by trade expansion. While openness to trade and FDI have distributional consequences, that is, there are 'winners' and 'losers' in the short run, it is also true to say that not all losers may come disproportionately from the disadvantaged group. To the extent that openness raises national income, it strengthens the fiscal ability of a society to provide safety nets or consider options to directly help the poor.

The development/modernisation hypothesis believes that, even if FDI initially stimulates growth in only some leading or favoured sectors, the growth in these sectors could in the long run facilitate more even income distribution via positive spillover effects. In fact, Authukorala and Menon (1997) show how FDI-related export-led industrialisation in Malaysia has generated employment opportunities and reduced income inequality. However, available data do not allow a carefully considered assessment of welfare consequences of recent globalisation and liberalisation for different socio-economic groups in Malaysia. Such an attempt may be futile as it will not be possible to separate the effects due to globalisation per se as opposed to domestic rapid economic growth or other government policies which are not related to globalisation efforts either as a response or a consequence of globalisation.

Besides attracting FDI into the country, Malaysia has also embarked on developing by investing abroad. The seventh MP set the tone for outward FDI to encourage local investors to invest abroad and form strategic alliances and establish networks with foreign partners. Government's incentives such as tax abatement on income earned overseas, tax deduction for pre-operating business expenditure, and tax incentives to acquire foreign-owned companies, are quite generous in this regard. Moreover, since November 1995, a Malaysia–Singapore Third Country Business Development Fund was established to help Malaysians and Singaporean enterprises to cooperate and identify business opportunities in 'third countries'.

It can be seen from Table 7.3 that outward FDI stock has been steadily increasing except for a sharp fall in 2004. But according to Economic Report 2005/06, FDI inflows abroad (as opposed to FDI stock in Table 7.3) was RM12.9 billion in 2005, a 2.5-fold increase from 2003. The pattern of Malaysia's FDI abroad so far indicates Singapore as the biggest recipient (due to the close proximity of the two countries and the historical and economic ties that they have enjoyed for more than 40 years) followed by Hong Kong (the bulk of it is to take advantage of the Chinese market) and mostly Asia, the US and UK. In general, Malaysia is active in the oil and gas sector, construction sector (related to large infrastructure, roads and highway projects), and overseas investments in the manufacturing sector are led by the semiconductor and other electronic components. It is expected that in the next few years, Malaysian MNCs will gather serious momentum.

Table 7.3   Outward FDI in Malaysia

	Outward FDI stock (Million US$)	Percentage of outward FDI stock to GDP
1980	197	0.8
1985	1374	4.3
1990	2671	6.1
1995	11143	12.5
2000	21 276	23.6
2004	13 796	11.7

Source: World Investment Report, various issues.

Lastly, short-term capital flows, mainly portfolio funds, also move in and out of the country freely. In fact, the World Bank and IMF have long been advocating the liberalisation of capital markets, including the establishment of stock markets and those for derivative financial instruments, largely ignoring the arguments for financial repression and restraint advocated by developments in information economics (Stiglitz 1989). There is a significant body of persuasive contrarian literature raising serious doubts about the nature and contribution of equity financing to late industrialisation (Singh 1994). But these institutions have recently conceded that short-term capital market liberalisation can lead to more economic instability. Malaysia has followed a gradual approach in its financial liberalisation reform, taking a 'stop–and–go approach' to completely liberalise its interest rates. But the financial crisis of 1997/98 led to the re-regulation of the financial system for a short period and transformed the domestic banking system from one that was highly fragmented comprising 54 banking institutions to 10 domestic banking groups. Liberalisation and restructuring efforts related to prudential policies are back on track with the launch of the Financial Sector Master Plan in 2001. In 2005, Malaysia opened its capital market to wholly foreign-owned participation in stockbroking and futures trading, to increase liquidity and risk management activity.

7.3.2   Trade

Malaysia embarked on the export-oriented strategy as early as the 1970s and this was strengthened by the FDI attracted into the country. In 2004, Malaysia was the 19th largest trading nation in the world. With rapid industrialisation and the onset of globalisation, the composition of exports within manufacturing has however changed, apart from the decline in agricultural commodities export. Table 7.4 shows an increasing share in high technology exports from Malaysia and this is comparable to the developed economies and the first-tier NIEs (except for Hong Kong) and Japan (although the decline in the trend after 2000 is a worldwide trend). However, the export manufacturing base has in a sense narrowed with the electrical and electronic exports accounting for 65 per cent of the total export of manufactured goods while that of the chemical and petroleum products' share decreased from 32 per cent in 1970 to 10 per cent in 2004. Nevertheless, excessive trade diversification is to be avoided as distortions to international trade and market-oriented resource allocation that run counter to a country's comparative advantage in trying to diversify exports can have adverse effects on economic efficiency and growth performance.

Table 7.4   Share of high technology exports in total manufactured exports (%)

	1990	2000	2004
Germany	11	18	17
Japan	24	28	24
UK	24	30	24
US	34	35	32
Australia	12	15	14
Hong Kong	12*	24	32
Singapore	40	63	59
South Korea	18	35	33
China	6*	19	30
Malaysia	38	60	55
Thailand	21	33	30

Note: * refers to 1992.

Source: World Development Indicators.

For Malaysia, to keep exporting high-technology-intensive exports is an attractive option as they offer better prospects for future growth because their products tend to grow faster in trade (Lall 2000). Lall further notes that such exports not only tend to be highly income elastic, create new demand and substitute faster for older products, but they also have greater potential for further learning because they offer more scope for applying new scientific knowledge.

The rapid development in exports has however led to an increasing dependence on imports instead of generating demand for local intermediate products. In fact, the share of the intermediate goods and capital goods of total merchandise imports is 86 per cent in 2004 (MITI 2004), much in line with an increased share of manufactured goods in total exports which stands at 79 per cent in 2004 (ibid). The high level of imports is however not necessarily unhealthy as Coe et al. (1997) find empirical evidence to support the view that developing countries could boost their TFP growth through R&D spillovers by increasing trade with industrial countries, and in particular by importing intermediate products and capital equipment embodying foreign knowledge. But Mahadevan (2004) warns that such productivity effects may take the form of unsustainable technological progress and declining technical efficiency (if workers lack adequate skills as is the case for Malaysia), resulting in insignificant, or otherwise negative impact on manufacturing TFP growth.

Given the importance of trade in the global environment, competitiveness is a key factor in sustaining economic growth. The Global Competitiveness Index ranked Malaysia 25th in 2005 and as seen in Table 7.5, this was ahead of the other competing developing countries. The Growth Competitiveness Index, on the other hand, measures the capacity of the economy to achieve sustained economic growth over the medium term, controlling for the current level of development. It considers the quality of the macroeconomic environment, the state of the country's public institutions and the level of technological readiness. While Malaysia's score for the first condition was 19, its overall rank of 24 as seen in Table 7.5 was better than Hong Kong and the other developing countries.

Table 7.5   Global and growth competitiveness index rank

	Global competitiveness index	Growth competitiveness index
	(out of 117 countries)	
Taiwan	8	5
Singapore	5	6
Australia	18	10
Japan	10	12
South Korea	19	17
Hong Kong	14	28
Malaysia	25	24
Thailand	33	36
India	45	50
Indonesia	69	74
China	48	49
Philippines	73	77

Source: The Global Competitiveness Report 2005-06.

Enhancing competition has become more urgent with increasing competition from emergent market economies such as Vietnam, China and India who are aggressively wooing FDI and expanding their trade opportunities. At the same time, these economies offer huge potential for electronic products and services as well as new trade and investment opportunities for Malaysia. Their trade and investment regimes will be more transparent and predictable and Malaysian exporters and investors will face less discrimination since these economies are WTO members. Equally important, Malaysian electronics firms may consider tapping into China's huge pool of low cost engineers and scientists and India's skilled IT workforce.

To remain ahead of the game to attract FDI, there is increasing pressure for Malaysia to establish competitive capabilities beyond cheap labour, such as having sufficient educated and skilled workers, high-quality infrastructure, local R&D capabilities, and strong entrepreneurial skills. These are necessary elements to increase the nation's technological absorptive capacity.

On the international scene, Malaysia also has to grapple with institutions such as WTO which is pushing economies to relax trade restrictions. In December 2005, the Sixth Ministerial Conference in Hong Kong, which reviewed the 2001 Doha Development Agenda, made limited progress in trying to balance the interests of both developing and developed countries. The negotiations in agriculture, services, market access for non-agriculture products and WTO dispute settlement procedures are still ongoing. There are yet to be clarifications on elements for a multilateral framework or rules on investment, competition policy, transparency in government procurement, trade facilitation and environment. For Malaysia, the challenge would be to use the post-Doha period to seek outcomes that further their trade interests in both developed and developing countries, and at the same time protect their ability to pursue developmental goals. In this regard, the second challenge is to equip oneself to participate actively and meaningfully at the international level by mastering negotiation skills, including the art of communication and persuasion. Proficiency in English is a necessity and the need to lobby and find alliances must be further developed.

Regional trade arrangements have also increasingly become a feature of globalisation. The AFTA has enabled the gradual reduction of the average common effective preferential rate for ASEAN-6 from 11.44 per cent in 1993 to 2.38 per cent in 2003 and this is targeted to be completely eliminated by 2010.[2] Import duties, on the other hand, are to be reduced to 0–5 per cent by 2008. And since 2005, Malaysia's automotive industry with its national car projects Proton and Perodua has had to cope with a rise in domestic car prices and improved access to competitors in its car market. Cars from ASEAN countries can be imported at the ASEAN CEPT rate of 5 per cent and this translates to a reduction of between 20 and 40 per cent on import duties, depending on the engine capacity of the car imported, while the import duties on non-ASEAN cars have been reduced between 5 per cent and 30%.[3] Other extensions under AFTA include cooperation in investment as well as industrial and specific sectoral cooperation in ICT, finance and agriculture, all of which can be expected to impact significantly in the economy's future.

Apart from regional trade agreements, following the collapse of the WTO talks at the ministerial meeting in Cancun in September 2003, there has however been a proliferation of bilateral free trade agreements set up between various countries and ASEAN, such as that with China in 2005 and South

Korea in 2006. While similar talks are expected to be concluded with India, Japan and the US in 2007, others with the European Union, Russia, and Australia and New Zealand are in the pipeline. It is however unclear at this stage how beneficial or significant these FTAs will be in providing a larger more diversified export market. Nevertheless, Malaysia's track record shows that her trade partners are well diversified and efforts are being made to enter non-traditional markets such as South and West Asia regions.

7.4 THE ROLE OF THE GOVERNMENT AND INDUSTRIAL POLICY

The role of the government can be quite a contentious issue as it is neither simple nor straightforward to judge the government's multifaceted functions. However, it would be difficult to deny that a significant part of Malaysia's rise to a high middle-income economy today is attributable to some of the policies undertaken by the interventionist state government. Even in earlier times, the government's commitment to prioritising objectives in its 5-year economic plans was clear although this was not always optimal. For instance, minimising racial tension was considered most important in the 1970s but this policy of rent allocation to the bumiputeras (detailed in Chapter 6) had little to do with economic efficiency (Jomo 1997).

While some of the industrial policies of the government in the past may not have been successful, this does not preclude the government's role in the current development stage. As Malaysia is a late industrialiser, its intrusive government's role is justified as Amsden (1995) asserts that a government's role increases, the later in time a country industrialises and the further away it is located from the world technological frontier. Booth (1999) in fact praises the Malaysian government's capability in coherent policy formulation and implementation in the face of external shocks and her ability to maintain the momentum of growth over several decades. This is seen in the swift way in which the negative impact of SARS was mitigated as well as the handling of the 1997/98 Asian financial crisis.

Lall (1995), on the other hand, explains that previous failure of the government policies was due to the poor design of these policies and that the political economy of Malaysia at the time dictated a different and apparently less effective set of interventions. Some of these failures include the failure of the take off of heavy industries which were promoted in the early 1980s. This partly took the form of the 'Look East Policy' adopted in late 1981 where massive projects with Japan on construction and joint ventures in the heavy industries took place. This policy which came to an abrupt end in 1984 was said to have not only resulted in a drain of Malaysian financial resources but also crowded out private investment (World Bank 1989).

The automobile manufacturing of the national car, Proton, was one of the products of this heavy industry promotion with protectionist tariffs of up to 300 per cent. Leutert and Sudhoff (1999) discuss how the unconditional protection given to Proton and to bumiputera suppliers have distorted economic incentives and prevented the progress of technological progress in the automotive industry. It is too early to tell how well this industry can fend for itself after the drastic cut in import duties in 2006.

Perhaps of some concern also is Malaysia's push to make Petronas, a home-grown wholly government owned national petroleum company, established in 1974, become a global player. It is unclear if this form of enterprise is another chaebol in the making, although the Korean government started grooming its chaebols before 1990 when globalisation took on a less definite stride. While Petronas bears the distinction of being the only Malaysian company on the Fortune 500 list, being government-owned, it has not been totally immune to government calls for financial help. In 1984 and 1989, the oil company's massive cash funds were used to save state-owned Bank Bumiputera from collapse and bailed out the debt-laden shipping company, Konsortium Perkapalan Berhad.

The latest concern in the line of government projects is the MSC, which has been identified as Malaysia's principal vehicle to leapfrog from the industrial to the post-industrial era as part of the big plan to attain developed status in 2020. The MSC is a striking state attempt to nurture a digital district which is all the more audacious considering Malaysia's standing as a second-tier NIE. Currently, both the economy's intelligent cities are underutilised with excess capacity and this is a sore sight to any passing visitor. Some suggest that the provision of tax and investment incentives to relocate to MSC has caused business diversion rather than creation (Australian Government 2005) and other sceptics say that the MSC may well be a white elephant project with a beautiful name and vision. Indergaard (2003), on the other hand, explains that the Malaysian state has continued to use its sovereignty in stabilising networks with a mix of regulation and subsidy and that consequently, MSC entrepreneurs have had more success even though they encountered international financial and political crises that their counterparts in Silicon Alley (situated in New York City) and other digital enclaves[4] that emerged during the 1990s, never faced.

One success of government intervention includes the development of agriculture and agroprocessing (Rock 2002). In particular, the imposition of higher duties on exports on crude palm oil in the mid 1970s stimulated massive investments in refining capacity. Intense competition, specialisation and excess refining capacity soon resulted in rapid technical progress, taking Malaysian palm oil refining to the world technological frontier in barely a decade (Gopal 1999). Other areas of success of government leadership include the emergence of Malaysia from the 1970s as a major offshore site for electronics assembly. Various incentives have been used to encourage foreign investors to transfer technology to Malaysian suppliers, some of whom have gone on to develop their own capabilities (Jomo and Felker 1999).

Needless to say, the overall domestic macroeconomic stability and political certainty in Malaysia is largely due to the type of government in place. While it is easy to go on providing examples of the two sides of the coin on government intervention, it does not add much to what is already known. What is important is, where is the government's role headed from this stage of Malaysia's development towards the goal of being a developed nation?

At various times since independence, the Malaysian government has targeted industries it believed would contribute to Malaysia's economic development, with varying degrees of success. Government attempts at influencing industry development and economic growth by 'picking winners' has been argued to be the second best method of ensuring efficient use of an economy's resources compared to market forces. This is not to say that the government's role should necessarily be diminished, but given Malaysia's current stage of economic development, a change in the nature of the government's role is timely and appropriate for the creation of an enabling environment to ensure that markets function well. This requires a move away from a top-driven approach, and a reduction in intervention as and when markets improve.

While some aspects of the changing role are evident, other aspects of the directive role of the government still persist. This is seen in the ninth MP where the push and hence generous incentives for various new growth areas such as nanotechnology, photonics, robotics, aerospace development, bioinformatics, digital content development, etc. have been set out. The cluster concept has also yet to lose its appeal (and neither have lessons of cluster governance from the MSC project been taken seriously) as there are plans for a digital media and creative zone in Cyberjaya. While the earlier push in the establishment of the ICT industry survived well with government intervention, the current push to advanced technologies industry require more than that. To sustain growth in these new industries, first, expertise in basic research to provide more radical or breakthrough solutions that anticipate future problems of industry is required. Second, private sector collaboration even in the early stages of establishing the new industries is necessary. The lack of these support mechanisms will impede the drive for a more vibrant and dynamic industrial sector. Stiff competition from Singapore, Japan and South Korea who enjoy first-mover advantage in some of the identified growth areas is another hurdle for Malaysia.

Appropriate management of the new push for rapid industrial transformation requires careful attention to the speed at which it is pursued. More specifically, one key challenge raised by several authors is the dire need to intensify critical mass for skilled workers in the area of high-level technical, engineering, science and IT. This is where transformation at an even faster pace is needed than in the past. Despite knowledge of this problem in government circles, it is not clear exactly what efforts are mounted by the government to popularise university-level enrolments in these areas. Until the government commits itself to a concrete strategy on this issue, mere provision of even sophisticated fiscal instruments for encouraging R&D or innovation is unlikely to bear fruit in the future.[5]

The second challenge, especially for the promotion of the new high technology industries, is to intensify efforts to improve government–business collaboration. There has been insufficient progress on this front despite the inception of 'Malaysia Incorporated' in 1983 whose aim was exactly that. More so now in the area of technology development, there must be a symbiotic system in place involving universities as well. Rasiah (2002) has indicated that unlike the Penang region, the co-location of key actors such as firms and government research institutes in the Klang valley cluster did not lead to much interaction. Actor competencies, habits and practices with respect to linkages, investment and learning are critical in determining the nature and extensiveness of their interactions (Mytleka and Barclay 2004). All three parties need to change their mindset and trust each other to work and cooperate, exchange and share information in order to create the right synergy to bring out the best in each other.

The area of policy coordination, on the other hand, has a different set of challenges. One is to ensure coordination between human capital and science and technology policies. While this will accelerate the economic growth process, their impacts are strongest when other crucial areas of public policy are equally well managed. That is, coordination with other economic policies is essential. In addition, effective policy implementation requires a two-pronged approach. One is the need to take into account the social, cultural, economic and political context in which the design and implementation of polices are to take place. Another is the need to reorganise duties and directives in various government institutions to avoid replication and reduce bureaucracy and red tape for policy implementation (Tham and Ragayah 2006) although some improvements in the revamp of the management structure with respect to science and technology have already taken place.[6]

Continuous monitoring of policy dynamics generated by the interaction between policies and the varied habits and practices of the key actors (comprising government, research universities, firms and the community) in the system, will be necessary to fine-tune policies for maximum impact. So too will learning and unlearning on the part of all actors, firms and policymakers, if a system is to evolve in response to new challenges (Mytleka and Barclay 2004). Consequently, governance needs to be open and transparent by engaging in the process of dialogue and working in the tensions of diversity and divergences in points of view.[7] And dynamism in the institutional framework is required to support the paradigm of managing business by continuously building capabilities that encourage flexibility to adapt to a changing future.

It is quite comforting to note on the other hand that the need for the supporting role of the government has to some extent been recognised in Malaysia. For instance, with the start of the privatisation policy in 1983, the public sector's role was scaled back to focus on strengthening the role of the private sector, but for some reason the Malaysian government still has a strong presence in the economy. In 2004, there were about 40 listed government-linked companies, accounting for 34 per cent of the total capitalisation of Bursa Malaysia,[8] and the government holds a majority stake in strategic national companies such as the airlines, telecommunications and electricity. In fact, the share of public investment in GDP has been higher and increasing more than the private investment share since 1999.

The dearth of private investment has, however, partly been compensated by FDI. Local investment is not only lacking but most of the companies are SMEs and hence quite disadvantaged in terms of competing with the bigger players. The Malaysian government has however provided many schemes, grants and incentives to develop the SME sector to enhance their ability and capacity to provide services and products in the supply chain.[9] In terms of technology development there has been some success in MNCs forming backward linkages with SMEs, especially in the electronics sector in the Penang region, but in general, there is room for a greater level of strategic alliance between the two players. It also does not help that the government's equity considerations ride high even in the support extended to SMEs. For instance, Reinhardt (2000) cites various studies which argue that the lack of the SME development was partly due to the government's desire to decrease the economic strength of the ethnic Chinese business sector. This is still apparent in the government's extension of services to bumiputera SMEs in at least three programmes, the Vendor Development Program, the Franchise Development Program and the Groom Big Program. The bias towards the establishment of a sustainable bumiputera commercial and industrial community is also supplemented in many other forms.[10] Surely such policy is restrictive on business activity and can focus entrepneurial effort on rent-seeking behaviour. To this extent, the policy may be counterproductive and even thwart the development of a vibrant and resilient bumiputera business community.

However, a recent survey of 93 managers in Malaysia showed that 90 per cent of them support government industrial policy and government's coordination of industries and fostering efforts at entrepreneurship (Mamman 2004). But the survey indicated that 75 per cent of the managers felt that government regulations of industry should be reduced to boost domestic capacity and competitiveness which is a top priority partly due to globalisation. A similar sentiment was echoed by the World Bank (2005). In fact, the extent of bureaucracy and red tape saw Malaysia positioned as 101 among 117 countries by *The Global Competitiveness Report 2005–06*. Table 7.6 shows some aspects of the business environment in Malaysia relative to other economies. It can be seen that the cost of doing business in Malaysia compares favourably with other regional economies although the costs to register a business are more than most other economies in the region.

Table 7.6   Doing business in 2005

	Time to start a business (days)	Cost to register a business (% of Gross National Income per capita)	Proce-dures to enforce a contract (number)	Cost to enforce a contract (% of Gross National Income per capita)
Malaysia	30	25	31	20
China	41	15	25	26
India	89	50	40	43
Indonesia	151	131	34	127
Korea	12	18	29	5
Taiwan	8	6	22	8
Singapore	8	1	23	14
Thailand	33	7	19	30
Australia	2	2	11	8

Source: The Global Competitiveness Report 2005–06.

7.5   THE POLITICAL AND SOCIO-CULTURAL ASPECTS OF GLOBALISATION

The economics of globalisation is often seen to focus on the increasing power of the market and the decreasing ability of governments to dictate economic policy, thereby diminishing national sovereignty. In the mid 1980s, globalisation simply meant being a trading state but a decade later, globalisation comes with a set of political correlates that many in East Asia will have difficulty adjusting to – the ideal of Western-style democracy, the emphasis on the sanctity of human rights, minimum labour standards, enforcing property rights and contracts through impartial, effective judicial systems, and ecological responsibility, among others. For instance, environmental groups like Greenpeace are now forging global alliances that transcend national and political boundaries. The Third World Network is another non-governmental organisation based in Malaysia that is concerned that well funded lobbyists from developed countries could have undue influence prejudicial to developing country interests.

Market forces underlying globalisation are held to be the route to prosperous economies which in turn maximise global economic welfare and wipe out corruption and cronyism. And the clarion call for good corporate governance and transparency that globalisation brings with it cannot be ignored in the new global order with the democracy of a free market system laced with rules of fair play and meritocracy. These features keep the economy in check and ensure that those serving the public interest do not put their private interests ahead of those of the nation and its citizens.

However, as discussed earlier, the role of the government is not necessarily diminished by globalisation but rather the form of government intervention takes on a new shape and different meaning. For instance, globalisation has promoted transnational crimes such as terrorism, cyber terrorism, smuggling of people, small arms trade, drug trafficking and money laundering, all of which threaten national security and hence have heightened the need for government action. The development of computers, satellites and the spread of intercontinental missile technology has extended the global reach of any potential military threat, inducing government action to strengthen military surveillance far more than before. Moreover, the activities of computer hackers and the development of computer crime illustrate the vulnerability of nations to globe-wide disruptive activities of individuals.

Globalisation has compelled Malaysia to move towards a more flexible labour market. This is particularly so as foreign workers have become the backbone of Malaysia's labour market and a major contributing factor to the country's economic success. Statistics on legal foreign unskilled workers in Malaysia put the figures for 2004 at 1.3 million, and if illegal workers are included the number rises to 2.5 million. Talib (2002) documents the extent to which national security came under threat with not just the negative activities (such as drug trafficking, people smuggling and prostitution) of these migrant workers, but also their involvement in internal affairs such as that in the 1999 demonstrations staged by the so-called *Reformasi* movement[11] to topple the elected government.

Another challenge for Malaysia in the face of globalisation is how to retain their highly skilled and talented citizens. In the past, appeals to nationalism and patriotism may have worked but today, job opportunities and higher pay elsewhere has led to increased migration helped by the ease of movement of people brought about by globalisation. The brain gain initiatives in place since 2004 have yet to see much success in retaining and attracting talented Malaysians back to the country.

In terms of demographic and ethnic imbalance, labour migration is also expected to upset the political scenario in Malaysia in the long run. Given the multi-ethnicity of Malaysia, each ethnic group is concerned with its numerical strength and as such, the influx of Indonesian labour with close socio-cultural ties with the Malays is viewed suspiciously by some non-Malay political entities. The accommodating attitude of the government towards immigrant labour is misconstrued as a deliberate attempt by the United Malaysian National Organisation to swamp the country with Indonesian Malays (Talib 2002).

Thus, the Malaysian government has to accept the fact that adapting to the economics of globalisation also means adapting to some aspects of the politics of globalisation but with the right attitude and a gradual and progressive approach.

Now we turn to some of the socio-cultural aspects of globalisation. Technology has now created the possibility and even the likelihood of a global culture. The internet, fax machines, satellites, and cable TV have swept away cultural boundaries. Some see this as enhancing cultural diversity through various manifestations of localisation, and helping to empower minorities and maintain threatened identities.[12] Others ask questions such as: will local cultures inevitably fall victim to a global 'consumer' culture? Will English eradicate weaker languages? Will consumer values overwhelm peoples' sense of community and social solidarity? Or, more optimistically, will a common culture lead the way to greater shared values and political unity? There are obviously more questions than answers in this subject matter.

Cultural globalisation refers to the unfettered flow of products (such as clothes, music, food and the like), information, images and ideas such as pornography, religious cults and extreme political ideologies through electronic and other media. More often than not, the expansion of culture across the globe is associated with the process of Westernisation. There is a fear of a shift from the emphasis on 'community interest' long held in Eastern values to that of 'right or interest' of individuals, particularly among the young generation. This is not to say that one set of values is better than the other, but different societies have evolved their own peculiar cultural and social systems to suit their own needs according to different environmental and historical circumstances. But can Malaysia choose Western technology and know-how without choosing Western values? I believe the jury is still out.

While some of these cross-cultural aspects may undermine the cultural foundation of the country, learning and understanding other cultures will help Malaysians to discern the good from the bad. Outright denial may raise curiosity and encourage people to try. Much can be learnt from Japan as a society that has been able to preserve its underlying cultural values and norms despite becoming a highly industrialised nation and at the same time becoming a major contributor to the current process of economic globalisation.

As globalisation is here to stay, the bottom line is for Malaysia to find ways to manage these external influences and ensure that they do not affect the unity and social fabric of the country. But ideologies that are consistent with the culture of the country for instance, in the form of Islam and religious fanaticism such as the infiltration of Al-Qedah, are difficult to control. In fact, among the foreign workers, a few have been known to spread deviant Islamic teachings such as those preached by the Naqshabandiah Sect (Talib 2002). Such religious backlash is especially dangerous for a multi-cultural society such as Malaysia.

A favourable social environment must prevail to allow the people to live and work in harmony while maintaining cultural diversity. A society with a culture that has a perpetual thirst for knowledge and information and a high regard for science and technology is more inclined to be inventive, creative and successful. Malaysia needs to strive to attain such a culture even if this means drawing from cross-cultural influences to better itself.

7.6 SUMMING UP THE MALAYSIAN CASE

Structural change can retard growth if its pace is too slow or its direction is inefficient, but at the same time it can contribute to growth if it improves the allocation of resources. In this regard, the move to a knowledge-driven economy per se is warranted in the post-industrial era as it is increasingly seen as an important source of economic growth and a basis for competitive advantage in the face of diminishing comparative advantage in traditional economic sectors. This is supported by Badawi's statement[13] that, 'globalisation and liberalisation draw us closer to more intense competition … we have no option but to move up the value chain. We have little choice but to transform again, to become a knowledge-based economy'.

There is however concern that in its pursuit of a developed country status, Malaysia's speed of structural transformation to the knowledge economy is maximal rather than optimal. Even the increasing difficulty of picking winners in the era of globalisation which is related to flexibility and not locking in resources and production systems does not appear to have slowed down Malaysia's move. Perhaps the new trade and investment rules under WTO can be counted as a blessing as it does not favour the nurturing of local industries by providing protection. But the downside under the new regime is that technological arrangements under the Trade Related Intellectual Property Rights have similar provisions restricting the imitation or reverse-engineering of foreign technologies. This will close an avenue for technology development that proved invaluable to Japan and NIEs like Korea and Taiwan during their earlier industrialisation process. On the other hand, the growing pressures to liberalise domestic markets for products, services and investment make it more difficult now to stay independent of MNCs.

Given its shaping potential, the impact of MNCs on future opportunities for catching up is much greater than its importance as a source of capital. At this stage of Malaysia's development, the government needs to adopt a targeted approach towards FDI, to ensure that MNCs have in place a plan for specific technology transfer or development that would benefit Malaysia. This means that close monitoring of the MNCs and appropriate support for the local firms should be priorities of the government. There is also a need to address the imbalance in incentives and support programmes offered to foreign firms as compared to local firms. It may be necessary for the government to start providing such opportunities to the MNCs for gains in technological development and diffusion to ripple through the domestic economy in the long run.

Thus, government intervention is particularly important because the type, degree and level of the intervention can positively influence the business environment. In particular, to ensure the sustainability of technological development in the K-economy, the government has a role of both a promoter and a regulator to manage the risks involved[14] and lead and facilitate the economy's development. However, when the environment changes and economic progress is made, the quasi-directive role needs to take on a different and more appropriate balance between intervention and support. Institutional mechanisms play a vital role in ensuring a transparent and objective assessment and evaluation of the government policies to work towards a more integrated approach in policy prescription. The critical success factors for this include political will and a dynamic institutional framework.

By and large, Malaysia has a fair chance of attaining its vision of becoming a developed country within 2020. This is so long as the government has put in place measures to address some of the problems by adopting a more balanced sectoral growth strategy, coordinating technology and human capital development policies, and studying poverty issues. But current evidence seems to indicate that the issues need to be tackled with more vigour and in a concerted manner by designing measures that are deeper and wider. While progressing to a developed nation status is a matter of time for Malaysia, it is however necessary that the transition to that status be kept smooth so that the growth momentum can be sustainable even after being classified as developed.

Hence the road to being a developed country has a different set of hurdles these days, given the confines and challenges of globalisation. Herein lies the lesson for any country – to recognise the need to be agile and flexible to match the changing circumstances as well as to exploit opportunities and respond to challenges. This requires direct effort on the part of the government, business and community at large to work hand-in-hand to effectively operate and gain in an optimal way and not be marginalised in the global environment.

NOTES

[1] One example was the start of an in-situ development approach in the form of Integrated Agricultural Development Project, which was aimed at increasing productivity in existing depressed rural areas, with a focus on the lower income groups in the less developed states of Kedah, Kelantan, Terengganu and Perlis.

[2] For Malaysia, the CEPT rate was 3.1 per cent in 2004 with about 99.3 per cent of its products included in the CEPT scheme.

[3] See *The New Straits Times* 23 March 2006.

[4] These include new media districts such as San Francisco's 'Multimedia Gulch' and the 'Digital Coast' of Los Angeles.

[5] The Global Competitiveness Report 2005-06 ranks Malaysia in the position of 40 out of 117 countries for innovation capability and this shows room for improvement.

[6] Mani (2002) notes improvements in the reconstitution of the National Council for Scientific Research and Development, the corporatisation of three research institutes (the Malaysian Institute of Microelectronic Systems, the Standards and Industrial Research Institute of Malaysia, and the Technology Park of Malaysia), and the creation of new institutions such as the National Information Technology Council, the Academy of Sciences and the Space Science Studies Centre.

[7] Transparency International ranked Malaysia 39 out of 146 economies in 2004, which is better than Korea, Italy and Greece but still lags behind a number of regional economies.

[8] Upon conversion to a public company, the Kuala Lumpur Stock Exchange became an exchange holding company and was renamed Bursa Malaysia on 20 April 2004.

[9] See http://www.smidec.gov.my for details.

[10] Concessionaries in any privatisation must allocate at least 30 per cent of contractual work to bumiputera individuals. New listing on Bursa Malaysia as well as acquisitions of domestic companies by local or foreign interests require an initial 30 per cent bumiputera equity ownership.

[11] This movement was the consequent of the 1998 expulsion and conviction of Anwar Ibrahim the former deputy prime minister and it manifested in the formation of the National Justice Party.

[12] The increased Thai links with the related Tai-lue communities in Laos, Burma, Vietnam and southern China are one example.

[13] Speech by Abdullah Badawi at the National Economic Action Council Dialogue Forum, 13 January 2004 in Putrajaya, Malaysia. See http://www.neac.gov.my

[14] For instance, ICT as a medium of change together with globalisation has its dangers – cybercrime, narcotics, terrorism, weapons, refugees and migrants all move back and forth faster and in greater numbers than in the past.

Bibliography

Abdullah, N. (1997) 'Measurement of Total Factor Productivity for the Malaysian Rice Sector', *IIUM Journal of Economics and Management*, vol.5, no.2: 67–95.

Alavi, R. (1996) *Industrialisation in Malaysia: Import Substitution and Infant Industry Performance*, London and New York: Routledge.

Amsden, A.H. (1995) 'Like the Rest: South-East Asia's Late Industrialisation', *Journal of International Development*, vol.7, no.5: 791–799.

— Goto, K. and Tschang, T. (2001) 'Do Foreign Companies Conduct R&D in Developing Countries?' *Asian Development Bank Institute Research Discussion Paper* No.14, Asian Development Bank Institute, Tokyo.

Anand, S. (1983) *Inequality and Poverty in Malaysia: Measurement and Decomposition*, London: Oxford University Press.

— and Kanbur, S. (1993) 'Inequality and Development: A Critique', *Journal of Development Economics*, vol.41: 19–43.

Ariff, M. and Lim, C.P. (1987) 'Foreign Investment in Malaysia', in Vincent Cable and Bishnodat Persaud (eds), *Developing With Foreign Investment*, London: Croom Helm.

Ariffin, N. and Figueiredo, P.N. (2004) 'Internationalization of Innovative Capabilities: Counter-evidence from the Electronics Industry in Malaysia and Brazil', *Oxford Development Studies*, vol.32, no.4: 559–583.

Arnade, C. (1998) 'Using a Programming Approach to Measure International Agricultural Efficiency and Productivity', *Journal of Agricultural Economics,* vol.49, no.1: 67–84.

Arora, A., Ganbardella, A. and Torrisis, S. (2001) 'In the Footsteps of Silicon Valley? Indian and Iris Software in the International Division of Labour', Stanford Institute for Economic Policy Research.

Aswicahyono, H. and Hill, H. (2002) 'Perspiration versus Inspiration in Asian Industrialisation: Indonesia Before the Crisis', *Journal of Development Studies*, vol.38, no.3: 138–163.

Athukorala, C. and Menon, J. (1997) 'Export-Led Industrialisation, Employment and Equity: The Malaysian Case', *Agenda*, vol.4, no.1: 63–76.

— (1999) 'Outward Orientation and Economic Development in Malaysia', *World Economy*, vol.22, no.8: 1119–1139.

Audretsch, D. (2002) 'The Dynamic Role of Small Firms: Evidence from US', *Small Business Economics*, vol.18, no.1/3: 13–40.

Australian Government (2005), *Malaysia: An Economy Transformed*, Department of Foreign Affairs and Trade, published by Monash International, Melbourne, Australia.

A.T. Kearney for various indexes, see www.atkearney.com

Awang, A. (2004) 'Human Capital and Technology Development in Malaysia', *International Education Journal*, vol.5, no.2: 239–246.

Bank Negara (2004a) *Annual Report 2003*, Malaysia.

— (2004b) *Monthly Statistical Bulletin March 2004*.

— (2005) *Annual Report 2004*.

Barro, R.J. (1999) *Inequality, Growth and Investment*, NBER Working Paper 7038.

— (2000) 'Inequality and Growth in a Panel of Countries', *Journal of Economic Growth*, vol.5, no.1: 5–32.

Bashir, M.S. and Rashid, Z.A. (2000) 'Labour Skill Content in Manufactures: The Case of Malaysia', in M.S. Habibullah (ed.), *ASEAN in an Interdependent World; Studies on Trade and Finance*, Burlington, USA: Ashgate.

Becker, G.S. (1964) *Human Capital*, New York: NBER.

Berndt, E.R. and Christensen, L.R. (1973) 'The Translog Function and the Substitution of Equipment, Structures, and Labour in US Manufacturing, 1929–68', *Journal of Econometrics*, vol.1, no.1: 81–113.

Best, M. (2001) *The New Competitive Advantage*, Oxford: Oxford University Press.

Bhagwati, J.N. (1984) 'Splintering and Disembodiment of Services and Developing Nations', *World Economy*, vol.7, no.2: 133–143.

Birdsall, N., Ross, D., and Sabot, R. (1995) 'Inequality and Growth Reconsidered: Lessons from East Asia', *The World Bank Economic Review*, vol.9, no.3: 477–508.

Booth, A. (1999) 'Initial Conditions and Miraculous Growth: Why is South East Asia Different From Taiwan and South Korea?', *World Development*, vol.27, no.2: 301–321.

Booth, A.L, Francesconi, M., and Frank, J. (2003) 'A Sticky Price Floors Model of Promotion, Pay and Gender', *European Economic Review*, vol.47: 295–322.

Bowie, A., (1988) 'Industrial Aspirations in a Divided Society: Malaysian Heavy Industries', Paper for Association of Asian Studies Annual Meeting, San Francisco, 25–27 Mar.

Brynjolfsson, E., Hitt, L. and Yang, S. (2002) 'Intangible Assets: Computers and Oganisational Capital', *Brookings Papers on Economic Activity 1*: 137–181.

Burnside, A.C., Eichenbaum, M.S. and Rebelo, S.T. (1996) 'Sectoral Solow Residuals', *European Economic Review*, vol.40: 861–869.

Castells, M. (1998) *End of Millennium*, Oxford: Blackwell.

Caves, R.E. and Barton, D.R. (1990) *Efficiency in US Manufacturing Industries*, Cambridge, MA: The MIT Press.

Charemza, W.W. and Deadman, D.F. (1992) *New Directions in Econometric Practice*, Aldershot, UK and Brookfield, US: Edward Elgar.

Chenery, H. Robinson, S. and Syrquin, M. (1986) *Industrialization and Growth: A Comparative Study*, Oxford, Oxford University Press.

Chuang, Y.C. and Lin, C.M. (1999) 'Foreign Direct Investment, R&D and Spillover Efficiency', *Journal of Development Studies*, vol.35, no.4: 117–137.

Coe, D., Helpman, E. and Hoffmaister, A. (1997) 'North–South R&D Spillovers', *The Economic Journal*, vol.107: 134–149.

Coelli, T. and Rao, P. (2005) 'Total Factor Productivity Growth in Agriculture: A Malmquist Index Analysis of 93 Countries, 1980–2000', *Agricultural Economics*, vol.32, no.1: 115–134.

Collins, S.M. and Bosworth, B.P. (1996) 'Economic Growth in East Asia: Accumulation versus Assimilation', *Brookings Papers on Economic Activity* 2: 135–203.

Cornwall, J. (1977) *Modern Capitalism: Its Growth and Transformation*, New York: St. Martin Press.

Dahlman, C., Ross-Larson, B. and Westphal, L. (1987) 'Managing Technological Development: Lessons from the Newly Industrializing Countries', *World Development*, vol.15, no.6: 759–775.

Dedrick, J. and Kraemer, K.L. (1998) *Asia's Computer Challenge: Threat or Opportunity for the United States and the World*, New York: Oxford University Press.

DeLong, J. and Summers, H. (1992) Equipment Investment and Economic Growth: How Strong is the Nexus? *Brookings Papers on Economic Activity* 2: 157–199.

Dempsey, G. (1999) 'Revisiting Intellectual Property Policy: Information Economics for the Information Age', *Prometheus*, vol.17: 33–30.

Department of Foreign Affairs and Trade (DFAT 2005), *Malaysia: An Economy Transformed*, Economic Analytical Unit, Australian Government.

Department of Statistics, *Malaysia Economic Statistics – Time Series 2002*, Department of Statistics, Malaysia.

– *Yearbook of Statistics*, various issues.

– (2005) *Agricultural Census*.

Diewert, W.E. and Wales, T.J., (1987) 'Flexible Functional Forms and Global Curvature Conditions', *Econometrica*, vol.55, no.1: 43-68.

Dolado, J.J. and Lükepohl. H. (1996) 'Making Wald Tests Work for Cointegrated VAR systems', *Econometrics Review*, vol. 15: 369–386.

Dollar, D. (1992) 'Outward-Oriented Economies Do Grow More Rapidly: Evidence from 95 LDCs', *Economic Development and Cultural Change*, vol. 40, no.3: 523–544.

Dowling, M. and Summers. P. (1998) 'Total Factor Productivity and Economic Growth – Issues for Asia', *Economic Record*, vol.74, no.225: 170–185.

Dowrick, S. (2004) 'Ideas and Education' in T. Ito and A.K. Rose (eds), *Growth and Productivity in East Asia*, London: University of Chicago Press.

Economic Planning Unit, National Printing, Kuala Lumpur.

— (1970) *The First Outline Perspective Plan 1970–1990.*

— (1971) *The Second Malaysian Plan 1971–1975.*

— (1973) *Mid-Term Review of the Second Malaysian Plan.*

— (1976) *The Third Malaysian Plan 1976–1980.*

— (1981) *The Fourth Malaysian Plan 1981–1985.*

— (1984) *Mid-Term Review of the Fourth Malaysian Plan.*

— (1986) *The Fifth Malaysian Plan 1986–1990.*

— (1989) *Mid-Term Review of The Fifth Malaysian Plan.*

— (1991a) *The Sixth Malaysian Plan 1991–1995.*

— (1991b) *The Second Outline Perspective Plan 1991–2000.*

— (1993) *Mid-Term Review of The Sixth Malaysian Plan.*

— (1996) *The Seventh Malaysian Plan 1996–2000.*

— (1999) *Mid-Term Review of The Seventh Malaysian Plan.*

— (2001a) *The Eighth Malaysian Plan 2001–2005.*

— (2001b) *The Third Outline Perspective Plan 2001–2010.*

— (2003) *Mid-Term Review of The Eighth Malaysian Plan.*

— (2004), *The Malaysian Quality of Life 2004 Report*, Prime Minister's Department, Malaysia.

— (2005a) *Knowledge Content in Key Economic Sectors in Malaysia 2004.*

— (2005b) *Malaysia: Achieving the Millennium Development Goals: Successes and Challenges.*

— (2006) *The Ninth Malaysian Plan 2006–2010.*

Englander, A. and Gurney, A. (1994) 'OECD Productivity Growth: Medium Term Trends', *OECD Economic Studies*, vol.22: 111–129.

Ernst, D. (2002) 'Global Production Networks in East Asia's Electronics Industry and Upgrading Perspectives in Malaysia', East-West Centre Working Paper no.44, East-West Centre.

Fare, R., Grosskopf, S. and Margaritis, D. (2001) 'APEC and the Asian Economic Crisis: Early Signals from Productivity Trends', *Asian Economic Journal*, vol.15, no.3: 325–341.

Färe, R., Grosskpof, S., Norris, M. and Zhang, Z. (1994) 'Productivity Growth, Technical Progress, and Efficiency Changes in Industrialised Countries', *American Economic Review*, vol.84: 66–83.

— and Mitomo, H. (2003) 'Explaining Digital Divide as a Consequence of Uneven Digital Opportunities Between Urban and Rural Areas', *Studies in Regional Science*, vol.33, no.3: 287–293.

Felipe, J. (1999) 'Total Factor Productivity Growth in East Asia: A Critical Survey', *Journal of Development Studies*, vol.35, no.4: 1–41.

Fields, G.S. (1980) *Poverty, Inequality and Development*, Cambridge: Cambridge University Press.

Fikri, K. (2004) 'Role of Finance in the Innovation Process', Paper Presented at the National Innovation Summit, Kuala Lumpur.

Fuchs, V.R. (1969) 'Comment', in L. Soltow (ed.), *Six Papers on the Size Distribution of Wealth and Income*, New York: NBER: 198–202.

Fulginiti, L.E. and Perrin, R.K. (1999) 'Have Price Policies Damaged LDC Agricultural Productivity?', *Contemporary Economic Policy*, vol.17, no.4: 469–475.

Gan, W.B., and Soon, Y.L. (1996) 'Input vs Productivity Driven Growth', Paper Presented at the 7th Malaysian Plan National Convention, Kuala Lumpur.

– and (1998) 'Explaining Malaysia's Economic Growth', *Research in Asian Economic Studies*, vol.8: 113–129.

Gemmell, N. (1991) 'Industrialisation, Catching Up and Economic Growth: A Comparative Study Across the World's Capitalist Economies', *The Economic Journal*, vol.101: 263–275.

Gholami, R., Lee, S.Y. and Heshmati, A. (2006) 'The Causal Relationship between Information and Communication Technology and Foreign Direct Investment', *The World Economy*, vol.29, no.1: 43–62.

Ghosh, B.N. and Chin, L.N. (1996) 'Small is Beautiful, Medium is Pretty: A Look at Malaysian Industries', *Asian Economies*, vol.25, no.1: 29–37.

Giles, J.A. and Williams, C. (2000) 'Export-led Growth: A Survey of the Empirical Literature and Some Non-Causality Results', *Journal of International Trade and Economic Development*, vol.9, no.3: 261–337.

Giroud, A. (2003) *Transnational Corporations, Technology and Economic Development*, Cheltenham, UK and Northampton, MA, USA: Edward Elgar.

Glyfason, T. and Zoega, G. (2001) 'Education, Social Equality and Economic Growth: A View of the Landscape', Paper Presented at the Conference on Globalisation, Inequality and Well-Being, available at http://www.hi.is/~gyflason

Gong, B.H. and Sickles, R.C. (1992) 'Finite Sample Evidence on the Performance of Stochastic Frontiers and Data Envelopment Analysis Using Panel Data', *Journal of Econometrics*, vol.51: 259–284.

Gopal, J. (1999) 'Malaysia's Palm Oil Refining Industry: Policy, Growth, Technical Change and Competitiveness', in K.S. Jomo, G. Falker and R. Rasiah (eds), *Industrial Technology Development in Malaysia*, London: Routledge.

Rasiah (eds), *Industrial Technology Development in Malaysia*, London: Routledge.

Granger, C.W.J. (1969) 'Investigating Causal Relations by Econometric Models and Cross-Spectral Methods', *Econometrica*, vol.37, no.3: 424–438.

Grifell-Tatje, E. and Lovell, C.A.K. (1995) 'A Note on the Malmquist Productivity Index', *Economic Letters*, vol.47: 169–175.

Griffiths, W.E. (1972) 'Estimation of Actual Response Coefficients in the Hildredth-Houck Random Coefficient Model', *Journal of The American Statistical Association*, vol.67: 633–635.

Griliches, Z. (1988) *Education and Productivity*, Oxford: Basil Blackwell.

Hamelink, C.J. (1997) 'New Information and Communication Technologies, Social Development and Cultural Change', vol.20, Discussion Paper no.86 June 1997, edited by United Nations Research Institute for Social Development.

Harvie, C. and Lee, B.C. (eds), (2005) *Sustaining Growth and Performance in East Asia: The Role of Small and Medium Sized Enterprises*, Cheltenham, UK and Northampton, MA, USA: Edward Elgar.

Hashim, S. (1998) *Income Inequality and Poverty in Malaysia*, Lanham, MD: Rowan and Littlefield Publishers.

Hassan, A.A. (2004) *Growth, Structural Change and Regional Inequality in Malaysia*, UK: Ashgate.

Hassan, O.R. and Salleh, A.M. (1991) 'Malays in Reserve Areas of Kuala Lumpur: How Poor Are They?', in M.Y. Johari (ed.), *Urban Poverty in Malaysia*, Institute for Development Studies, Kota Kinabalu, Malaysia.

Heckman, J. (1999) *Policies to Foster Human Capital*, NBER Working Paper No.8239.

Heeks, R. (2000) 'Information and Communications Technologies, Poverty and Development', vol.2000, Working Paper no.5, edited by Institute for Development Policy and Management, University of Manchester, UK.

Hildredth, C. and Houck, J.K. (1968) 'Some Estimators for Linear Model with Random Coefficients', *Journal of The American Statistical Association*, vol.63: 764–768.

Huff, T. (2001) 'Globalization and the Internet: Comparing the Middle Eastern and Malaysian Experiences', *Middle East Journal*, vol.3: 439–458.

Ibrahim, M. (1997a) 'Patterns and Variations in State Manufacturing Productivity', *IIUM Journal of Economics and Management*, vol.5, no.2: 39–65.

—— (1997b) 'Efficiency Performance in Malaysian Manufacturing Industries', *Pakistan Journal of Applied Economics*, vol.13, no.2: 227–243.

Idris, Z. (2004) 'Government Policy on ICT Research and Development', Seminar Mengenalpasti Peluang-peluang Pelaburna Dalam Industri ICT bagi GLCs, Ministry of Science of Technology and Innovation, 14 Dec. 2004.

International Labour Office (ILO) 1998, *World Employment Report 1998–99: Employability in the Global Economy: How Training Matters*, Geneva: ILO.

— (2004) *World Employment Report 2004–05: Employment, Productivity and Poverty Reduction.*

Islam, I. and Chowdhury, A. (1997) *Asia Pacific Economies: A Survey*, London: Routledge.

Ismail, R. and Zin, R. (2003) 'Earnings Differentials Determinants Between Skills in the Malaysian Manufacturing Sector', *Asian Economic Journal*, vol.17, no.4: 325–340.

Jajri, I. (2002) 'Input Elasticity of Substitution in the Malaysian Manufacturing Sector', *Malaysian Journal of Economic Studies*, vol.39, no.1/2: 33–46.

Jantti, M. and Danziger, S. (2000) 'Income Poverty in Advanced Countries', in A.B. Atkinson and F. Bourguignon (eds), *Handbook of Income Distribution*, vol.1, Amsterdam, North Holland.

Jenkins, G.P. and Lai, A. (1989) *Trade, Exchange Rate, and Agricultural Policies in Malaysia*, Washington DC: The World Bank.

Jha, S. (1996) 'The Kuznets Curve: A Reassessment', *World Development*, vol.24, no.4: 773–780.

Jomo, K.S. (ed.) (2003) *Manufacturing Competitiveness in Asia: How Internationally Competitive National Firms and Industries Developed in East Asia*, London and New York: Routledge.

— and Felker, G. (eds) (1999) *Technology, Competitiveness and the State*, London and New York: Routledge.

— (1997) *South East Asia's Misunderstood Miracle*, Boulder, CO: Westview Press.

Jussawalla, M. and Taylor, R. (eds) (2003) *Information Technology Parks of the Asia Pacific: Lessons for the Regional Digital Divide*, New York: M.E. Sharpe Inc.

Kakwani, N.C. and Pernia, E.M. (2000) 'What is Pro-poor Growth?', *Asian Development Review*, vol.18, no.1: 1–16.

Kalirajan, K.P. and Tse, K.Y. (1989) 'Technical Efficiency Measures for the Malaysian Food Manufacturing Industry', *The Developing Economies*, vol.27, no.2: 174–184.

Kalirajan, K.P. and Shand, R. (1994) *Economics in Disequilibrium: An Approach from the Frontier*, India: Macmillan.

Katib, M.N. and Matthew, K. (1999) 'A Non-Parametric Approach to Efficiency and Measurement in the Malaysian Banking Sector', *Singapore Economic Review*, vol.44, no.2: 89–114.

Kawai, H. (1994) 'International Comparative Analysis of Economic Growth: Trade Liberalization and Productivity', *The Developing Economies* vol.32, no.4: 373–397.

Kendrick, J.W. (1990) 'International Comparisons of Productivity Trends and Levels', *Atlantic Economic Journal*, vol.18, no.3: 42–54.

Kawai, H. (1994) 'International Comparative Analysis of Economic Growth: Trade Liberalization and Productivity', *The Developing Economies* vol.32, no.4: 373–397.

Kendrick, J.W. (1990) 'International Comparisons of Productivity Trends and Levels', *Atlantic Economic Journal*, vol.18, no.3: 42–54.

Kondo, M. (1999) 'Improving Malaysian Industrial Policies and Institutions', in Jomo and Felker (eds): 199–217.

Krugman, P. (1990) *The Age of Diminished Expectation*, Cambridge, MA: MIT Press.

— (1994)'The Myth of Asia's Miracle', *Foreign Affairs*, vol. 73 no.6: 62–78.

Kuznets, S. (1955) 'Economic Growth and Income Inequality', *American Economic Review*, vol.45, no.1: 1–28.

Lai, M.C. and Yap, S.F. (2004) 'Technology Development in Malaysia and the Newly Industrializing Economies: A Comparative Analysis', *Asia Pacific Development Journal*, vol.11, no.2: 53–80.

Lai, Y.W. and Narayanan, S., (1999) 'Technology Utilisation Levels and Choice', in K.S. Jomo, G. Felker and R. Rasiah (eds), *Industry Technology Development in Malaysia*, Routledge: London.

Laird, S. (1997) 'WTO Rules and Good Practice on Export Policy', Staff Working Policy, Trade Policy Review Document 9701, Geneva: WTO.

Lall, S. (1995) 'Malaysia: Industrial Success and The Role of the Government', *Journal of International Development* vol.7, no.5: 759–773.

— (1996) 'Technology Policy and Challenges', Paper presented at the Conference on 'Globalisation and Development: Lessons for the Malaysian Economy', Faculty of Economics and Administration, Kuala Lumpur, 12–13 Aug.

— (2000) 'The Technological Structure and Performance of Developing Country Manufactured Exports 1985–98', *Oxford Development Studies*, vol.28, no.3: 337–370.

Lattimore, R.A., Madge, B., Martin, A. and Mills, J. (1998) 'Designing Principles for Small Business Programs and Regulations', Staff Research Paper, Productivity Commission, Australia.

Lee, C. (2004) 'Regulating Competition in Malaysia', in P. Cook, C. Kirkpatrick, M. Minogue and D. Parker, (eds) *Leading Issues in Competition, Regulation and Development*, Cheltenham, UK and Northampton, MA, USA: Edward Elgar.

Lee, G. (2005) 'Direct versus Indirect International R&D Spillovers', *Information Economics and Policy*, vol.17: 334–348.

Lee, H. and Khatri, Y. (2003) *Information Technology and Productivity Growth in Asia*, IMF Working Paper 03/15.

Leutert, H.G. and Sudhoff, R. (1999) 'Technology Capapcity Building in the Malaysian Automotive Industry', K.S. Jomo, G. Felker and R. Rasiah (eds), *Industry Technology Development in Malaysia: Industry and Firm Studies* Routledge: London and New York.

— (1987) 'Growth and Slowdown in Advanced Capitalist Economies: Techniques of Quantitative Assessment', *Journal of Economic Literature*, vol.25, no.2: 649–698.

Magnani, E. (2003) 'The Productivity Slowdown: Sectoral Re-allocations and the Growth of Atypical Employment', *Journal of Productivity Analysis*, vol.20, no.2: 121–142.

Mahadevan, R. (2000) 'How Productive is Foreign Direct Investment in the Malaysian Manufacturing Sector?', *Indian Journal of Quantitative Economics*, vol.15, no.1&2: 1–29.

— (2001) 'Assessing the Output and Productivity Growth of Malaysia's Manufacturing Sector', *Journal of Asian Economics*, vol.12, no.4: 587–597.

— (2002a) 'What Is and Is Not Measured by the Total Factor Productivity Growth Studies in Malaysia?', *Malaysian Journal of Economic Studies*, vol.39, no.1&2: 21–31.

— (2002b) 'Is There a Real TFP Growth Measure for Malaysia's Manufacturing Sector?', *ASEAN Economic Bulletin*, vol.19, no.2: 178–190.

— (2003) 'To Measure or Not To Measure TFP Growth?', *Oxford Development Studies*, vol.31, no.3: 365–378.

— (2004) *The Economics of Productivity in Asia and Australia*, Cheltenham, UK and Morthampton, MA, USA: Edward Elgar.

— (2005) 'Malaysia in the Era of Globalisation', in C. Tisdell (ed.), *Globalisation and World Economic Policies: Studies Highlighting Effects and Policy Responses of Nations and Country Groups*, New Delhi: Serial Publication.

Malaysian Science and Technology Centre (MASTIC), Malaysia.

— (2003) *National Survey of Innovation 2000–2001*.

— (2004) *National Survey of Research and Development Report 2004*.

— (2005a) *Malaysian Science and Technology Indicators 2004 Report*.

— (2005b) *Public Awareness of Science and Technology in Malaysia 2004*.

Malaysian Quality of Life Report 2004, downloadable from http://www.epu.jpm.my

Mamman, A. (2004) 'Managerial Perspectives on Government Intervention in Malaysia: Implications for International Business', *Competition and Change*, vol.8, no.2: 137–152.

Mani, S. (2002) *Government, Innovation and Technology Policy: An International Comparative Analysis*, Cheltenham, UK and Northampton, MA, USA: Edward Elgar.

Marwah, K. and Tavakoli, A. (2004) 'The Effect of Foreign Capital and Imports on Economic Growth: Further Evidence from Four Asian Countries', *Journal of Asian Economics*, vol.15: 399–413.

Mathison, S. (2003) *Digital Dividends for the Poor*, Global Knowledge Partnership Secretariat, Technology Park Malaysia, Kuala Lumpur. Available at http://www.globalknowledge.org

Marwah, K. and Tavakoli, A. (2004) 'The Effect of Foreign Capital and Imports on Economic Growth: Further Evidence from Four Asian Countries', *Journal of Asian Economics*, vol.15: 399–413.

Mathison, S. (2003) *Digital Dividends for the Poor*, Global Knowledge Partnership Secretariat, Technology Park Malaysia, Kuala Lumpur. Available at http://www.globalknowledge.org

McKay, H. (2001) 'Productivity and the Penetration of Information Technology', *Economic Papers*, vol.20, no.4: 26–35.

Menon, J. (1998) 'Total Factor Productivity Growth in Foreign and Domestic Firms in Malaysian Manufacturing', *Journal of Asian Economics*, vol.9, no.2: 251–280.

Ministry of Agriculture (1999) *Third National Agricultural Policy 1998–2010*, Ministry of Agriculture, Malaysia.

Ministry of Finance, *Economic Report*, various years, Kuala Lumpur, Ministry of Finance, Malaysia.

Ministry of Human Resources, *Annual Report 2004*, Kuala Lumpur, Ministry of Human Resources, Malaysia.

Ministry of International Trade and Industry (MITI), *Ministry of International Trade and Industry Report*, various issues, Kuala Lumpur, MITI, Malaysia.

— (1996) *The Second Industrial Master Plan 1996–2005*.

— (2000) 'Manufacturing Sector: Policy Measures and Initiatives', *MITI Report*.

— (2006) *The Third Industrial Master Plan 2006–2020*.

Ministry of Science, Technology and Environment (MOSTE) (2003) *The Second National Science and Technology Policy*, Kuala Lumpur, MOSTE, Malaysia.

Mody, A. and Yilmaz, M. (2002) 'Imported Machinery and Export Competitiveness', *The World Bank Economic Review*, vol.16, no.1: 23–48.

Mowery, D.C. and Oxley, J.E. (1995) 'Inward Technology Transfer and Competitiveness: The Role of National Innovation Systems', *Cambridge Economic Journal*, vol.19, no.1: 67–93.

MSC Impact Survey (various years), downloadable from http://www.msc.com.my

Mundlak, Y. (1988) 'Endogenous Technology and the Measurement of Productivity' in S.M. Capalbo, and J.M. Antle (eds), *Agricultural Productivity: Measurement and Explanation*, Resources for the Future, Washington, DC.

Mytelka, L.K. and Barclay, L.A. (2004) 'Using Foreign Investment Strategically for Innovation', *The European Journal of Development Research*, vol.16, no.3: 531–560.

Nagy, H. (2003) 'Why ICT Matters for Growth and Poverty Reduction?', See http://www.developmentgateway.org/node/133833/sdm/blob?pid=4037

Nambiar, S. (1998) 'State and Firm Technology Transfer: The Case of the Malaysian Electronics and Electrical Industry', *Asian Economies*, vol.27, no.3: 42–55.

National Productivity Corporation of Malaysia, *Productivity Report*, various years, Kuala Lumpur: Ampang Press Sdn.Bhd.

Naziruddin, A. (1997) 'Measurement of Total Factor Productivity for the Malaysian Rice Sector', *IIUM Journal of Economics and Management*, vol.5, no.2: 67–95.

Nehru, V. and Dhareshwar, A. (1993) 'A New Database on Physical Capital Stock: Sources, Methodology and Results', *Revista de Analisis Economico*, vol.8, no.1: 37–59.

—— (1994) 'New Estimates of Total Factor Productivity Growth for Developing and Industrial Countries', World Bank Policy Research Paper No.1313.

Nelson, R. (ed.) (1993) *National Innovation Systems: A Comparative Analysis*, New York: Oxford University Press.

Nishimizu, M. and Page, J. (1982) 'Total Factor Productivity Growth, Technological Progress and Technical Efficiency Change: Yugoslavia 1965–78', *The Economic Journal*, vol.92, no.368: 920–936.

Noor, H.M., Clarke, R. and Driffield, N. (2002) 'Multinational Enterprises and Technological Effort by Local Firms: A Case Study of the Malaysian Electronic and Electrical Industry', *Journal of Development Studies*, vol.38, no.6: 129–141.

OECD (2000) 'Local Partnerships, Clusters and SME Globalisation', Workshop Paper No.2, Bologna Meeting, Paris: OECD.

Oguchi, N., Amdzah, N.A., Bakar, Z., Abidin, R.Z. and Shafii, M. (2002) 'Productivity of Foreign and Domestic Firms in the Malaysian Manufacturing Industry', *Asian Economic Journal*, vol.16, no.3: 215–228.

Okabe, M. (2002) 'International R&D Spillovers and Trade Expansion: Evidence from East Asian Economies', *ASEAN Economic Bulletin*, vol.19, no.2: 141–154.

Okamoto, Y. (1994) 'Impact of Trade and FDI Liberalization Policies on the Malaysian Economy', *The Developing Economies*, vol.32, no.4: 460–478.

Okuda, H. and Hashimoto, H. (2004) 'Estimating Cost Functions of Malaysian Commercial Banks: The Differential Effects of Size, Location, and Ownership', *Asian Economic Journal*, vol.18, no.3: 233–259.

Onn, F.C. (1989) 'Kemiskinan Bandar di Malaysia: Profil dan Kedudukan pada Pertengahan 1980', *Ilmu Masyarakat*, vol.15: 43–58.

Othman, J. and Jusoh, M. (2001) 'Factor Shares, Productivity, and Sustainability of Growth in the Malaysian Agricultural Sector', *ASEAN Economic Bulletin*, vol.18, no.3: 320–333.

Pacific Economic Outlook (2000) *Productivity Growth and Industrial Structure in the Pacific Region*, Pacific Economic Cooperation Council, Japan Committee for Pacific Economic Outlook.

Perotti, R. (1996) 'Growth, Income Distribution, and Democracy', *Journal of Economic Growth*, vol.1, no.2: 149–187.

Perumal, M. (1989) 'Economic Growth and Income Inequality in Malaysia, 1957–84', *Singapore Economic Review*, vol.34, no.2: 33–46.

Pacific Economic Outlook (2000) *Productivity Growth and Industrial Structure in the Pacific Region*, Pacific Economic Cooperation Council, Japan Committee for Pacific Economic Outlook.

Perotti, R. (1996) 'Growth, Income Distribution, and Democracy', *Journal of Economic Growth*, vol.1, no.2: 149–187.

Perumal, M. (1989) 'Economic Growth and Income Inequality in Malaysia, 1957–84', *Singapore Economic Review*, vol.34, no.2: 33–46.

— (1992) 'New Budget Standard Poverty Lines for Malaysia', *Review of Income and Wealth*, vol.38, no.3: 341–353.

Pillai, P. (1995) 'Malaysia', in *ASEAN Economic Bulletin* (Special issue on Labour Migration in Asia), vol.12, no.2: 221–236.

Pratten, C. (1971) *Economies of Scale in Manufacturing Industry*, Cambridge: Cambridge University Press.

Quibria, M.G. and Tschang, T. (2001) 'Information and Communication Technology and Poverty: An Asian Perspective', ADB Institute Working Paper 12.

Ragayah, H.M.Z. (2005) 'Revisiting Urban Poverty and the Issue of Social Protection in Malaysia', in Zhang Yun Ling (ed.), *Emerging Urban Poverty and Social Safety Net in East Asia*, Beijing: World Affairs Press.

— (2003) 'The U-Turn in Malaysian Income Inequalities: Some Possible Explanations?', IKMAS Research Notes.

— Ismail, R. and Shari, I. (2000) 'The Impact of Industrialisation on Income Distribution in Malaysia', Paper presented at the East Asian Economic Association in Nov 2000 in Singapore.

Rahman, A.A. (1998) 'Economic Reforms and Agricultural Development in Malaysia', *ASEAN Economic Bulletin*, vol.15, no.1: 59–76.

Ram, R. (1988) 'Economic Development and Income Inequality: Further Evidence on the U Curve Hypothesis', *World Development*, vol.16, no.11: 1371–1375.

Rao, V.V. Bhanoji and Lee, C. (1995) 'Sources of Growth in the Singapore Economy and its Manufacturing and Service Sectors', *Singapore Economic Review*, vol.40, no.1: 83–115.

Rasiah, R. (1995) *Foreign Capital and Industrialization in Malaysia*, London: Macmillan Press.

— and Osman-Rani, H. (1995) *Enterprise Training and Productivity in Malaysian Manufacturing*, Paper presented at the World Bank Conference on Enterprise Training and Productivity, Washington DC, June 12–13.

— and Shari, I. (2001) 'Market, Government and Malaysia's New Economic Policy', *Cambridge Journal of Economics*, vol.25: 57–78.

— (2002) 'Systematic Coordination and the Development of Human Capital: Knowledge Flows in Malaysia's TNC-Driven Electronic Clusters', *Transnational Corporations*, vol.11, no.3: 89–130.

— (2003a) 'Foreign Ownership, Technology and Electronics Exports from Malaysia and Thailand', *Journal of Asian Economics*, vol.14: 785–811.

Reinhardt, N. (2000) 'Back to Basics in Malaysia and Thailand: The Role of Resource-Based Exports in Their Export-Led Growth', *World Development*, vol.28, no.1: 57–77.

Rock, M.T. (2002) 'Exploring the Impact of Selective Interventions in Agriculture on the Growth of Manufactures in Indonesia, Malaysia, and Thailand', *Journal of International Development*, vol.14, no.4: 485–510.

Salleh, I. (1995) 'Foreign Direct Investment and Technology Transfer in the Malaysian Electronics Industry', in *The New Wave of Foreign Direct Investment in Asia* (Compiled by Nomura Research Institute and Institute of Southeast Asian Studies).

— and Meyanathan, S.D. (1993) *The Lessons of East Asia: Malaysia Growth, Equity and Structural Transformation*, Washington, DC: World Bank.

Sarel, M. (1997) 'Growth and Productivity in ASEAN Countries', IMF Working Paper 97/97.

Scherer, F. (1993) 'Changing Perspectives on the Firm Size Problem', in Z.J. Acs and D.B. Audretsch (eds), *Innovation and Technological Change: An International Comparison*, Ann Arbor: University of Michigan Press.

Shari, I. (2000) 'Economic Growth and Income Inequality in Malaysia, 1971–95', *Journal of the Asia Pacific Economy*, vol.5, no.1/2: 112–124.

Shiong, T.T. (1997) 'Measuring the Benefits and Costs of Foreign Direct Investment With Reference to Malaysia', *Asian Economic Journal*, vol.11, no.3: 227–241.

Sims, C.A. (1972) 'Money, Income and Causality', *American Economic Review*, vol.62, no.4: 540–552.

Singh, A. (1994) 'Openness and the Market-friendly Approach to Development: Learning the Right Lessons from Development Experience', *World Development*, vol.22, no.12: 1811–1823.

Siwar, C. and Kasim, M.Y. (1997) 'Urban Development and Urban Poverty in Malaysia', *International Journal of Social Economics*, vol.24, no.12: 1524–1535.

— and Rahman, A.A. (1999) 'The Prospects of Agriculture Institutions', Paper presented at Seminar on Repositioning of the Agriculture Industry in the Next Millennium at the Universiti Putra Malaysia, Serdang, on the 13–14 July 1999.

Snodgrass, D. (1980) *Inequality and Economic Development in Malaysia*, Kuala Lumpur: Oxford University Press.

Solow, R.M. (1994) 'Perspectives on Growth Theory', *Journal of Economic Perspectives*, vol.8, no.1: 45–54.

Somun, H. (2003) *Mahathir: The Secret of Success*, Malaysia: Pelanduk Publications.

Stiglitz, J. (1998) 'Towards a New Paradigm for Development: Strategies, Policies and Processes', Paper presented as Prebisch Lecture at UNCTAD, Geneva.

Somun, H. (2003) *Mahathir: The Secret of Success*, Malaysia: Pelanduk Publications.

Stiglitz, J. (1998) 'Towards a New Paradigm for Development: Strategies, Policies and Processes', Paper presented as Prebisch Lecture at UNCTAD, Geneva.

Talib, M. (2002) 'Foreign Workforce: Balancing Economic and Security Interests', Paper presented at the 7th National Civil Service Conference, Kuala Lumpur, Malaysia.

— and Batra, G. (1995) *Enterprise Training in Developing Countries: Incidence, Productivity Effects and Policy Implications*, Washington D.C., The World Bank.

Tan, H.W. and Gill, I.S. (2000) 'Malaysia', in I. Gill, F. Fluitman and A. Dar (eds), *Vocational Education and Training Reform: Matching skills to Markets and Budgets*, New York: Oxford University Press.

Tham, S.Y. (1995) 'Productivity, Growth and Development in Malaysia', *The Singapore Economic Review*, vol.40, no.1: 41–63.

— (1996) 'Productivity and Competitiveness of Malaysian Manufacturing Sector', Paper presented at the 7th Malaysian Plan National Convention, Kuala Lumpur, 5–7 Aug 96.

— and Ragayah, H.M.Z. (2006) 'Moving Towards High-Tech Industrialisation', in Y.P. Chu, and H. Hill (eds), *The East Asian High-Tech Drive*, Cheltenham, UK and Northampton, MA, USA: Edward Elgar.

Thiruchelvam, K. (1999) 'Managing Research Utilisation in Malaysia', in K.S. Jomo and G. Falker (eds), *Technology, Competitiveness and the State*, London and New York: Routledge.

Toda, H. and Phillips, P.C.B. (1993), 'Vector Autoregressions and Causality', *Econometrica*, vol.61, no.6: 1367–1393.

— and Yamamoto, T. (1995) 'Statistical Inference in Vector Autoregressions with Possibly Integrated Processes', *Journal of Econometrics*, vol.66: 225–250.

Tori, I. (2003) 'The Mechanism for State-led Creation of Malaysia's Middle Class', *The Developing Economies*, vol.51, no.2: 221–242.

Townsend, P. (1979) *Poverty in the United Kingdom: A Survey of Household Resources and Standards of Living*, Harmondsworth: Penguin Books.

Tybout, J. (1990) 'Making Noisy Data Sing: Estimating Production Technologies in Developing Countries', *Journal of Econometrics*, vol.53: 25–44.

United National Conference on Trade and Development (UNCTAD) *World Investment Report*, various issues, New York and Geneva: United Nations.

— (2005) *Information Economy Report 2005*.

United Nations Development Program (UNDP) (1994) *Technology Transfer to Malaysia: The Electronics and Electrical Goods Sector and the Supporting Industries in Penang*, United Nations Development Program, Kuala Lumpur.

Vernon, R. (1966) 'International Investment and International Trade in the Product Cycle', *Quarterly Journal of Economics*, vol.80, no.2: 190–207.

Wah, L.Y. (1997) 'Employment Effects of Output and Technological Progress in Malaysian Manufacturing', *Journal of Development Studies*, vol.33, no.3: 411– 420.

Wahab, A.A. (2003) *A Complexity Approach to National IT Policy Making: The Case of Malaysia's Multimedia Super Corridor*, Unpublished PhD Thesis, University of Queensland.

Wales, T.J. (1987) 'Flexible Functional Forms and Global Curvature Conditions', *Econometrica*, vol.55, no.1: 43–68.

Wolff, E. (2000) 'Human Capital Investment and Economic Growth: Exploring the Cross-Country Evidence', *Structural Change and Economic Dynamics*, vol.11: 433–472.

— (2002) 'Productivity, Computerization, and Skill Change', NBER Working Paper 8743.

Wong, P.K. (2002) 'ICT Production and Diffusion in Asia: Digital Dividends or Digital Divide?', *Information Economics and Policy*, vol.14: 167–187.

World Bank, Washington, DC.

— (1989) *Malaysia: Matching Risks and Rewards in a Mixed Economy.*

— (1993) *The East Asian Miracle*, New York: Oxford University Press.

— (1995) *Malaysia Meeting Labour Needs: More Workers and Better Skills.*

— *World Development Report 1995: Workers in an Integrating World*, New York: Oxford University Press.

— (1997) *Malaysia Enterprise Training, Technology, and Productivity.*

— (1998) *World Development Report 1998–99: Knowledge for Development.*

— (2000) *World Development Report 2000: Attacking Poverty.*

— (2004a) *SME, Growth and Poverty*, Public Policy for the Private Sector Viewpoint Note No.268.

— (2004b) *World Development Indicators 2004.*

— (2005) *Malaysia: Firm Competitiveness, Investment Climate and Growth.*

World Economic Forum, *The Global Competitiveness Report 2005–06*, UK: Palgrave Macmillan.

— *The Global Technology Report,* various years.

Young, A. (1995) 'The Tyranny of Numbers: Confronting the Statistical Realities of the East Asian Growth Experience', *Quarterly Journal of Economics*, vol.110, no.3: 641–680.

Yusof (2001) 'Income Distribution in Malaysia', in C. Barlow (ed.), *Modern Malaysia in the Global Economy: Political and Social Change into the 21st Century*, Cheltenham, UK and Northampton, MA, USA: Edward Elgar.

Zapata, H.O. and Rambaldi, A.N. (1997) 'Monte Carlo Evidence on Cointegration and Causation', *Oxford Bulletin of Economics and Statistics*, vol.59, no.2: 285–298.

Zapata, H.O. and Rambaldi, A.N. (1997) 'Monte Carlo Evidence on Cointegration and Causation', *Oxford Bulletin of Economics and Statistics*, vol.59, no.2: 285–298.

Index

213